Right on Time!

The Complete Guide for Time-Pressured Managers

Lester R. Bittel

Professor of Management Emeritus
and Virginia Eminent Scholar
James Madison University

McGraw-Hill, Inc.

New York   St. Louis   San Francisco   Auckland   Bogotá
Caracas   Hamburg   Lisbon   London   Madrid
Mexico   Milan   Montreal   New Delhi   Paris
San Juan   São Paulo   Singapore
Sydney   Tokyo   Toronto

Library of Congress Cataloging-in-Publication Data

Bittel, Lester R.
    Right on time! : the complete guide for time-pressured managers /
Lester R. Bittel.
        p.   cm.
    Includes index.
    ISBN 0-07-005584-X :   — ISBN 0-07-005585-8 (pbk.) :
    1. Time management.   I. Title.
HD69.T54B54   1991
658.4'093—dc20   90-45591
                                                                            CIP

1 2 3 4 5 6 7 8 9 0 DOC/DOC 9 5 4 3 2 1 0

ISBN 0-07-005584-X {HC}
ISBN 0-07-005585-8 {PBK}

*The sponsoring editor for this book was William A. Sabin, the editing
supervisors were Olive Collen and Alfred Bernardi, the designer was Susan
Maksuta, and the production supervisor was Suzanne W. Babeuf. It was set in
Baskerville by McGraw-Hill's Professional Publishing composition unit.*

Printed and bound by R. R. Donnelley & Sons Company.

Contents

Part 3. Managing Organizational Time

Preface

No one has to tell *you* about time pressure. You could probably write a book about it. It has hit you from every side, and it finds new ways to harass and frustrate you each day. In general, the pressure to squeeze more out of your already limited time gets greater—not weaker.

Because of your sophistication about time, I've tried to write a book that doesn't slight your knowledge or experience in the matter. And I've tried not to repeat the time-worn advice that you've heard so often, although much of it has probably been good. Instead, in this book I give you a fresh—and I hope a deeper and more useful—perspective on the management of time.

A Personal and Professional Guide

Part 1 treats time in its most urgent and personal form. It provides an extensive array of practical techniques for getting control of your own time so that you waste less of it and get maximum use out of more of it.

Part 2 shifts your focus to ways and means of getting the most out of the time of your immediate support staff. It will help you make time-saving work assignments and extend the time available for innovation and creativity.

Part 3 deals extensively with your responsibilities for effectively managing time in an organizational setting. It provides you with a professional approach to time conservation, along with dozens of proven methods for shortening the time it takes to perform the vital business functions.

Unique Features in Each Chapter

Each chapter offers a number of features designed to enhance your understanding and to facilitate your application of the time-saving ideas presented. Among these features are:

Time Sights.   Self-appraisals that help you judge where you stand on the matter of time and what you may want to do about it. Time Sights appear in the first five chapters.

Time Bytes.   Brief but real case examples showing how individuals and organizations are currently handling the time problem.

Practice Times.   Self-directed exercises that enable you to experiment with, and test your proficiency in, selected time-saving techniques.

Time Checks.   "Action-plan" checklists to help you plan a course of action based upon the material in the chapter.

Lester R. Bittel

PART 1
Managing Your Own Time

1
Gauging Time's Impact on You

How to anticipate the impact of time upon your personal and professional performance, and how to sharpen your responses to it

Come what, come may,
Time and the hour
Runs through the roughest day.
WILLIAM SHAKESPEARE
Macbeth

Do you really want to be smart about time? Are you serious when you say that you want to hold time in your grasp—to be *right* on time? If you are, the answers are easy. You'll find the most important ones in the list below, with dozens more in the chapters to come. The catch, of course, is that it will take more than good intentions to carry out the advice so as to get time in your hands.

The Twelve Keys to Time Mastery

Let's put everything up front. I'll tell you the main secrets of time control right away. Later on, I'll reinforce this advice with detailed explanations and practical guidelines for you to follow.

The 12 most important things that you must learn how to do in order to be a master of time are listed below.

1. *Find out where your time goes.*   You can do this in any of three ways. (a) You can make an *activities time analysis*—the most systematic and thorough approach. Chapter 2 will show you exactly how to do it. (b) You can keep a *daily log* of your activities. This is the simplest approach, and Chapter 3 covers it. (c) Or you can *"sample"* your time using an easy shortcut, as fully explained in Chapter 6.

2. *Learn why your time goes where it does.*   You should treat time as your personal capital, and should invest mainly in activities that can pay off handsomely. Otherwise you may fritter away your time in nonproductive activities. The *time-use matrix* in Chapter 2 will show you how to make the distinction between productive and nonproductive use of time.

3. *Minimize your time commitments.*   Smart people don't take on more work than they can comfortably handle. They avoid overcommitment, especially in the kinds of *deadline traps* identified in Chapter 3. You, too, should try to limit your activities to those that fit in with the goals and the *daily agenda* established during your *individual time-planning* sessions, as described in Chapter 3.

4. *Sort out what needs to be done now from what can wait until later.*   Not everything need be done today. Nevertheless, you don't want to set aside important, urgent matters. You can make appropriate determinations through a system of *prioritizing* (Chapter 2). Or you can use the 80-20 rule of *ABC analysis* (Chapter 5) to separate the vital few demands upon your time from the trivial many.

5. *Cut down on time-wasting activities.*   A great many of the time problems we face are of our own making. It's a hard fact of life that we waste more time in trivial pursuits than we invest in useful ones. Chapter 3 will show you how to recognize the most common time wasters in your life and provide you with a three-part program to eliminate them.

6. *Be ruthless about distractions.*   If you are to cut down on time wasters, you're going to have to be ruthless with situations that—and people who—would intrude upon your personal time. This means that you won't always be the most popular person on your block, but Chapter 3 will show you how to avoid diversions that steal your time, and

you'll be offered a menu of 12 ways to *protect your personal time* with the least offense to others.

7. *Locate information in a hurry.* Studies show that searching for, and handling, information occupies up to 20 percent of your time. Chapter 4 provides you with three valuable assists: (a) a *seven-step procedure* for speeding your search for the information you need to manage your job; (b) a technique for setting up your own *personalized information system*, and (c) 12 ways to *stem the flow of paperwork* across your desk.

8. *Build a time control plan that fits your job and your own unique personality.* Based upon a knowledge of how time influences your life (as discussed later in this chapter), you'll discover several ways to get control of your time (Chapter 3). These include preparing a *daily agenda*, a five-point *planning check chart*, and a *block-time budget.*

9. *Break the procrastination habit.* Procrastination, an insidious temptation, is putting off difficult or unpleasant tasks. It plagues all of us, and it may be the greatest time waster of them all. Chapter 5 will show you how to identify the *causes* of procrastination, erect *barriers* to its temptations, and apply *five tips* for breaking the habit.

10. *Use other people's time to your advantage.* The greater your responsibilities, the clearer it will become to you that you cannot do it all by yourself. You must find ways to get others to help you—willingly—to get your work done. The secret lies in delegating to others those of your tasks that they are capable of carrying out. Ways and means of successful *delegation* are supplied in Chapter 6, along with instructions for using a widely used, but little-publicized, technique called *management by exception (MBE).* Also, in Chapter 7, you'll be given insights into *expectancy theory* so that you can use time to motivate employees and other people.

11. *Be creative with the use of your time.* Traditional ways of doing things are often accepted as the only ways, despite their declining effectiveness. Accordingly, you may discover that your time is being consumed by tasks and procedures that are no longer efficient. You can discard these costly habits and replace them with more time-effective methods by exploiting the ideas suggested in Chapter 8.

12. *Add hours to your time budget by working smarter, not harder.* Modern technology—including the telephone, electronic mail, and the fax machine—is at your fingertips to help you accomplish more in less time. There are also dozens of other practical ways to apply leverage to your time inputs, and thus to add hours to your outputs. Among these techniques are five ways to *read faster and better* (Chapter 4) and a mul-

titude of suggestions for *improving the time-use productivity* of employees, facilities and equipment, energy and utilities, and materials and supplies (Chapter 10). That's not all. Chapter 11 will show you how to create *time-saving production schedules* and to keep them on time, and Chapter 12 will brief you on dozens of ways for *conserving time in key business functions*. Application of these ideas will advance your career by demonstrating your proficiency in time management.

Winners and Losers in the Time Game

Time is the agent—or the bedeviler—of all people. Time is also the great leveler. No person has more of it each day than any other person. Every day the universe allots 24 hours for the use of every person—every manager or professional, technician or laborer, salesperson or private person. Why then is it that only a few rare successful individuals are in command of their time? Why is it that most of us have to submit to the will of time—and, as a consequence, fail to attain our potential? Perhaps it is because those who master time understand the secrets of its power, while those who succumb to time misunderstand the essential features of its power.

Losing, When Time Is Your Adversary

When Rudyard Kipling, in his poem "If," spoke of the demands of the "unforgiving minute," he was observing that time often shuts the door on an activity before you can complete it. For instance, how often have you heard yourself making remarks like these?

If only I had enough time.

Time ran out.

I couldn't make the deadline.

Time was too short.

We almost finished it.

The place was closed when I got there.

I didn't make my request in time.

We should have started sooner.

All these remarks are testimony to time as an enemy, as an essentially unfriendly factor you must cope with. And if that were not enough, time can cruelly punish your failures to meet its demands. For example, time pressures, more often than anything else but money problems, are cited as a source of stress. As a manager or a professional, you know the "loser's" feeling:

How can I juggle all these balls at the same time?

Which assignment should come first?

I can't do three things at once.

I don't have enough time to come up for air.

One more day like this and I'll be ready for the mental ward.

I can't sleep thinking about tomorrow's deadlines.

The time squeeze has my nerves in an iron grip.

Winning, by Making Time Your Ally

Conversely, it is time that enables you to get things done. You can't use a magic wand to work instant miracles. But what you do have is time at your disposal—to fulfill a plan, complete a schedule, or meet a delivery. Every day, effective managers say things like these:

We planned far enough ahead to be sure that our strategy would have time to develop.

We'll make money on this job because our time estimates were realistic.

If we keep up with this pace, we'll easily meet our deadline.

This project will finish on schedule because we have allowed for possible delays.

We're OK because we asked for enough time before we accepted the order.

Our product-release date was chosen to accommodate our projected manufacturing-cycle time.

Our financing has been spread out over a period of time to reduce repayment pressures.

Managing Time Can Cut Both Ways

It should be obvious from the above remarks that time can be duplicitous. That is, when it is managed poorly, it is unforgiving and punishing. When it is managed well, however, it yields accomplishments and rewards. How can this be? Let's take a closer look to see what *you* can do to avoid having time as your opponent:

1. Anticipate time constraints and factor them into your plans. That way you can avoid having time run out, missing deadlines, or finding that time was too short.

2. Construct realistic schedules so that you won't have to "juggle all those balls" or do three things at once.

3. Plan for early starts, to make sure that jobs are completed (not "almost finished"), or that the place you are going is open when you get there, not closed.

4. Preset priorities for your time so that you won't have to make judgments under pressure about "which assignment should come first."

5. Make allowances for time constraints so that you can place your requests "on time" and ask for "enough time" before agreeing to a commitment.

TIME SIGHT: A Self-Appraisal

How Responsive Are You to Time
Factors?

Listed below are a number of statements that reflect awareness of, and responsiveness to, the time factors in life. Read each statement. Then place a check mark in the column to the right that best matches your feeling about that statement. After you finish, check your answers with the scoring procedure and interpretation provided at the end of this exercise.

	Agree	Disagree	Neither agree nor disagree
1. I tend to see time as an adversary.	____	____	____
2. Generally speaking, I make good use of my time.	____	____	____
3. Too much emphasis is placed on being on time.	____	____	____
4. Accuracy should take precedence over quickness.	____	____	____

5. I always have more to do than I have time to do it in. _____ _____ _____

6. I pride myself on meeting my deadlines. _____ _____ _____

7. It bothers me when I see people wasting time. _____ _____ _____

8. I almost never fall behind in my work. _____ _____ _____

9. Compared with others I work with, I am very quick. _____ _____ _____

10. My boss doesn't allow enough time for the work that is to be done. _____ _____ _____

11. Project plans should allow for delays. _____ _____ _____

12. I am rarely late for an appointment. _____ _____ _____

13. There's no problem if a job falls behind schedule; I can always get caught up by working overtime. _____ _____ _____

14. I make a point of beating the time allowed for my job assignments. _____ _____ _____

15. I always wear a wristwatch and consult it frequently. _____ _____ _____

16. I rarely get excited if my airplane is delayed. _____ _____ _____

17. My estimates of the time needed to do a job are usually right on the money. _____ _____ _____

18. Saving time is low on my priority list. _____ _____ _____

19. I'm laid back when it comes to time pressures. _____ _____ _____

20. The day is often over before I realize it. _____ _____ _____

Scoring. Give yourself 1 point for each of the following statements that you *agreed* with: 2, 6, 7, 8, 9, 11, 12, 14, 15, 17. Give yourself 1 point for each of the following statements that you *disagreed* with: 1, 3, 4, 5, 10, 13, 16, 18, 19, 20. (You get no points for statements that you neither agreed nor disagreed with.)

Interpretation. If you scored between 16 and 20 points, you are highly responsive to time passage and its demands. If you scored between 10 and 15 points, your responsiveness in time-related matters probably suffers a little. If you scored less than 10 points, your responsiveness is likely to be sluggish; you can expect criticism in this regard not only at work, but also in your private life. *Caveat*: This self-appraisal is provided only as a rough check of your responsiveness to time; it is not necessarily a predictor of your success or failure. Furthermore, your choice of the most responsive answer to any one question might easily be defended as more appropriate than the author's; it is the aggregate of your responses that is significant.

Getting Time in Hand

To manage time is to be able to evaluate its potential and its constraints, to anticipate whatever factors influence its use, and to develop and implement methods that both conserve and exploit its advantages. Otherwise, time manages you, often with unhappy results for you and your organization. Generally speaking, you will manage time well if you can master the four skills described below.

Controlling the Use of Time

Avoid wasted motions and distracting efforts. Workers should not retrace their steps. Jobs should be done right the first time so that they do not have to be done over. You must control intrusions. Other people in your organization can—and will—make inordinate demands upon your own work time, as well as the time of your facilities and your work force. You must learn when to say no. You can't be overprotective of your resources, but neither can you afford to allow others to dissipate them.

Making Time Work for You

Time is a commodity, and a most valuable one. Once consumed, it can never be tapped again. On the other hand, it is renewed each day. Time misused yesterday need not be the pattern for today or tomorrow. As John Wayne, in *The Cowboys*, said to his posse when they wanted to sleep late while on the trail, "You're burning daylight." Neither should *you* burn "daylight"—valuable time—on the job; instead, you should make time work for you and your organization. Time is not meant just to be "filled," although that is what happens all too often at work. That's the essence of clock watching, boondoggling, and other make-work activities. Employees who don't use their time productively are not necessarily lazy or disinterested. More likely, they are poorly managed. Employees cannot use their time well if they must wait for assignments or materials or equipment, or if tasks are not properly designed and arranged. The guideline, for your employees and for yourself, is that time should always be utilized to accomplish an objective. If you—or they—ask, "Why am I doing this?" and you cannot provide a convincing answer, you can be sure that you are not making time work to your advantage. Conditions are worse still, of course, when the implication is "I have nothing worthwhile to do."

TIME BYTE 1-1

Faster Product Rollout

Under former president Michel C. Bergerac, Revlon took from 2 to 5 years to introduce a new product. This, among other things, led to his ouster. His successor, Ron Perelmann, moved much faster. Time to bring a new product to market was cut in half. Said a company spokesperson, "The new Revlon doesn't wait for years to make a decision and miss the market in the process." For example, when Revlon got wind that a competitor was about to roll out its own version of Revlon's yet-to-be released *No Color* mascara before Revlon had planned, Revlon overnight sent 70,000 tubes to drugstores for a preemptive strike. *In today's competitive world, the fable of the tortoise and the hare has become an anachronism: the race will now almost always go to the swiftest.*

"Strategies: The Changes at Revlon Are More than Just Cosmetic," *Business Week*, Nov. 20, 1989, p. 74.

Applying Time Strategically

Time has been characterized by some observers as a "moving stream." Such observers often imply that some places in the current of time are more opportune for immersion than others. From a practical point of view, this means that the timing of a venture can be of vital strategic significance. First consider a small example. If you wish to register a complaint about damage, you should do it as soon as possible after the damage has occurred. If too much time elapses, your chances of obtaining restitution are slim. You will have missed the opportune time to be legally effective.

Now consider a strategic example. Two competing toiletries firms have detected a market opportunity for a new hand cream. Company A begins to develop a product and a marketing plan on its usual slow schedule—with due deliberation. Company B gives the emerging market its highest priority and is able to place a new product in the market within 6 months. As a consequence, company B gets a foothold in the market before company A's equally good product makes its debut. The faster-moving company has seized the opportunity; the slower one has missed its chance. The moral is reflected in old sayings, such as "Strike while the iron is hot" and "Timing is everything."

Of course it isn't all that simple. There have been innumerable instances in which a company has introduced a product into a market that wasn't ready for it, and the venture has failed miserably. Such a failure is made even more bitter when, a few years later, another company brings an almost identical product into the market and meets with incredible success. You may say of the first company, "It was ahead of its time." The successful company gets applause, however, with the saying, "Its timing was perfect."

TIME BYTE 1-2
Slow Reaction Time

When auto sales in the United States surged in the third quarter of 1989, Detroit automakers were hypnotized by their success. They were so bedazzled, however, that they did not watch the dismaying climb in inventories that took place in the fourth quarter of that year. An economist who studies auto sales observed at the time that the auto industry was in a recession and didn't recognize it. Most worrisome was that the industry didn't react fast enough to the sales slump. By 1990, things were getting worse, and all the rebates and discounts in the world were not cutting far into the inventories standing on dealers' lots. Inevitably, plants were closed temporarily and layoffs occurred. *Slow-moving organizations—and people—are usually the ones who are also the last to become aware of changes.*

"Economic Trends: Detroit Hasn't Downshifted Fast Enough," *Business Week*, Dec. 4, 1989, p. 24.

Respecting the Pace of Time

For practical purposes, time is absolute—that is, a day is a day, an hour an hour, a minute a minute—but our perception of time is far from constant. You needn't be told how slowly time seems to pass when you're bored or waiting for quitting time or a holiday. And you can well remember how quickly time passes when you're occupied with something enjoyable. Monotonous, mindless work can seem endless. On the other hand, time flies when the work is interesting and challenging. All of us, then, respond to time subjectively. We live according to inner clocks that deeply reflect our personalities, experiences, environments, and genetic makeups. It's easy to see that, whatever the cause may be, some people perform best in the morning, and others get up to par only as the day wears on. Managers and professionals must take into account both the situation and the pace at which other people do their best work. Sometimes it is most productive to maintain a steady day-long pace, at other times one must "turn on the after-burners," and there are also times when it is preferable to fall back to a less demanding pace.

Rhythm, too, plays its part. Individuals and teams reach their peak performance when they "move to a beat," when their rhythms are "in sync." You observe this most often in sports, when a team is said to have "momentum." You recognize this euphoric condition in yourself when you can say, "When I'm hot, I'm hot!"

Living Well With Time

There is a growing awareness that the way we perceive time has a dramatic influence on our behavior. And you will not be able to control it, master it, pace it, or use it as a strategic factor unless you understand its impact on your life, both independently and as a member of an organization. Let's examine the four principal ways that time makes an impact upon you.

TIME BYTE 1-3

When Does Time Run Out?

For Armand Hammer, the energetic chief executive of Occidental Petroleum Corp, never! At 91, the billionaire executive was still going strong. After receiving a pacemaker, he was back on the job within 4 days—working his usual schedule. This meant flying to the Soviet Union to inspect a joint-venture fertilizer plant. Hammer, a peripatetic person if there ever was one, kept on going simply because he had so much yet to do in his life, and he was fearful that time would run out. This man with the Midas touch had already achieved many goals—entrepreneur extraordinaire, chief of a $20 billion corporation, medical doctor, philanthropist, art collector, globe trotting diplomat, and shrewd deal maker. *Not everyone is so lucky, of course. For most of us, the time will always be short.*

"The Teflon Tycoon," by Cindy Skrzycki, *The Washington Post*, Dec. 11, 1989, p. H1.

Physical Impact

This is a primary concern. You need to know how time influences your behavior and also how you can factor time into your plans. Accordingly, you must provide answers to such questions as:

What are the time factors that regulate your life?

What schedules dictate your personal affairs?

What job-related schedules are imposed upon you?

When does your workday begin and end?

What clocks and calendars trigger your actions and measure your progress?

What do you know about the past that you can use to plan your future?

How predictable is the sequence of events that influences your life—at home and at work?

With what other people and organizations must you coordinate your activities and plans?

Only by knowing the extent of these rational, measurable time factors—and their effect upon your behavior and the behavior of others with whom you interact—can you begin to get a handle on time itself. In Practice Time 1-2, you'll be shown a technique for obtaining some fairly accurate answers to these questions about yourself.

Psychological Impact

For many people, emotional concerns are the major factor in determining the impact of time on their lives. Time, with its inexorably forward movement, loads stresses of all kinds onto individuals and onto organizations as well. Psychological impact can be judged by the answers to questions like these:

How worried am I when I am late for a personal appointment?

How annoyed am I when others fail to keep a date with me?

How upset am I when I find that I can't meet a deadline at work?

What kind of stress do I feel when I realize that I am gradually falling behind with my job responsibilities?

What kind of pressure do I feel at work when others, such as subordinates who report to me or associates with whom I share a commitment, don't perform up to established time standards?

How realistic is my sense of time? Are my estimates for completing a task usually reliable?

To what extent do I feel that I have time in hand as opposed to its getting away from me?

Here again, a knowledge of how you—and others—react to time constraints and pressures will provide a basis for developing skills and techniques to accommodate and control these factors. The Time Sight Self-Appraisal on pages 8–10 will help to give you an idea of just how stressful time may be in your life.

TIME BYTE 1-4

Maybe They're Right

Italian businesspeople say that Americans are in too much of a hurry. They don't take enough time to talk with their Italian colleagues so as to learn how to work together. "American style," these executives say, "is too combative; a cooperative negotiating stance would be more welcome and more successful." The Italian nationals say, "We allow ourselves to be influenced by your culture. You should do the same." *It certainly makes no sense to hurry up, only to have to wait later on. Perhaps all of us do too much of that.*

"Global Perspective," *Management Development Report*, (*ASTD*), fall 1989, p. 5.

Philosophical Impact

Besides emotional reactions, another important aspect of dealing with time is the way in which we integrate time factors into our outlook. This is largely an intellectual activity, though many people don't think about it much. Others adopt time-honored views as their philosophy. Many of us accept as our guidelines one or more of these sayings:

Time and tide wait for no man.

You only live once.

The future lies in the past.

All in good time.

One must take time by the forelock.

There will be enough time to sleep.

There's a time for all things.

Time is fleeting.

Time is short.

As you can see, some philosophies are confident and optimistic, others are careless with time, and still others are fearful about it. Regardless of the validity of a particular viewpoint, what is important is that all individuals, wittingly or unknowingly, adopt a viewpoint that helps them to cope best with time.

Biological Impact

The life sciences indicate that each human being has his or her own biological clock. This inner clock seems to establish a daily cycle that influences, if not controls, the person's body temperature and metabolic rate. Attempts to isolate the portion of the brain that establishes these cycles have not been particularly successful. Nevertheless, there is good evidence that *alpha rhythms* (electrical impulses in the brain) vibrate at about 10 cycles per second and are apparently unique to each individual. Your own body probably reflects these rhythms and the effects of your unique biological clock. Accordingly, there are times of day when your performance is keen and other times when, no matter how hard you try, you can't bring yourself up to standard.

Do you remember the Three Mile Island nuclear meltdown and the Chernobyl disaster? The former took place at 4 a.m. and the latter at 1:23 a.m. Chronobiologists speculate that it may be no coincidence that both accidents occurred in early morning. They believe that both occurrences are related to biological rhythms that slow down the alertness of most workers at times when they might normally be sleeping.

Scientific explanations aside, you will want to determine the answers to questions about the biological impact of time on your body, and as a consequence, your performance. For example:

What time of day are you likely to be most productive?

What time of day are you likely to be least effective?

What have you observed about the biological clocks of those with whom you work? To what extent are their biological clocks problematic for you?

Since the work environment is typically much affected by time factors, there is often little that can be done to adjust an organization's work schedules to accommodate the infinite variations of biological rhythms present within a work force. It will make sense, nevertheless, for you to look for opportunities to try either of the following measures:

1. *Anticipate your high and low performance periods during the day, and seek to strike an average rate that meets the job's overall time requirements.*
2. *Rearrange your workday so that you can do highly demanding tasks during your peak periods and less demanding tasks during your below-par periods.*

When you are responsible for planning the work of others, you can make similar accommodations, so long as you don't lose control of an operation or upset the necessary coordination between task sequences.

How Time Slips Away

Just how much time is at your disposal? How much time is there in a minute? An hour? A day? A week? A month? A year? Your lifetime? You may not have thought much about time from this standpoint, but you'll be surprised by the insights that such an examination can provide.

All the Livelong Day

A once-popular folk song had the refrain, "I've been working on the railroad/All the livelong day." It may have felt that way to railroad workers who worked 12-hour days, but like everyone else, they also lived a life away from work. In this regard, how would you break up the times of your day? In all probability you measure your day not by the hours so much as by what you do during various segments of it. That is a useful approach. Consider, for example, the activities shown in Table 1-1. Try to estimate how many hours you spend on each activity as compared with the arbitrary numbers of target hours displayed there.

If you have a reasonably normal life, two-thirds of your time—about 16 hours—is spent away from your employment. From that figure, it appears that time for working (as distinct from time for "being") is mighty slim. Even the 8 hours devoted exclusively to employment is reduced by break time and social—or gossip—time, as well as by the inevitable waiting time. No wonder most people feel pressured on the job; there simply isn't a lot of time available for work.

Looking at the other side of your ledger, you see that there isn't much leisure time, either. Once you get enough sleep and take time to eat properly, keep yourself clean, and travel to and from work, you have

Table 1-1. Where Your Time Goes

Daily activity (Monday–Friday)	No. of hours	
	Target	Actual
Utility time		
Sleeping	8	_____
Bathing, dressing, etc.	½	_____
Eating	1½	_____
Traveling	1½	_____
Total utility time	11½	_____
Employment time		
Working	7	_____
Break	½	_____
Waiting	¼	_____
Socializing	¼	_____
Total employment time	8	_____
Discretionary (leisure) time		
TV	1	_____
Athletic and health activities	½	_____
Hobby, housework, etc.	1	_____
Family and social activities	2	_____
Total discretionary time	4½	_____
Total	24	24

only four and a half hours of discretionary time. It follows that how you spend that time is as important to you as how you spend your time at work.

TIME BYTE 1-5
Merging of Home and Work Time

For some people, it is increasingly difficult to separate the time demands at work from those at home. (See Practice Time 1-2 at the end of this chapter.) According to Link Resources, a market research firm, 23 percent of the total labor force in the United States was working at home in 1989. These 26 million people include the self-employed, salaried employees who work at home on or off company time, contract workers, and free-lancers. The number of work-at-homers increased about 7 percent per year during the last part of the decade. Reasons for the increase include the entrepreneurial boom of the 1980s and the wide availability of electronic tools such as computers and facsimile machines, which make work at home a practical option. *An unanswered question is: Does this merging of work and home sites increase or decrease time pressures?*

"Memo: Home Sweet Home/Office," *Management Development Report, ASTD*, fall 1989, p. 5.

___

As Time Goes By

Philosophers and strategists would say that focusing on hours and days is being overly concerned with *microtime*. We should also be concerned, they say, with weeks, months, and years—*macrotime*. This is true, of course. And the higher the level of your advancement in an organization, the longer view of time you must take. First-line supervisors, for example, are mostly worried about how well they and their workers perform against daily or weekly schedules. Middle managers direct their efforts toward coordinating monthly, quarterly, and yearly schedules. Top-level executives are much more likely to develop plans for 1 to 5 years.

In your personal life as well, you'll need to keep your eye not only on days and minutes, but also on the long-term passage of time. Otherwise, time will get away from you. The month will conclude with unfinished objectives. The year will end unsatisfactorily and lead only to a new set of unfulfilled resolutions for the year to come. To avoid such disappointments, you'll want to plan your time according to these three guidelines:

1. Look to the month and year ahead to develop a context for your daily activities. This may require nothing more than notations on your calendar. The plan need not be rigid, but it ought to be explicit enough so that you know (a) exactly what commitments (milestones) must be met and (b) the time constraints that are likely to be imposed on your daily and weekly plans.

2. Focus your strongest attention on your daily activities, rigorously adhering to time standards that you have established as reasonable. When daily plans are met, there is a great likelihood that monthly and yearly plans will be, too.

3. Periodically, check your progress against the milestones that you marked on your calendar. Determine the relationship of improper progress to your daily activities. When these activities are at fault, direct your efforts toward improving the productive utilization of your time.

Three Guidelines for Personal Time Management

The time in your hands is limited. It needs careful management, and it needs a perspective based upon its duration. Generally speaking, you should approach time management according to the following schedule:

1. Use minutes as (a) the building blocks for measuring the effectiveness of your use of time and (b) a basis for planning for improvement in productivity.
2. Use your days as a ledger against which to account for the use of your time.
3. Use months and years to mark your commitments and obligations and to check your progress toward these milestones.

Putting a Higher Price on Your Time

When it comes to our employment, most of us feel undervalued and underpaid. How can that be? Employers in today's tight labor market have to pay wages and salaries that reflect supply and demand. You'll probably accept that fact. At the same time, however, you'll argue quite rightly that many people with half your talent get paid lots more for their time, often within the same organization. Part of the reason for this injustice can be attributed to unfortunate circumstances, company politics, or simply not being there at the right time. The rest probably lies within you. Either you have persistently undervalued your time, or you haven't made a persuasive case for its worth, or you haven't found a way to improve its value. The last reason is often the most valid one, and it is one you can do something about.

How to Judge the Worth of Your Time

Let's start by taking a look at the factors influencing the price that is placed on a person's time, as shown in Table 1-2. A good argument can be made for some of these factors. Others might rightfully be challenged as irrelevant—even if they are valued in the labor market.

Note that the factors putting the highest price on a person's time are occupational skill and performance. Potential for advancement (which can often be equated to knowledge of industry, company, profession, or occupation) is given only a medium value, along with education and experience, and sometimes length of service in the occupation. Certain factors, once more highly valued and better priced, have fallen from fa-

Table 1-2. Factors That Influence the Worth of Your Time

Factors affecting the value of your time	Influence on time-price		
	Low	Medium	High
Attendance record	x		
Education		x	
Experience		x	
Particular occupational skill			x
Performance on the job			x
Potential for advancement		x	
Length of service in occupation		x	
Length of service with employer	x		
Loyalty to employer	x		

vor. These include length of service with the employer, attendance, and loyalty. Too many individuals rely upon these factors for their bargaining chips. What they should be doing is improving their occupational skills and demonstrating their proficiency by a high level of performance on the job.

Productive Performance

In the long run, your time is valued most highly and paid for accordingly when you are able to deliver more value per minute, hour, day, month, and year—either as (1) more value than the established standards call for or (2) more value than others performing the same work can deliver. That is the sine qua non—the "without which, nothing"—of performance. Note that the premium for your time is based upon value, not just output. *Maximum value is usually achieved by combining high output with high quality, often along with reduced costs or reduced help from others.* There are finite limits on how much you can improve your productivity by simply working harder. You will surely improve your productivity and add value to your time, however, if you learn to work smarter at what you are doing. To accomplish this end, you can:

- Sharpen and broaden your occupational skills.

- Improve your knowledge base, especially in relation to your occupation.

- Apply your skills and knowledge to purposeful activities, while abandoning wasteful efforts.

- Devote your time to achieving objectives that your company and your boss deem to be important.

Time as an Investment

Finally, you must recognize that time is the universal form of measure used in the material world. Couched in financial terms, time is "capital." You have as much of it as anyone else on earth. Your 24 hours each day are yours to invest wisely or to spend foolishly. Businesses look at time this way, and they also judge their employees in the same light. Whether you work for someone or someone works for you—or even if you are not employed—management of time to purposeful ends will spell the difference between success and failure, profit and loss, satisfaction or dissatisfaction. This conclusion about time's pivotal place in your life leads to four dictums:

1. Time should never be spent; it should always be invested. When time is wasted—that is, when time is used to serve no purpose—it is spent, not invested. It pays no interest and no dividend. There are no capital gains.

2. Time that is invested in work and employment should be aimed at improving its productivity—accomplishing more in fewer hours.

3. Time that is invested in your utilities (as defined in Table 1-1) should be aimed at strengthening your personal support system.

4. The discretionary time available to you should be invested in: (a) building friendships and cementing family ties; (b) maintaining your health; (c) improving your skills and knowledge and contributing to the good of your home and your community; and (d) relaxing in ways that refresh your body, mind, and spirit.

 PRACTICE TIME 1-1: A Self-Directed Exercise

Awareness Time

Assignment: Answer the following questions without looking at the answers in the commentary below.

1. How long does a traffic light stay red?_____
2. How long does a TV commercial last on a late-night movie?_____
3. How long will it take you to read aloud a five-page double-spaced, typed speech?_____

Commentary

1. Average time for a red light is 30 seconds. A very few are set at 15 seconds, and many are as long as 60 seconds. Of course, the greater your hurry, the longer the light seems to stay red.

2. Late-night commercials tend to be much longer than those shown

during the day. Daytime commercials run from 15 to 60 seconds; most last 30 seconds. Nighttime ads are much longer on average; direct-response commercials (those with 800 numbers) run more like 120 seconds, because of the belief that it takes 2 minutes or more to really catch the viewer's attention strongly enough to stimulate an immediate telephone response.

3. We hope that you didn't say 5 minutes or less. You'd have to read at breakneck speed to make that time. Eight minutes is more like it. You can figure on about one and a half minutes a page. If you are pausing for emphasis and working on voice projection, 2 minutes a page is about right. If you read more slowly than that, you may find your audience getting restless and impatient.

PRACTICE TIME 1-2: A Self-Directed Exercise

Time Demands Imposed by Your Regular and Recurring Responsibilities and Commitments

Assignment: Listed below are a number of typical responsibilities and commitments that can make demands upon your personal and professional time. Use this list as a basis for preparing a checklist of your own commitments. For each item, indicate for yourself the extent to which that particular responsibility makes a demand upon your time. Add as many items as you believe are recurring duties. For the time being, don't include occasional or exceptional items.

	Extent of demand on your time			
	Major	Moderate	Minor	None
Weekday Responsibilities: Personal				
1. Laundry	___	___	___	___
2. Food shopping	___	___	___	___
3. Food preparation	___	___	___	___
4. Housekeeping	___	___	___	___
5. Routines, such as garbage disposal	___	___	___	___
6. Other	___	___	___	___
Weekend Responsibilities: Personal				
7. Lawn and garden maintenance	___	___	___	___
8. Household shopping	___	___	___	___
9. Household maintenance and repairs	___	___	___	___

10. Banking and bill payments   ____ ____ ____ ____

11. Auto maintenance   ____ ____ ____ ____

12. Religious services   ____ ____ ____ ____

13. Other   ____ ____ ____ ____

Daily Responsibilities: Employment-Related

14. Routine job duties   ____ ____ ____ ____

15. Daily paperwork   ____ ____ ____ ____

16. Staff meetings   ____ ____ ____ ____

17. Committee assignments   ____ ____ ____ ____

18. Special projects   ____ ____ ____ ____

19. Report preparation   ____ ____ ____ ____

20. Job-related travel   ____ ____ ____ ____

21. Other   ____ ____ ____ ____

Commentary: Many of your responsibilities and commitments are inescapable. Only you can identify them. Of course, if you can eliminate any of these or have someone else handle them, such action will reduce the demands upon your time. Nevertheless, your list helps to establish the constraints that your duties and responsibilities—at home and at work—place upon your time. In effect, you will have constructed a set of time-related planning premises.

TIME CHECK

Use this action-plan checklist to verify your understanding of the various concepts, ideas, and techniques presented in this chapter and to indicate any need for further action on your part.

	Applies to your situation		Schedule for action	
	Yes	No	Yes	No
1. Time is an adversary when poorly managed.	____	____	____	____
2. Time can be an ally when properly utilized.	____	____	____	____
3. Control your use of time by avoiding waste effort and motion.	____	____	____	____
4. Time is best employed when it serves to attain an objective.	____	____	____	____

5. Apply time strategically by gauging your timing to the potential risks and rewards of a particular situation.   ____ ____ ____ ____

6. Vary the pace of time according to your own inclinations and those of the people who work with you, always seeking the most harmonious rhythms.   ____ ____ ____ ____

7. Regulate your life to accommodate the unique ways in which you respond to the four pressures of time: physical, psychological, philosophical, and biological.   ____ ____ ____ ____

8. Know where your daily time goes: utility time, employment time, and discretionary time.   ____ ____ ____ ____

9. Be aware of, and make notations about, the major time-related commitments you will face during the next year.   ____ ____ ____ ____

10. Use your minutes as building blocks for time improvement, days as a time-ledger account, and months and years to mark your commitments and to check progress toward them.   ____ ____ ____ ____

11. Recognize that you increase the value of your professional time by making it more productive in the service of company goals.   ____ ____ ____ ____

12. Acknowledge that time is capital and should be invested with regard for the value of its potential returns.   ____ ____ ____ ____

2
Achieving Mastery Over Time

How to change your ways so that time becomes a tool rather than a tyrant

We all of us complain of the shortness of time and yet have much more than we know what to do with. We are always complaining that the days are few, and acting as though there would be no end to them.   SENECA

Mastery of time will not by itself bring success to your career and personal life. Advancement of many kinds, however, depends on getting the important things done on time. Consciously planning and controlling your use of time makes you better able to meet deadlines and schedules. To accomplish your goals, you must allow sufficient time for performance. Wasting time, overcommitting yourself, and devoting large amounts of time and energy to low-priority, secondary tasks are tremendous obstacles to achievement.

Understanding the nature of the time available for productive activity is the critical first step in making better use of time. It is a natural human tendency to consider time as a given; we unwittingly push time to a back shelf in the management of our lives. Allowing time to pass by "as it will" can be destructive.

Giving conscious thought to the use of time will pay you well. You will

then be able to give the activities that have highest priority for you sufficient time for completion. That, perhaps, is the greatest reward of
time mastery: *time to accomplish the things you want to do.*

Your Time-Perception Identity

Your ability to manage time and to plan goals that can be achieved
within given times depends partly on the way you experience the passage of time. To find out how you perceive time, do the self-appraisal
tests in the Time Sight. After you have completed the tests and digested
their meaning, you will have a clearer insight into what you must do to
attain time mastery.

TIME SIGHT: A Self-Appraisal

Which Type of Time Person Are You?

This self-appraisal will help you to determine (1) which category of time
perception you fall into and therefore (2) which approach to time mastery
is most appropriate for you.

Instructions: There are three parts to this exercise. For the first part, you
will need the wristwatch or clock you normally use, as well as a radio,
television set, or telephone. You will also need someone to assist you for
about a half-hour with part C.

Part A. Check Your Watch. Write down the following numbers:

1. The time shown on my watch is _____.
2. The correct time (according to a radio, television, or telephone service report) is _____.
3. My watch is (accurate, fast, slow) _____.   *a li'l fast*

Part B. History. Respond to each of the following events by writing down
the month and year in which you think it occurred. Do not consult any
references or ask anyone for help. If you don't know the correct date,
guess.

1. The meltdown of the Three Mile Island nuclear reactor:_____   10/??
2. The first landing of a man on the moon:_____   10/69
3. The Pan Am 747 aircraft disaster at Lockerbie, Scotland:_____   8/88
4. President Richard M. Nixon's resignation:_____   6/76
5. Dr. Martin Luther King's assassination:_____   ?/66

Part C. The Empty Room. Ask someone to help you with this test. Tell your helper that you will sit alone in an empty room, and that he or she should call you sometime during the next half-hour. Your helper should record the time you went into the room and how long you have been in the room at the time he or she calls.

Before entering the room, remove your wristwatch, and make sure that there is no clock, radio, or television set running. Do not work or read. Tune out everything and just sit.

When your helper calls, estimate how long you have been in the room. Then ask how long you have actually been there. Make a record of your estimate, and whether it was accurate or was longer or shorter than the true time.

Interpretation: These exercises give some indication of your orientation toward time. They roughly distinguish between two types of time perceptions:

P   The view that there are a great many important things to be done and that time is limited

Q   The feeling that time is in great supply and that there is no need to rush to get things done

Part A. People with marked type P perceptions often set their watches a few minutes fast. This seems to give them a feeling that there is more time and that they are less likely to be late for appointments and for meeting short deadlines. People with type Q perceptions are more likely to be forgiving of a slow watch.

Part B. These are the correct answers: (1) March 1979; (2) July 1969; (3) December 1988; (4) August 1974; (5) April 1968. Type P perceivers tend to estimate these events as occurring more recently than they actually did. Type Q perceivers are more likely to assign more distant times to past events.

Part C. Type P perceivers often grossly overestimate how long they have been doing nothing. Time that is not filled with activities seems to pass very slowly for such people. Type Q perceivers tend to underestimate the time spent in the room.

In each of the three exercises, accuracy—correct or fast watch, proper dates, and accurate estimation—is more associated with type P perception than with type Q.

Important Implications

People who have type P time perception—who feel that there is much to be done and little time to do it in—need to firmly limit the number of activities that they schedule. Their drive to accomplish so much can lead them to take on too many projects; as a result, few activities will get the time and energy they deserve. People who have type Q time perception—who believe that there is plenty of time and no rush to get things done—tend to procrastinate. Time seems to stretch out before them in great abundance; if you are a type Q time perceiver, it is easy to have that third cup of coffee and promise yourself that you'll get started soon.

Insight into your own perceptions of time can provide guidance in planning and using your personal time. Whichever kind of time perceiver you are, type P or type Q, you can recognize your habits and inclinations—and their inherent shortcomings—and try to manage your time more effectively.

When you have managerial responsibilities, the implications are even broader. Not only must you make corrective adjustments for your own time perceptions; you will also have to be alert to, and compensate for, the time perceptions of your subordinates. This is why it is so necessary for a manager to have skills in communications, instruction, motivation, and control.

Time-Use Categories

A healthy awareness of time and its uses can be strengthened by reviewing uses of time according to their contribution to the achievement of goals. The guiding principle is this: *manage time in order to accomplish what you want*. As an extension of this principle, consider the following general categories of time use:

1. *Major uses.*   Everyone needs adequate time for the major, or fundamental, accomplishments of life. Of course, people's definitions of *fundamental* differ. For most people, though, work and career are high on the list of major uses of time. You may also consider utility time and discretionary time (discussed in Chapter 1) to be major uses. Family time usually needs to be protected, too, including time for activities with your spouse or partner and your children. Community, religious, civic, and charitable activities are major time uses for many people; time for such activities must be budgeted because such activities can be quite time-consuming. Recreation of some sort should be a major activity for everyone, although it may often be slighted. The fulfilling use of leisure time is fun and satisfying in itself; it can also recharge your batteries to provide more energy for other major undertakings.

2. *Minor uses.*   For most people, minor uses of time revolve around the "maintenance" or "utility" activities of life. For example, it is very difficult to make time spent commuting to work a productive activity. Activities such as doing the laundry, shopping for necessities like food

and clothing, and running routine errands can absorb large blocks of time if not carefully managed. Eating can be major or minor according to the orientation of the individual. For some people, eating is a rather elaborate process that provides great pleasure, conversation, and quality time with family or friends. For others, eating is a necessity to be disposed of as quickly as possible.

3. *Productive uses.*   In the present context, productive uses of time include all time that is devoted, with some focus, to the things you want to accomplish. *Productive use,* in an important, more restricted sense, also refers to time use in which your efforts contribute directly to meeting significant goals, rather than just "keeping busy." This distinction can readily be observed in work situations. Some of the things you do simply keep you busy without really accomplishing much. Take, for example, poring over the mail, even when there is nothing important in it, or attending conferences that don't relate to the goals of your job, or gathering information for other people that they should have acquired or maintained for themselves. These are examples of activities that keep you busy but do not contribute to your goals. In contrast are the critical activities that determine whether the work you do makes an essential contribution to your organization. Does a production supervisor get employees to work effectively enough to produce the required output on time and under budget? Does the architect finish the building design when promised and in a sound, buildable form? Does a clerk keep the filing current, with few or no misfilings? Does a delivery driver make calls as scheduled, driving safely and protecting the truck and the goods to be delivered?

4. *Nonproductive uses.*   Nonproductive uses of time do not contribute to what you wish to accomplish. Watching a football game on television and walking for hours in the woods are not *non*productive if these are activities you have chosen as important *and* if pursuing these activities does not prevent you from achieving critical career and personal goals. The truly nonproductive activity simply wastes time—that is, you are neither enjoying yourself nor accomplishing the essential work of life. Nonproductive time use can become more common than you might think. Even in the structured environment of normal work for pay, many tasks contribute little or nothing either to the real work goals of the organization or to your personal goals. Managers, in particular, must identify these wasteful, meaningless activities and root them out.

The Time-Use Matrix

As the matrix in Figure 2-1 shows, it pays to focus your efforts on the first quadrant of time use, where time is invested in major uses and for

	Productive uses	Nonproductive uses
Major uses	First Quadrant	Third Quadrant
Minor uses	Second Quadrant	Fourth Quadrant

Four categories of time-use according to their
contribution toward the attainment of goals.

Figure 2-1. Time-use matrix.

productive purposes. At the other extreme, you should eliminate all usages that fall into the third and fourth quadrants, but especially those in the third quadrant, major nonproductive activities. The amount of time invested in the second quadrant should be appropriate for productive, but minor, uses.

Activities-Time Analysis

The different categories of uses of time introduce a critical topic in time planning and management: recognizing and responding to priorities. Setting priorities is important because one surefire way to improve your use of time is to devote the majority of your available time to work or activities that are genuinely important. Identifying major and minor activities and productive and nonproductive tasks is the beginning of this process.

Thorough time planning, however, calls for analysis in more depth. The analysis method shown here will help you to take control of the routine and recurring demands of life. It will also help you to sort out the specific tasks that confront you, and guide you toward devoting more time to the most important tasks.

Activities-Time Analysis

At its most basic, activities-time analysis consists of making a list of all your tasks—whether recurring or unique—and evaluating each task. By doing this, you develop for yourself a guide for deciding how much time to devote to each task and when to devote the time. The concept was first introduced by R. Alec Mackenzie as a technique for identifying what he called *time traps*.* Later, George Odiorne, a major advocate of management by objectives (MBO), suggested that activities-time analysis be used for avoiding what he called *the activity trap*.† Odiorne's term implies that far too many activities are performed for the sake of being active, rather than for their importance to accomplishing goals.

Activities-time analysis is a procedure for time planning that is useful in a number of different contexts. Here we will apply the method in a formal work environment, but you can use it to plan any other kind of time use.

Establishing Priorities for Use of Your Time

The Five-Step Procedure

For an overview of an activities-time analysis, look at the worksheet in Figure 2-2. It provides a format for analysis of all the activities that occupy a person's work time. Among other things the worksheet provides columns for rating each activity according to its (1) intrinsic importance, (2) urgency, (3) potential for delegation, and (4) needed frequency of communication—along with (5) the key people with whom communication must be maintained. Don't be overwhelmed by what may appear to be a complex task. The five-step procedure below will show you how to make each entry.

The initial ratings you enter for each activity can then be used to assign priorities. The process for making the assignments is explained after the five-step procedure, in the section entitled "Setting Priorities."

In Practice Time 2-1 at the end of this chapter, you'll have an opportunity to prepare and evaluate a complete activities-time analysis of your own. For the time being, just read through the steps below, and compare them with the sample entries in Figure 2-2.

Step 1. *Make a list of all the activities you must perform.* Your list should include your formal job duties; special projects you wish to complete; your responses to routine requests for information or work, made by others in the organization; and any other tasks you do. By the time your list is complete, it should be a pretty good description of your job.

*R. Alec Mackenzie, *The Time Trap: How to Get More Done in Less Time*, AMACOM, New York, 1972, p. 26.

†George Odiorne, *The Activity Trap: How to Avoid It and How to Get Out of It*, Harper and Row, New York, 1974.

	Step 1	Step 2		Step 3	Step 4	Step 5	
	Time Demand Ratings						
Activity Number and Description	Intrinsic Importance 1 2 3 4	Urgency 1 2 3 4	Potential for Delegation 1 2	Communications Frequency 1 2 3 4	Key People for Communications	Priority 1 2 3 4	Person to Whom Task Is to Be Delegated
1 Review incoming orders	X	X	X(2)	X(1)	Martin	X(1)	Order Clerk
2 Check project VF	X(3)	X(3)	X(1)	X(4)	Alice	X(4)	
3 Weekly business lunch	X(3)	X(1)	X(2)	X(4)	Jones	X(3)	Sales promo prep
4 Telephone key clients	X(1)	X(1)	X(1)	X(2)	Tony + Jones	X(1)	
5 Prepare long-range plan	X(1)	X(4)	X(1)	X(4)	Naomi	X(2)	

Figure 2-2. Activities-time analysis.

In this first step, ignore priority, importance, the amount of time each takes, and so on. Simply list the activities in whatever order they occur to you.

> Marcia, sales manager for an office supplies company, listed the sample entries in Figure 2-2: (1) Review incoming orders for indications of a need to change production schedules. (2) Check progress of project F (redesign of call-report forms). (3) Attend weekly luncheons of the local business association. (4) Make follow-up telephone calls to clients who may be considering shifting to other suppliers. (5) Prepare a long-range marketing plan.

Step 2. *Rate each listed activity according to its intrinsic importance.* Use the intrinsic importance scale in Figure 2-3 to judge the relative importance of these activities and to assign an importance number to each. Not all activities are equally important; certainly not all deserve a top rating. The probability is that some activities will fall under each point. Use your best judgment to estimate how important each activity is to you personally and to the company. *For each activity, ask these questions*: Does this really matter? How directly does the activity contribute to meeting goals that count? Be candid and objective.

> As shown in Figure 2-2, Marcia assigned rather high intrinsic importance ratings to activities 1, 4, and 5 but gave lower ratings to 2 and 3.

Step 3. *Rate each activity according to its urgency.* The urgency scale (Figure 2-4) ranges from "very urgent" for tasks that must be com-

Very Important (Clearly Critical to Essential Goals)	Important (Should Be Done)	Important (Useful but Possibly Not Essential)	Unimportant (Not Necessary to Do)
1	2	3	4

Definition of ratings

1. Very Important activities have a certain, direct effect on goals that have priority for you and your company. If these activities are not performed, critical performance goals will be missed.

2. Important activities contribute to goals, but the consequences of neglecting them are less certain and immediate than are the consequences of neglecting very important activities.

3. Not so important activities are discretionary. They provide valuable or useful output but can be dispensed with in an emergency. Neglecting these activities will not necessarily cause you to miss high-level goals.

4. Unimportant activities do not contribute to essential goals at all, even though this may not be immediately obvious. Careful thought on the question "Will it make an important difference if I don't do this ?" will help identify these time-wasters.

Figure 2-3. Intrinsic importance scale.

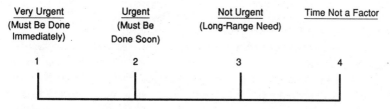

Figure 2-4. Urgency scale.

pleted immediately to "time not a factor." *Urgency* relates to how long the activity can be delayed without causing goals to be missed.

Note that some tasks may be very important but not at all urgent. They must be carefully done *sometime*, but it is not critical whether they are completed next week or next month. Thoroughness may be more important for such tasks than quickness. A study of methods in an already efficient operation, for example, might bring about improvements, but it should not receive priority over tasks needed to maintain current efficiency.

> As you can see in Figure 2-2, the sales manager assigned urgency rating 1 to activities 1, 3, and 4 but indicated that time was not particularly pressing for either activity 2 or activity 5.

Step 4. *Rate each task according to its potential for being delegated.* Assignment of a task to another person, usually a subordinate, who can be expected to perform that task effectively, is *delegation*. In rating the delegation potential of your activities, the first question to answer for each activity is: Should you personally be responsible for this activity? If not, you should assign it to someone else within your scope of authority. If it is, however, appropriate for you to retain responsibility for the activity, consider the scale in Figure 2-5: You must do some activities yourself, whereas other activities can be effectively done by other people. Two points, however, always affect the decision to delegate: (a) whether or not someone within your scope of authority is qualified to undertake the activity and (b) whether or not the qualified person is available and has the time.

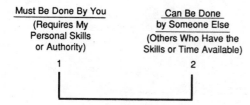

Figure 2-5. Potential-for-delegation scale.

Marcia saw potential for delegation of activity 1 to an order clerk and activity 3 to the sales promotion supervisor, as shown in Figure 2-2.

Step 5. *Rate each task according to its communications requirements.* At this point, you need to do two things: (a) For each activity on your list, identify the key people with whom (or function with which) you must communicate in order for that particular task to be completed successfully and on time. (b) For each of these people (not for the activity), rate the frequency with which communication is necessary. Consult the communications contact scale in Figure 2-6 for a description of frequency ratings.

This evaluation is critical to time mastery, even in supposedly minor situations, so you should try to be as specific as possible. Communication is often the missing link that prevents successful completion of an activity. Caveat: Strictly speaking, this rating is intended to help you identify critical communications contacts with others who can advance or obstruct your deadlines. This is not to say, however, that the social pleasures of working in an organization are to be ruthlessly eliminated. Instead, such prioritizing should encourage the attitude "Work is work," and should help to shift social contacts to time periods that will not interfere with effective performance.

Marcia decided (see Figure 2-2) that information about activity 1 must be communicated every day—a rating of 1—to Martin in the production department. For the progress report, activity 2, she assigned a communications rating of 3, assuring regular but infrequent contact with Alice, the sales supervisor to whom the project itself had already been delegated. To weekly lunches, activity 3, she assigned a rating of 4, in order to keep Jones, the general manager, informed about local developments. She assigned a rating of 2 to activity 4, telephone calls to Tony, the financial manager, and Jones, the general manager. To the long-range marketing plan, activity 5, she assigned a rating of 4, to indicate her intentions of checking in occasionally with Naomi, who coordinates strategic planning for the company.

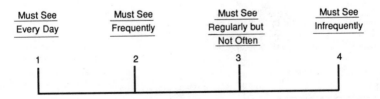

Figure 2-6. Communications frequency scale.

TIME BYTE 2-1

Even the Big Boys Forget

When General Motors announced its massive reorganization strategy in 1984, it forgot one big thing: to make the strategy work, the plan had to be communicated to everyone responsible for its coordination. Five years later (the completion date for the plan), nothing much that was good had been accomplished. Not only that, the auto maker's share of the market had declined from 44.1 percent to 34.2 percent. Another indicator showed that while GM had invested $40 billion during the decade to improve productivity, its productivity had risen only 5 percent compared with a 40 percent improvement at Ford Motor Company. Said GM's chairman Roger B. Smith, in commenting on the difficulty he and other top GM executives encountered in getting the company's middle managers to coordinate the program, "There was a problem of communication." *Communication is time-consuming, but—without it— time is often wasted in the long run.*

"Study: GM Program a Costly Mistake," by Warren Brown, *The Washington Post*, Jan. 3, 1990, p. C1.

Setting Priorities

You have just walked through a step-by-step demonstration of a detailed procedure for activities-time analysis. Now let's summarize what this process has accomplished so far. For each activity on the sales manager's list in Figure 2-2, there are now four ratings, one each for importance, urgency, potential for delegation, and frequency of communications. In addition, Marcia has identified the key people with whom these communications must be maintained.

Now comes crunch time. She must make the vital decisions that will integrate the four-part ratings for each activity into a single ranking of priority for that activity. She can do this by taking the steps listed below, using the format in Figure 2-2. You will be doing it too, in Practice Time 2-1.

1. *Prioritize your activities.* Assign to each activity one of the following priorities:

Priority 1. Highest priority. Activities that are both important and urgent.

Priority 2. Importance priority. Activities that are high only in importance.

Priority 3. Urgency priority. Activities that are high only in urgency.

Priority 4. Lowest priority. Activities that are neither highly important nor immediately urgent.

The definitions in the list above imply absolute distinctions of importance and urgency, but assigning priorities is a decision-making process,
and judgment is required.

> As shown in Figure 2-2, the sales manager made the following priority
> assignments: Priority 1 for activities 1 and 4, daily sales-order reviews and
> telephone calls to clients thinking of shifting to other suppliers. Priority 2
> for activity 5, long-range marketing plan. Priority 3 for activity 3, weekly
> lunch meetings. Priority 4 for activity 2, checking the progress of the call-
> report redesign project.

2. *Seek opportunities to delegate.*   Next, compare your prioritized list
with your notations of delegation potential. Delegate tasks that can be
reliably handled by others, even if the tasks are important and urgent.
You may be tempted, understandably, to reserve these vital activities for
yourself so as to ensure that they are handled properly. Don't make this
common mistake! It will block your path to time mastery. Delegation of
such activities removes some of the most time-consuming, stressful tasks
from your personal list, leaving you free to vigorously attack other activities that you cannot delegate. Write the names of people to whom
you are delegating tasks in the right-hand column of the table.

> Figure 2-2 shows that Marcia has chosen to delegate activity 1 to the sales
> order clerk and activity 3 to the sales promotion supervisor. Incidentally,
> the sales manager enjoyed attending the local meetings, but she realized
> that—although they are important to the company—the meetings were an
> unnecessary drain on her time, especially since her responsibilities are now
> national rather than local.

3. *Develop a communications strategy.*   Don't make this step too com-
plicated. All that is needed is a realistic but simple strategy for ensuring
that the necessary communications take place. Don't get bogged down
by listing specific hours and minutes, but do block out times in your
daily work schedule for the recurrent contacts required. (This strategy
is not shown in Figure 2-2.)

4. *Reconstruct your activities list.*   Now you should strip from your
prioritized list the activities that you have decided to delegate, and rearrange the remaining tasks in order of priority, from highest to lowest.
Your stripped-down and rearranged list will give you a powerful planning tool for managing your work. Not only will your activities be in
priority order but the list will now include only tasks that must be handled by you personally. First, list the *priority 1 tasks* that are critical to
goals and that must be attended to immediately. Next, write the *priority
2 items* that control the results you are responsible for but that have less
time urgency. *Priority 3 tasks* come next; these may have less importance but need to be disposed of quite soon. Last, list the *priority 4 items*,

which will get your attention only if time remains after the higher-priority activities have been completed.

Your future time-planning efforts should be applied to this list of prioritized activities and duties. Practice Time 2-1 (at the end of this chapter) will give you an opportunity to try your skills at analyzing and prioritizing a list of your daily—as opposed to your overall—activities.

Marcia's next step is to rearrange the five activities analyzed in Figure 2-2 according to their priorities:

Activity number and description	Priority
4. Telephone key clients.	1
5. Prepare long-range plan.	2
2. Check project F.	4
1. Review incoming orders.	4
3. Weekly business lunch.	4

Activities 1 and 3 might have been dropped from her list, since they have been delegated to others. However, she decided to retain them, with priority 4, for occasional checking, because she will still be accountable for their accomplishment.

Handling the Crises

No matter how carefully you plan your time, situations will frequently arise that demand your immediate attention. Such situations are very hard on a time budget and will disrupt your most rationalized priorities. For this reason, think carefully before agreeing to requests that "can't wait" or reacting to work stamped "Rush," or even to requests labeled "ASAP" (for "as soon as possible"). Two general kinds of crisis conditions exist, and each requires a different solution.

1. *Are crises routine in your work?* Do you spend much of your time responding to emergencies and putting out fires? If so, either or both of two conditions exist: (a) your own management style may be ineffective, (b) the crises are caused by poor management on the part of others. If you are at fault, you'll need to look for ways to improve your management techniques. If the fault lies elsewhere, you may have an uphill struggle. Often the best you can do is to try to seek some mutual approach for improving the coordination of operations between your department and others with which yours is interdependent. If the source of the problem is your boss, you might try demonstrating the costliness

of the crises. Failing that, you may need to put yourself in a new environment—that is, maybe you should get a different job—to achieve better time use and more solid accomplishments.

TIME BYTE 2-2
Quiet Time

A research study performed in 1989 points to the value of "quiet time" in the lives of managers and professionals. While the study was made of top corporate executives, the results can be applied to a broad spectrum of what Peter Drucker calls "knowledge workers." A major conclusion was that "quiet plays a profound and active part in the methods and thinking" of these kinds of people. Most of them try to schedule a time during the day during which quiet can be maintained. If quiet is not available at the office, many try to arrange quiet away from work, usually at home. Some seize undisturbed quiet time while commuting or when traveling by air. *Quiet* is an elusive and ambiguous term, however, with many definitions. *In the main, quiet means far more than simply freedom from the clatter of noise or the ring of the telephone. More often, it is defined as an opportunity for seclusion—a time when the mind can focus, undistracted.*

"The Power of Quiet," a study commissioned by Northwestern Mutual Life Insurance Company, Milwaukee, Wisconsin, and written by Thomas J. O'Hanlon.

---

2. *Are the crises that arise important?*   Remember the distinction between *important* and *urgent*. Something that is important has a direct, known effect on achievement of central goals. Something that is urgent must be done right away to avoid an undesirable consequence. Experience repeatedly shows that urgent matters tend to be comparatively unimportant. Generally, decisions or programs of true consequence allow time for thorough study and informed reaction. The implication is that you should refuse urgent but unimportant requests, or refer them to someone else. When you do an excellent job with important things, you won't be severely criticized for not jumping to respond to urgent but trivial matters.

Minimizing the Time Wasters

So far this chapter has emphasized a structured, rational approach to time management, and for good reason. Genuine mastery of time must be built upon careful analysis, realistic plans, and systematic controls. This requires a considerable amount of front-end loading to develop your own time-management strategy. Nevertheless, myriad small things can—and do—nibble away at your most carefully laid plans. Time-wasting practices creep into every life and into all organizations. Often these practices become deeply embedded in the life style of the individual or in the culture of the organization. Changing these habits is not easy and may require challenging the status quo—which, itself, can be time-consuming. When taken as a whole, however, the dozens of seemingly innocuous time wasters can destroy your time budget. Accordingly, it is just as worthwhile to identify and control time wasters as it is to focus on creating productive time. It follows that if the extent of wasted time can be reduced, more time will then be available for your prioritized activities.

Sources of Wasted Time

Hundreds of studies have been done of time lost in various occupational categories. The three categories discussed below have emerged most often as the major culprits.

1. *Slow starts.*   Many people are slow in beginning their workdays. They are also slow in getting up to speed after coffee breaks and lunch. They may also delay before undertaking responsible work, especially projects that involve considerable effort and risk. Coffee breaks and socializing may use up increased amounts of their time, along with unnecessary reading or research and other forms of procrastination. Managers who set good examples by prompt starts and decisive movement into new projects are a leading force in motivating their subordinates to get off the mark quickly.

2. *Disorganization.*   Disorganization is reflected in (a) allowing workplaces to become cluttered, (b) trying to handle many issues at a time, without being able to do justice to any one of them, (c) having to deal with too many people with conflicting interests, and (d) devoting major efforts to minor tasks. Plans and controls are likely to be respected and adhered to by rational people. Many people, however, especially those who are creative, seem to dislike structure. Not only are they unable to organize structure for themselves, but also they actively resist the conformity that structure demands of them. As a consequence, management is faced with the difficult task of creating and maintaining the necessary degree of order in the work environment without stifling the creative work of people who don't like the confinement of structure.

3. *Diversion.*   Employees often wait to do things that are more appealing than the assigned work. The result is work time frittered away

on unnecessary socializing, personal affairs, and hobbies and outside interests. These distractions, though often initiated by employees who are less than devoted, impinge upon the time of others who are more fully motivated. Managers and employees alike are susceptible to such distractions. It is a management responsibility, however, to find ways to minimize them.

Commonly Encountered Time Wasters

Many lists of common time wasters have been developed from studies of employees engaging in what might otherwise be productive work. The list below is just a sample. In all probability, you can add to it from your own experience.

- Absence of plans
- Procrastination
- Indecision
- Mistakes
- Misplaced materials
- Make-work projects
- Paper shuffling
- Ineffective meetings
- Unnecessary meetings
- Misunderstood communication
- Poor coordination
- Unspecified priorities
- Lack of concrete goals
- Obscure procedures
- Inefficient filing systems
- Cluttered workplaces
- Socializing
- Roaming
- Failure to delegate
- Perfectionism
- Too much memo writing
- Unselective reading

- Failure to listen
- Overconcern with details
- Management by crisis
- Conflicting policies
- Telephone interruptions
- Unimportant tasks

Cutting Down on Wasted Time

Wasted time, like productive time, is best approached by a carefully conceived program. The three steps listed below are a good approach.

1. *Identify the sources of wasted time—both in your work and in your personal affairs.* Then find answers to these questions: What causes you to lose valuable time? What is the scope of this problem? How much productive time is lost by it? How deeply does it cut into your leisure time?

2. *Plan specific actions to reduce the extent of wasted time.* Divide the problem into (a) time you waste and (b) time others waste. Begin by setting goals, in terms of *causes* to eliminate and *time* to be saved. Then specify how you will accomplish these goals by changing your habits and exercising discipline over your behavior. For others under your authority or influence, develop a program of organization, training, motivation, and time control. Commit your goals and plans to writing.

3. *Implement your planned actions.* This will require initiative and persistence on your part. No matter how strongly motivated you may be in this regard, others will need a lot of persuasion; perhaps they will even have to be dragged along. Maintain a chart of the progress toward your goals, weekly and monthly. This will discourage backsliding.

In addition, there are dozens of tips and techniques for dealing with specific time wasters throughout this text. Sample them from time to time for inspiration and for revitalizing your attack on time wasters.

PRACTICE TIME 2-1: A Self-Directed Exercise
Assessing the Daily Grind

Assignment: This chapter presented an orderly procedure for evaluating the routine, recurring activities of a job. The processes of analyzing activities and setting priorities also made it possible to evaluate a job in terms of its time demands. Combined, these two processes are a powerful and versatile tool for gaining mastery over personal and work-related time. The example used in the chapter was sales manager, but the processes are the same for any job.

In the assignment that follows, you'll get an opportunity to practice a second, equally important application: *sorting out the work to be accomplished in a single day on the job.* The procedures are essentially the same as those illustrated in the chapter, but the application is more focused. As you work through the assignment, record all your entries on a copy of Table PT 2-1.

Step 1. *Make a list of all the activities you must do tomorrow.* Be as detailed as you can. In this first step, provide as complete a picture as possible of all your projected activities for the day.

If you work in an office, consider all the items in your in-basket. Include the notations on your calendar for appointments and meetings. List the people you plan to talk with, the reports or tallies you will work on, and the routine work you must do.

If you work in another setting, such as manufacturing, consider all your interactions, such as arranging for materials, dispatching, giving directions, and responding to requests.

Step 2. *Apply the four analysis ratings to each activity.* Place check marks for each activity in the appropriate columns of the table. Intrinsic importance, urgency, potential for delegation, and need for communication with others are the four analysis ratings you will be working with. (See step 5 below for special instructions about how to fill in the "Communications frequency" and "Key people communications" columns.)

Step 3. *Set priorities for the items on your list.* Place a check mark for each activity in the "Priority" column in the table.

Step 4. *Eliminate all activities that you have identified as having a potential for delegation.* Try not to equivocate about decisions you made earlier. Identify the exact person who will handle each delegated activity tomorrow.

Step 5. *Estimate the time needed for each communication.* You'll need not only to identify frequency and the key contact for each communication need, but also to estimate the time to be allowed for that contact. Since you are analyzing only one day's activities, you need only indicate in the "Communications frequency" column that a contact must be made tomorrow. The amount of time to be budgeted for that contact, however, is very important. For example, to rate a conference called by your boss on the terms of a proposed contract to be sent tomorrow, your notation might be: "Communications frequency—1; Key people for communication—my boss"; and then add an estimate of the time needed for the meeting as "½ hour." This often-overlooked figure can become a major factor in planning tomorrow's activities.

Step 6. *Reconstruct your list to reflect steps 4 and 5.* This is an optional clean-up job. You may want to use a fresh copy of the table to rearrange your stripped-down list in order of your priority groupings.

Table PT 2-1. Activities-Time Analysis and Prioritizing Worksheet

Time Demand Ratings

Activity Number and Description	a Intrinsic Importance 1 2 3 4	b Urgency 1 2 3 4	c Potential for Delegation 1 2	d Communications Frequency 1 2 3 4	Key People for Communications	e Priority 1 2 3 4	Person to Whom Task Is to Be Delegated

aIntrinsic importance scale: 1 = very important, 2 = important, 3 = not so important, 4 = unimportant.

bUrgency scale: 1 = very urgent, 2 = urgent, 3 = not so urgent, 4 = time not a factor.

cPotential-for-delegation scale: 1 = must be done by you, 2 = can be done by someone else.

dCommunications frequency scale: 1 = must communicate every day, 2 = must communicate frequently, 3 = must communicate regularly but not often, 4 = must communicate infrequently.

ePriority scale: 1 = highest priority, 2 = importance priority, 3 = urgency priority, 4 = lowest priority.

Place activities with priority 1 rankings at the top, and continue listing your activities in order of priority, ending with your lowest-priority items at the bottom.

Commentary: The emphasis in this exercise is on learning how to identify your daily routines and to assign priorities to them according to their demand upon your time and the time of others for whom you are responsible. This is not a block-time budget, which will be discussed in Chapter 3. Your prioritized list, however, forms the basis for all your time-related planning. It will help you to (1) establish orderly and realistic routines for meeting your goals and deadlines, (2) make appropriate decisions when time-disrupting crises arise, and (3) minimize the debilitating occurrence of time wasters.

TIME CHECK

Use this action-plan checklist to verify your understanding of the various concepts, ideas, and techniques presented in this chapter and to indicate any need for further action on your part.

	Applies to your situation		Schedule for action	
	Yes	No	Yes	No
1. An assessment of your characteristic perception of time—either (P) much to do and little time for it or (Q) loads of time and no hurry to get things done.	____	____	____	____
2. An understanding of the value derived from looking at your time usage according to how well it serves your goals: major use, minor use, productive use, and unproductive use.	____	____	____	____
3. Completion of a five-step activities-time analysis, in which you list all your activities and rank each according to its intrinsic importance, urgency, potential for delegation, and need for communication with others.	____	____	____	____

4. Assignment of priorities for each of your activities according to four ratings: highest priority, importance priority, urgency priority, and lowest priority. ____ ____ ____ ____

5. As an integral part of your setting of priorities, (a) opportunities are sought for delegation and (b) communications strategy is developed for time management. ____ ____ ____ ____

6. Separation of crises into (a) those that should be eliminated by better management and (b) those that should be responded to only when their importance is genuine. ____ ____ ____ ____

7. Identification of major sources of wasted time—slow starts, disorganization, and diversion. ____ ____ ____ ____

8. Implementation of an ongoing, goal-related program to minimize time wasters in your personal life and in your organization as a whole. ____ ____ ____ ____

3
Planning and Controlling Your Own Time

How to create time-saving plans and keep them on track so that you reach your goals

The best laid plans o'mice and men
gang aft a-gley.   ROBERT BURNS

You must keep your goals in sight,
labor toward them day and night.
                    WITTNER BYNNER
                    Wisdom

Effective visions prepare for the future,
but honor the past.   TOM PETERS
                    Thriving on Chaos

Perhaps better planning is where mastery of time should really begin. Planning is usually thought of as being concerned with missions, strategies, goals, policies, plans, procedures, schedules, and budgets. Nowhere does the word "time" appear. Yet, planning is time-oriented and time-driven. It looks to the future, and it is propelled by the past. Plans are made for today and tomorrow, next week and next month, a year ahead or 5 years from now. Paradoxically, however, most plans are launched with a keen regard for what happened last week, last month, a year ago. In the great majority of cases, events, data, and trends that began 5 or 10 years ago are taken into account. Plans and planning, then, are not only deeply influenced by an awareness of time; they are inseparable from it.

Planning also goes hand in hand with controlling. Whereas plans point the way toward attainment of your goals, controls provide the guidance that keeps these plans on track.

Plans and Goals

In its simplest form, the planning process enables you (1) to establish goals and (2) to develop plans for reaching them. Realistic goals have deadlines. As a consequence, plans must incorporate timetables and specify completion dates. The timing of goals and the making of time-tables are the plans that can change your dreams to reality.

Timing of Goals

In order to fully understand the place of goals in the planning process, you must start at the end and work backward. You engage in planning only because you want to get somewhere or get something. But how are these somewheres or somethings determined? Look at it this way. Your plan calls for having your car packed by 5 p.m. so that you can be at the airport by 6 p.m. so that you can be in Dallas by 9 p.m. so that you can call on a client in his office at 9 a.m. tomorrow to close a sale. Your major concern is with the sale. That's your "something." Closing the sale is your goal. Dallas and the client's office tomorrow at 9 a.m. are the "somewhere." That's the deadline part of your goal. Planners describe both the somewhere and the something variously as goals, objectives, targets, and missions. These variations have nuances, but for the most part the nuances are not important. What is important is the time dimension of a goal, which is the time (or date) of expected attainment or completion.

A certain convention has grown up around the time dimension of goals. Typically, the following definitions prevail:

Short-range goals are usually set for up to and including a year ahead.

Long-range goals are ordinarily set for over 1 year and up to 5 years into the future.

Notwithstanding the convention, perceptions of these terms will vary according to the individuals concerned and the situations that confront them. In your personal life, *long range*—so far as your bank account goes—may very well mean next month. For your next vacation, however, *long range* may mean 12 months. *Short range* may mean what you plan to do this weekend. Or take a business situation. First-line supervisors may never be concerned with what is conventionally termed long range: for them, short range is tomorrow and long range is next month. On the other hand, highly placed executives may pay no attention whatsoever to short-range goals and concentrate exclusively on goals from 2 to 5 years into the future.

TIME SIGHT: A Self-Appraisal
How Hot a Planner Are You?

The way individuals create and react to the plans and schedules that govern their time can tell a lot about them. This self-appraisal may help you to understand your own practices better—and perhaps to improve them.

Instructions. For each of the actions or practices listed below, place a check mark in the column to the right that best reflects your reaction to it.

	Would do most of the time	Would do rarely, if ever
1. Before making a plan, decide exactly on the goal to be attained.	_____	_____
2. Concentrate exclusively on long-range goals.	_____	_____
3. Allow for seasonal peaks and valleys when extrapolating historical data to make a forecast.	_____	_____
4. Check the feasibility of a goal and its deadline before accepting it.	_____	_____
5. Readily say "yes" when asked to accept an assignment, regardless of your other commitments.	_____	_____
6. Add a safety factor when estimating a completion date.	_____	_____

7. Set goals a little bit higher each time the job is repeated so that you can show continual improvement. _____ _____

8. Prepare a daily agenda of things to be done and their priorities. _____ _____

9. Arrange your schedule so as to eliminate the need for a desk calendar or an appointment book. _____ _____

10. Attach a time factor, such as a completion date or deadline, to the goals that you establish. _____ _____

11. Arrive at work about a half-hour early. _____ _____

12. Sacrifice a lesser deadline in favor of a more important one. _____ _____

13. Check the readiness of your resources before you begin working on an activity. _____ _____

14. Place planning higher on your list of daily priorities than your regular, routine assignments. _____ _____

15. Eliminate all idle time from your schedule. _____ _____

Scoring. Give yourself 1 point for each of the following practices you *would do most of the time*: 1, 3, 4, 6, 8, 10, 11, 12, 13. Give yourself 1 point for each of the following practices that you *would do rarely, if ever*: 2, 5, 7, 9, 14, 15.

Interpretation. A score of from 13 to 15 puts you in the echelon of super planners. A score of from 10 to 12 implies that you may stumble occasionally in meeting scheduled deadlines. A score of anything under 10 is liable to put you in the class of people whom others don't like to depend upon for meeting their commitments.

Time Forecasts

When setting the time dimension for a goal, you are faced with two questions:

- How soon do I want to attain this goal? Or, in an organizational setting: How soon must it be accomplished?

- How feasible is this deadline, given the resources that are available?

You can readily sense that the answers to these questions are often contradictory. As a consequence, they often pose two more difficult questions:

1. Could the deadline be met by applying additional resources?

2. Are the additional resources available and affordable?

A starting point in solving this dilemma of contradictions is to base the time dimensions of your goals on reliable forecasts. Too often, there is a temptation to set a deadline without any justification other than a wish for gratification sooner rather than later. Organizational deadlines are often no better. They are similarly unreasoned and unjustified. In fact, completely reliable forecasts are rare.

TIME BYTE 3-1

Personal Prompters

In order to speed up the time needed to complete your daily activities, the American Society for Training and Development (ASTD) suggests the use of *job aids*. These can be prepared in a number of formats such as:

- Checklists in which sequence of tasks is not important
- "Cookbooks," or step-by-step procedures
- Decision guides, or flowcharts with options to guide choices
- Worksheets on which responses that will be needed for future reference may be documented
- Sourcebooks, such as vendors' catalogs that contain detailed product and price data

These prompters keep job-related data close at hand and reduce time wasted in hunting for information that you use regularly in your work.

"Job Aids: 'Just-in-Time' for Managers," *Management Development Report,* American Society for Training and Development, Alexandria, Va., fall 1989, p. 7.

A systematic approach to forecasting, however, reduces the chances of error. *For instance, when setting goals for the future, you should*:

1. Make allowances for seasonal influences.

2. Be alert to trends that indicate an acceleration or a slowing down of events.

3. Not accept data at face value. Statistical analysis often shows that casual interpretations are misleading. There is always the possibility for chance variations to appear significant when, in fact, they are meaningless.

4. Avoid jumping to conclusions about relationships between one set of

conditions and another. For instance, you may conclude that traffic is slow this summer because of added commuters from a nearby vacation resort. Investigation, however, may show that the real problem is a bottleneck caused by a bridge that is under repair. If you were to base your commuting time every summer on the former assumption, you'd be making a time-wasting error.

To get more extensive guidance on this extremely important matter, be sure to look at Chapter 11, Improving Scheduling Time.

Avoiding the Deadline Trap

Time forecasts lead to the setting of completion dates and deadlines. Once they are established, however, deadlines are hard to back away from. Patently, this is unfair, given the number of variables and uncertain circumstances that influence a time forecast. The deadline trap is very real indeed. Accordingly, you are urged to be cautious in either assigning or accepting a deadline. Try these buffers:

1. *Don't say "yes" too quickly.* It may make you popular to agree to an impossible deadline—but you won't be so popular when you miss the deadline. Promising and not delivering is worse than not taking on the job in the first place.

2. *Check your resources beforehand.* Make your acceptance of a deadline dependent upon provision of the resources needed to meet the completion time.

3. *Don't overcommit yourself.* Taken one at a time, the deadlines for a number of projects or assignments may be feasible; taken together, they may more than exhaust your time and resources.

4. *Review your dependence upon others beforehand.* There are a lot of contingencies to consider in setting a deadline, and the reliability of other people about meeting their commitments is often the most important variable.

5. *Don't shoot too high.* You're more liable to be criticized for missing a deadline than for setting one that's too conservative.

6. *Don't automatically up the ante on your last performance.* If you cut 2 days from a completion date last month, it does not necessarily follow that you can cut 2 more days the next time around.

7. *Always apply a safety factor.* The unforeseen and the imponderables will always be out there in the future. It is simply prudent to extend your time estimates anywhere from 10 to 30 percent. Similarly, safety factors should be applied to deadlines promised by others. If

the promise is for completion of a job upon which you depend in 10 days, add 3 or more days to your expectation for its receipt.

Goals and MBO

Increasingly, managers at all levels are confronted with—or asked to develop—a series of time-related performance goals. Especially at the middle and upper levels of management, the formal or informal process used is management by objectives (MBO). In an MBO program, the subordinate and his or her superior negotiate a set of individual (or departmental) performance goals to be attained within a designated time period, usually 1 year. After the negotiation is agreed upon, the subordinate is left pretty much alone except for any coaching he or she may request. At the end of the designated time period, the subordinate's performance is compared with the agreed-upon goals. The degree of attainment often becomes a major determinant of salary and advancement. A set of MBO performance goals for a marketing manager is shown in Table 3-1.

Personal Time Planning

To be effective, plans for use of your personal time must be reduced to writing. There are a number of simple formats that you can employ to advantage.

1. *Prepare a daily agenda.* This can be done on a form, as illustrated in Figure 3-1, or you can do it on the back of an envelope while

Table 3-1. Performance Goals for a Marketing Manager

Departmental goals to be achieved during the next 12 months	
Goal	Targeted completion date
1. Increase sales revenues by 15%.	December 31
2. Reduce sales travel expenses by 10%.	December 31
3. Maintain advertising expenses at 12% of sales revenues.	December 31
4. Revise existing marketing plan.	March 31
5. Oversee introduction of new product.	May 1
6. Prepare trade-show exhibit.	June 15
7. Conduct market survey.	July 31
8. Hire three new sales representatives.	August 15
9. Conduct sales meeting at trade show.	September 5
10. Visit one sales region per month.	December 31

Daily Agenda of Things to Be Done	
Priority Assigned	Date: *Monday*
⑦ ✓	*Prepare purchase requisition for supplier*
⑥	*Talk to Charlie about absences*
② ✓	*Make sure that Product A schedule is started by noon*
① ✓	*Check to see whether Smith order was shipped on Friday*
⑤	*Call maintenance about leaking oil line*
⑨	*Get figures from Design on new tolerances*
④ ✓	*Start labor gang on cleanup of shed*
⑧	*See whether materials for new product line have arrived*
③ ✓	*Complete summary report for Accounting*
√	• Check things done today. • Enter undone projects on tomorrow's agenda.

Figure 3-1. Daily agenda priority list.

you're having breakfast. It's better, of course, if the agenda is prepared on each afternoon for the next day (or on a Friday afternoon for the following Monday). A daily agenda is simply a list of (a) the important tasks that you must do, along with (b) an informal priority number assigned to each item. As the week progresses, at the end of each day, you scratch off each completed task and update the list—and the priorities—for the next day.

2. *Maintain an appointment calendar.* An open-face calendar that displays a full month is preferable to the closed-book type; its advantage is that you can see 4 weeks at a glance. On the calendar, note all important events, appointments, deadlines, and other similar commitments. Most important, *for every deadline date*—such as for the completion of a report—*also mark the date on which you must begin* to prepare the report, gather relevant information, etc. One of the greatest time-study experts who ever lived, Phil Carroll, once said, "You don't miss the trolley [today, of course, he would have said 'airplane'] because you can't run fast enough; it's because you don't start soon enough!"

WHAT	Objectives	Specifications
		Cost and price limits
WHERE	Locale	Delivery point
WHEN	Time elapsed	Starting date
		Completion date
HOW	Tactics	• Methods
	Strategy	• Procedures
		• Sequence
WHO	Responsibility	• Authority
		• Control
		• Assignment

Figure 3-2. Five-point planning chart.

3. *Double-check your plans.*   The five-point planning chart shown in Figure 3-2 is especially designed to help you make sure that you haven't overlooked an important element in your plans or schedules. The chart points out the items that every plan and schedule ought to include:

> *What* specifies the goal or objective to be accomplished, often including quality and cost or price specifications.

> *Where* indicates the locale at which the task is to be performed or the place to which the finished product or service is to be delivered.

> *When* stipulates not only the completion time or date, but also the starting time or date.

> *How* prescribes the strategy and tactics of the plan and, most important, the methods, procedures, and sequences that must be followed in carrying it out.

> *Who* assigns the responsibility for implementing the plan, and also delegates authority and control over the necessary resources.

Keeping Your Plans on Time

Personal time has a way of creating leaks in the best of plans. These leaks drain away time that is better placed in service of your time schedule. Fortunately, there are several things you can do to plug these leaks:

- *Start early.*   Many personal time problems can be minimized by beginning the workday a few minutes early. A great many executives testify to this. They say that they can accomplish more by getting to work a half-hour early in the morning than they can during any 2 or 3 hours during the day.

- *Decide quickly on small things.*   Most problems do not require a lot of time for a decision. On small matters, especially, there is rarely justification for asking for time to think them over. A prompt "yes" or "no" saves time since it allows you to dispose of the matter without having to return to it later.

- *Control the telephone.* There is probably no demon more liable to chew up personal time than the telephone. Often, what begins as a brief exchange of business information degenerates into 15 minutes of irrelevant gossip. The telephone also wastes time when you allow a nonurgent call to interrupt a meeting or a business session with an employee or associate. Such calls can better be handled by saying, "Please call back later" or "I'll return your call in 15 minutes."

- *Limit chitchat.* There is nothing like a 20-minute conversation about the weekend's entertainments to put you behind schedule the first thing on a Monday morning. It is difficult, of course, to sense when to lend an interested ear and when to cut a conversation short. It's probably best to develop a routine way of handling such situations by saying, "I'd love to hear about it at lunch," or "Let's get together during the coffee break, if we can, so that I can hear the whole story."

- *Discourage interruptions.* Don't be carried away with the urge to establish an open-door policy. You can be assured that the callers will not be considerate of your time. It's better to establish a daily routine that is recognized and respected by others. With such a routine, employees and associates know in advance when you will be free and when you will be occupied and cannot be disturbed—except in an emergency.

TIME BYTE 3-2

Start Meetings on Time, Too

We've all heard that the best way to get your workday off on the right foot is to start on time. It's surprising, however, how seldom this advice is followed in other situations. It is especially true of meetings: internal committee meetings, meetings of charitable and civic groups, and professional seminars. George David Kieffer, a lawyer and president of an investment company, however, is firm in his advice to meeting coordinators: "Starting on time is the first test of your control. It sets a subconscious expectation about your ability to perform throughout the meeting. If you can't do the first thing you said you were going to do (start on time), why should your leadership be taken seriously? There will always be a tendency to put off starting the meeting until a few latecomers arrive. Don't succumb. When you begin starting on time, you'll be surprised at how quickly people arrive on time." *Formal or informal meetings that you start on time are likely to end on time, too.*

"Making a More Effective Meeting," by George David Kieffer, *Marriott Portfolio,* January/February 1990, p. 52.

Time Control

You control time the same way that you control anything else. The control process involves three sequential steps:

1. *Establish a time goal (deadline or time frame) for the particular activity you wish to keep under control.* Your goals should be fixed in your mind and entered on a calendar or in an appointment book. If your activity is part of a larger organizational plan, the deadline may also be displayed on a production control chart.

2. *Measure progress toward the goal or deadline.* This can be accomplished in many ways, such as glancing at your watch, checking your appointment calendar, or examining a production control chart.

3. *Take action to keep progress moving as expected.* Such facilitating, or corrective, action requires that you change your present approach to speed up the progress. Adding resources is one way. For instance, you may get help from someone else, gain access to faster equipment, or delegate a portion of the work to a subordinate. These are all *positive* actions. Sometimes, however, corrective action is *negative.* You may, for example, have to pass up one appointment in favor of another. Or, if you observe a delay in a work-related activity, you may have to assign it a higher priority at the expense of another activity. Suppose, for example, that you have five deadlines to meet by Friday and you are falling behind in two of them. If no additional help is available, you may have to choose which three or four deadlines you will surely meet, recognizing that you may be late with one or two others.

Timing of Controls

Generally speaking, you can exert control of an activity at any of three stages: (1) at the point at which it begins, (2) at key make-or-break points during the activity, and (3) upon completion of the activity. *Preventive controls*—those that check the status of your resources before you begin—are great time savers. They ensure that all is in readiness before you expend effort and energy. *Operating controls*—those applied selectively during the activity—help to keep things moving on track and according to schedule. These controls give you an opportunity to speed up the process while there may still be time to meet your deadlines. *Postoperative controls*—those applied after the activity has been completed—are the least effective from a time-control standpoint. They are too late to do much good about your deadlines. Such controls do have a secondary value, however. If a final product—such as a report—is involved and you detect a serious error in it, you will have a chance to save the time and energy that might otherwise be wasted in delivering and retrieving an unacceptable product.

Controlling Personal Time

Time control requires that you keep track of two things: (1) the deadline you are shooting for and (2) the time frame in which you expect to start and finish the activity. Technically, this time frame is called a *time standard*. To control time effectively, you ought to set some sort of time standard for every item on your daily agenda. It need not be painstakingly accurate. A rough estimate will do. For example, you might say that commuting to work ought to take a half-hour of your time. If, over a period of a week or so, however, you find that it takes 45 minutes, it's a signal that you should look for ways to shorten that time—by leaving ahead of the rush-hour traffic, for example. Or, if you block out 15 minutes each morning for paperwork and then find that 45 minutes is more like it, you're faced with a dilemma. Should you increase the time standard? Or should you try to get the paperwork done more quickly?

Block-Time Budget

You can exert more precise control of your activities if you place your time standard estimates in a format like the block-time budget, illustrated in Figure 3-3. This kind of personal time budget will commit you to a structured control of your time during an entire week. You can use the block-time budget as a control framework into which your daily agenda priority list must fit. Note that the block-time budget in Figure 3-3 establishes four categories of time blocks:

Routine Work.   This includes preparation of employee time and payroll sheets, routine paperwork, checking logbooks and production reports, and answering mail. Most budgets for managerial and professional workers allocate from 10 to 20 percent of time to routine work.

Regular Duties.   These are the tasks that make up the core of your job and are truly most important. You should try to block out from 50 to 75 percent of your time for these responsibilities. You should exercise time control here in order to ensure that time allocated for regular duties is, in fact, available and being used for that purpose.

Special Assignments.   It is realistic to budget about 10 percent of your time for meetings, committee work, and special assignments. This is an

	Monday	Tuesday	Wednesday	Thursday	Friday
8	Routine	Routine	Routine	Routine	Routine
9 10	Inspection and supervision of operations	Individual work with staff **Regular**	Inspection and supervision of operations	Individual work with staff **Regular**	**Special work**
		Inspection and supervision of operations	**Regular**	Control studies and reports	Inspection and supervision of operations **Regular**
11 12	**Regular**	**Regular**	Division staff meeting **Regular**	**Regular**	Department staff meeting **Regular**
1	L	U	N	C	H
2	Interviews and contacts **Regular**	Interviews and contacts **Regular**	Interviews and contacts **Regular**	Interviews and contacts **Regular**	**Creative work**
3 4	Planning and organizing **Planning work**	Inspection and supervision of operations **Regular**	**Special work**	Inspection and supervision of operations **Regular**	
5	Routine	Routine	Routine	Routine	Routine

Figure 3-3. Block-time budget.

area in which time control is essential. Work on special assignments will help your career, but if you're not careful, such work will eat away ravenously at your available time. Accordingly, it doesn't pay to be too willing a volunteer.

Planning and Creative Work. Planning provides the groundwork for control, so you must be careful not to give planning short shrift in your time budget. It is also important to allot some time on a regular basis for creative activities. This is when you look for ways to smooth out work flow and to investigate new techniques for doing things. This time block should also include time for thought, reflection, and self-improvement. To be realistic, you'll be lucky if you can squeeze out 5 percent of your available time for planning and creative work. If you can't work this in during your 40-hour week, you may have to do it before or after work.

Your Own Time Audit

Your time budget for your own work time should not be something that is prepared once, and then relegated to your desk drawer. Instead, your block-time budget should be used as the basis for an occasional audit of how well you are controlling your work time. Twice a year for this audit is about right. You need not be so precise in gathering your data that you begin all over again with another activities-time analysis (Figure 2-2 in Chapter 2). The audit should be thorough enough, however, to give you a reasonably accurate measure of the distribution of your work in the four categories of your block-time budget. (A work-sampling study, as described in Chapter 6, simplifies and speeds the audit enormously.)

The variances revealed by the audit will quickly tell you (1) whether or not you are staying within your weekly time budget and (2) whether or not your budget should be changed to reflect the true demands of your job. If, for example, you have reduced the hours you spend each week on routine work and transferred that time to any of the three other categories in your block-time budget, that's great! If, however, you find that you are stealing time from your regular duties to work on special assignments, you must take action to get your time for regular duties under control. On the other hand, if you discover that the demands of your job have shifted so that you ought to devote a larger amount of your time to planning, then your budget should be adjusted to reflect that fact.

TIME BYTE 3-3

Time Budget in a Shoebox

Wouldn't you know that the ubiquitous computer would like to take over your time-management chores? That's what a number of ingenious software programs now offer. One popular program, *Shoebox 1 Plus*, takes over once you've filled out your calendar and plugged it into your personal computer (PC). If you request reminder flags, *Shoebox* will automatically set up a tickler program. When your calendar seems booked solid months in advance, the program riffles through the days and finds an open time block. And, of course, your calendar can be called up to the PC screen instantly, even in the midst of whatever other program you're working with. *It looks as if the days of back-of-an-envelope plans and a marked-up calendar are doomed.*

"High Tech Cures for the Time Crunch," by Roxane Farmanfarmaian, *Psychology Today*, March 1989, p. 46.

Time-Saving Controls

Your time gets out of control because it is misplaced on activities that do not fit your time budget. Time traps are so ever-present that you must continually guard against them. Fortunately, there are a number of time-saving techniques that help to alert you to time traps and suggest ways to avoid them. At the risk of being repetitious, many of the most useful techniques are provided in this checklist:

- *Control the telephone.*   Whenever possible, have someone else answer your telephone and screen your calls. Set aside one time during the day when you make and receive calls. Give priority to what you are doing, not to a ringing telephone.

- *Control social visiting.*   Don't make extended conversations comfortable for the other person. Say that you're busy at the moment, or offer to schedule an appointment. Shorten conversations by excusing yourself to go to the washroom or by having your secretary interrupt after a prearranged period. Limit physical access as a buffer to casual visitors.

- *Expect to be able to control only about 50 percent of your time during a particular day, but insist on devoting that time to productive activities.*

- *Expect idle time to crop up when you least expect it.*   Accordingly, keep a block of productive activities in reserve for those opportunities. Or prepare to move up other deadlines to fill these gaps.

- *Increase the extent of your delegations.*   Assign routine work and unexceptional decisions to subordinates. Try to delegate one additional task each week.

- *Avoid activities that offer a low payoff.*   Refuse to accept them or delegate them to subordinates.

- *Check your time estimates.*   Periodically assess how your estimates are working out, to see if they were realistic. Adjust your time budget accordingly.

- *Expect a 20 percent—or more—slippage in most time schedules.*   Perfection may be planned, but it rarely occurs.

- *Don't overcommit your time.*   Not only does slippage occur in your plans, but there will always be new and unexpected demands placed upon you.

- *Understand that every completion deadline invokes a related starting deadline.*   Don't let the starting time pass without beginning the work.

- *Make a habit of deciding quickly on small matters.* There are a great many small matters to deal with, and an occasional misfire among them won't cause much damage.

- *Form the "completion" habit.* Whenever possible, finish one task before starting another.

PRACTICE TIME 3-1: A Self-Directed Exercise
The Beginning and the End

Many of your activities involve sequential steps from point to point until the entire job or task is completed. This is especially true of a project that requires you to complete phase A, for example, before you can start phase B, and to complete phase B before you can begin phase C, and so on. This creates a difficult problem in time planning because you must set the project completion date far enough ahead to allow time to complete each separate phase. This exercise will show you how to accomplish this goal, using a wall calendar.

Background. You have been assigned to prepare a vendor-rating program for the purchasing department of your organization. It must be on-stream and fully functioning as soon as possible, and today is February 15. You've thought through the phases needed to complete this assignment and come up with the following time estimates for the steps involved in development of the vendor-rating program.

	Estimated number of weeks needed
Step 1. Design vendor-rating form.	2
Step 2. Present tentative specifications to suppliers for their suggestions.	2
Step 3. Gather suggestions from suppliers, consolidate them, and present them to purchasing manager for approval.	4
Step 4. Revise vendor-rating form. Confirm with suppliers. Present to purchasing manager and general manager for approval.	2
Step 5. Formally announce installation date to suppliers and to company's production, receiving, and quality control departments.	2

You've examined the process and have concluded that each phase must be completed before the next one can begin. You also know that other commitments will prevent you from starting this project until March 1.

Assignment. Using the calendar provided in Figure PT 3-1, prepare a plan for this project. Enter on the calendar the beginning and ending dates for each phase. A new phase cannot begin on the same date that the previous one is completed, and the project can only be active on weekdays. For planning purposes, first enter your dates here:

Phase	Starting date	Completion date
1	___	___
2	___	___
3	___	___
4	___	___
5	___	___

	Monday	Tuesday	Wednesday	Thursday	Friday
March	1	2	3	4	5
	8	9	10	11	12
	15	16	17	18	19
	22	23	24	25	26
	29	30	31		

	Monday	Tuesday	Wednesday	Thursday	Friday
April				1	2
	5	6	7	8	9
	12	13	14	15	16
	19	20	21	22	23
	26	27	28	29	30

	Monday	Tuesday	Wednesday	Thursday	Friday
May	3	4	5	6	7
	10	11	12	13	14
	17	18	19	20	21
	24	25	26	27	28
	31				

Figure PT 3-1. Calendar control chart.

Commentary. Starting and completion dates are as follows: phase 1—March 1, March 12; phase 2—March 15, March 26; phase 3—March 29, April 23; phase 4—April 26, May 7; phase 5—May 10, May 21. This exercise illustrates the value of taking into account starting dates as well as completion dates when preparing time schedules. The time needed to complete this project might have been shortened, of course, if there had been some way of beginning some phases before the previous ones were completed. Chapter 11 will show you how this can be done.

TIME CHECK

Use the action-plan checklist below to verify your understanding of the various concepts, ideas, and techniques presented in this chapter and to indicate any need for further action on your part.

	Applies to your situation		Schedule for action	
	Yes	No	Yes	No
1. A distinction made between short-range and long-range goals, with proper attention given to both.	____	____	____	____
2. Recognition that the first step in planning is selection of goals, and that the selection should be based upon systematic forecasts.	____	____	____	____
3. Assignment of completion dates or deadlines to all goals.	____	____	____	____
4. Avoidance of deadline traps by checking resources beforehand, guarding against overcommitments, minimizing dependence on others, and applying a safety factor.	____	____	____	____
5. Preparation of a set of time-related goals (within or without a formal MBO program), at the beginning of each year.	____	____	____	____
6. Preparation of a daily agenda, with associated priorities.	____	____	____	____
7. Maintenance of a desk calendar or appointment book.	____	____	____	____

8. Auditing your plans, using the "what, where, when, how, who" approach.   ____ ____ ____ ____

9. Time schedules kept on target by starting each day early, deciding quickly on small things, controlling the telephone, limiting chitchat, and discouraging interruptions.   ____ ____ ____ ____

10. Knowledge of the time-control process: (a) setting of time goals or standards, (b) measurement of progress toward goals and standards, and (c) action to keep progress moving as expected.   ____ ____ ____ ____

11. Awareness of the importance of timing in applying (a) preventive controls, (b) operating controls, and (c) postoperative controls.   ____ ____ ____ ____

12. Preparation of a time budget (block-time budget) to plan and control the use of your own work time according to (a) routine work, (b) regular work, (c) special assignments, and (d) planning and creative work.   ____ ____ ____ ____

13. Periodic auditing of the way you actually spend your time as compared with your time budget.   ____ ____ ____ ____

14. Regular application of a number of time-saving controls over your own time.   ____ ____ ____ ____

4
Managing Your Information-Handling Time

How to use an information system to manage your time wisely and cut down on your paperwork

*Knowledge is of two kinds: we know a subject
ourselves, or we know where we can find
information upon it.*   SAMUEL JOHNSON

Information Overload

There's hardly a person today who doesn't suffer from information overload. At home, it's TV and radio news, newspapers, magazines, books, and the daily assault of direct mail. At work, it's a similar story: memos and letters piling up in your in-basket, hand-delivered printouts of yesterday's computer runs, a desk drawer jammed with policy manuals and operations procedures, and a shelfful of reference books and handbooks. What's a person to do? The solution is simple, at least in theory. Block out what's of no use. Retain only what's important. Speed up your assimilation of its content. In practice, of course, this is all very difficult to achieve.

Time-Consuming Exchanges

A study conducted by Booz, Allen & Hamilton Inc. in 1984 showed that managerial and professional people spend about 21 percent of their work time on document-related activities, but only 8 percent of the time on analysis. The situation is worse for knowledge workers down the line. They spend twice as much time composing documents as managers do. And it will come as no surprise that managers and upper-level professionals spend 40 to 60 percent of their time in person-to-person information exchanges, either in casual encounters, on the telephone, or in formal meetings—in their own offices or in scheduled briefings and seminars. The purpose of all this, one supposes, is to obtain or exchange information. But at what a cost in time—anywhere from 60 to 80 percent of a manager's or professional's working hours.

High-Tech Answers

Long-range, at least, it appears that the major villain—computers and advancements in information tecnology—may hold the conceptual answers, if not the practical solutions. Information scientists predict that the problem of overload will be solved by (1) the incredible speed of data manipulation and (2) the narrowing of the gap between the person seeking the information and the information source.

The person-to-source gap is also narrowing rapidly. Such narrowing depends upon removal of middle persons and/or media from the process. Direct marketing, for example, eliminates the personal salesperson. Videotaping a college course can eliminate the lecturer and the classroom. Computer typesetting eliminates the typesetting house. The technical term for such elimination is *disintermediation*. Consider what the long-distance telephone accomplishes. Routinely, it puts two voices, separated by thousands of miles, into instant and immediate contact. Another giant step forward is that data collected at a point of contact, such as a supermarket checkout counter or a factory work station, can now be instantly identified, collected, and transmitted to an inventory-control center. A dramatic narrowing of the person-to-source gap also takes place when a PC is connected by a modem to any of the hundreds of databases already in operation. There's no denying that computer-assisted, on-line, real-time systems are bringing information seekers closer and closer to the source—and doing it at almost breakneck speeds.

TIME BYTE 4-1

20,000 Bits of Information...in 4 Seconds

When John Deere's agricultural equipment dealers need service
information, they have almost instant access to 20,000 recorded solutions
to previously encountered problems. Deere operates 10 dealer technical
assistance centers (DTACs) aimed at helping customers speed up
equipment repairs. In just 4 seconds, DTAC's computers can retrieve
trouble-shooting information that once required days, sometimes weeks,
to locate in manuals and files scattered all over the company's dozens of
operating locations. *High-tech will do its part: the rest is up to you.*

Deere & Company 1989 Annual Report, Moline, Iowa, p. 19.

Personal Guidelines

As exciting as the high-tech developments are, the practical solutions
to the problems of everyday information management are likely to
come from individual, personal approaches. Information technology,
seen in proper perspective, is just another tool to be managed. It is a
valuable and highly complex tool, of course. But for all its time-
saving potential, information technology is a very time-consuming resource at present. Accordingly, we need (1) first to get a firm grip on
our information sources and their potential value and (2) then to develop a set of fundamental approaches for utilizing these resources in
the most time-productive way. That's the path you'll be shown in this
chapter.

TIME SIGHT: A Self-Appraisal

How Fast a Paper Shuffler Are You?

The flow of information inundates some people. They are buried by a
paperwork snowstorm. Others seem to be able to shuffle paper fast
enough to avoid such disasters. They do this not for bureaucratic reasons
but in order to make the best use of the wealth of information available
with the least inroads on their time. This exercise is provided to give you
some idea of where you stand when it comes to having the "information
smarts."

Instructions. For each statement in the left-hand column, place a check
mark in the column to the right that best expresses your reaction.

	Least like me	Neither least nor most like me	Most like me
A. You place highest priority on reviewing information that relates to output, quality, and costs.	_____	_____	_____
B. You pay little attention to historical records since they offer very little help in solving current problems.	_____	_____	_____
C. You defer examination of daily operating reports until the end of the week; that way, you won't be distracted by daily fluctuations.	_____	_____	_____
D. When confronted by a problem that you haven't faced before, you look first for information about how someone else has solved a similar problem.	_____	_____	_____
E. In your search for problem-solving information, you rely on your instincts about where best to find it.	_____	_____	_____
F. When you discover an information source, you tell the supplier, "Give me everything you've got."	_____	_____	_____
G. You've learned that when it comes to retaining paperwork, you'd better hang on to everything, since sooner or later someone will want it.	_____	_____	_____
H. Your motto is, "Act fast on important paperwork."	_____	_____	_____
I. You treat all information that goes through your hands with equal accuracy, precision, and care.	_____	_____	_____
J. When you read for information, you find that it pays to study every line of the text so that you don't miss something important.	_____	_____	_____

Scoring. Each check mark is worth 1, 2, or 3 points, based upon the following table:

	Least like me	Neither least nor most like me	Most like me
A	1	2	3
B	3	2	1

C	3	2	1
D	1	2	3
E	3	2	1
F	3	2	1
G	3	2	1
H	1	2	3
I	3	2	1
J	3	2	1

Caveat. Scores are based on speed in assimilating, utilizing, and/or disposing of information, rather than on a fully comprehensive weighing of all factors that might or might not apply in a given situation.

Interpretation. You're a world-class information handler if you scored from 24 to 30. From 17 to 23, you're still in the minor leagues. Under 17, you're going to get buried in an information overload.

Information at the Ready

In the midst of the information revolution, the practical concepts about information remain pretty much the same. First of all, information might just as well be called *data, intelligence,* or *knowledge.* There has been a traditional distinction, however, between data and information, although most people no longer observe it. *Information* was defined as processed data—data made useful—and *data* was thought to consist primarily of numbers or other quantitative designations. Today, the two terms are commonly interchangeable.

Classes of Information

From a practical point of view, it helps to classify the information to which you are exposed in the following ways.

1. *Current operating information*—the information you need—at work or at home—to keep on top of things, to order supplies when you need them, and to settle accounts when they are due. In most business situations, operating information is routinely provided, or passed on, in printed formats. Such current information can be divided into two groups, listed below.
   a. *Information received.* Pay close attention to these high-priority items:
   (1) Operating or production schedules

(2) Standards and specifications

(3) Expense and equipment-utilization budgets

(4) Sales and income budgets, if they pertain

b. *Information generated.* Be accurate and prompt in collecting and transmitting these high-priority items:

(1) Records of what was produced and when and how much of it was produced

(2) Reports of how the output may have varied from quality standards

(3) Expenditures of resources, especially for labor-hours, equipment utilization, utilities consumption, and other out-of-pocket or direct expenses such as traveling and operating supplies

The above items are in the mainstream and warrant the bulk of your daily time and attention. Of course, dozens of other bits of information also impinge upon current activities. These include policy memorandums as well as rules and regulations for safety, security, and data processing. You cannot disregard these, but they are not usually so important as information that has to do directly with output, quality, and costs—and ultimately with profits.

2. *Problem-solving and resource information*—the kind of nonurgent information that you should collect and retain more or less permanently. Much of the data can be copied or removed from current operating information. The balance must be gathered selectively from the wealth of information sources that surround you. This information will take time to accumulate, index, and file, but it has large and continuing payoffs. It is valuable because it will help you with the following activities.

a. *Confirming past history.* Almost all problem-solving attempts begin with assembling the facts. In far too many instances, the only facts examined are the obvious or hastily—and dimly—recollected ones. "Let's see," says the inventory manager, "I think that's the same kind of shipment that was late the last time." Was it? Time flies and memories are short—and often unreliable. A look at your retained records can verify recollections or provide information that has been completely forgotten.

b. *Finding standard solutions.* Solving the same problem over and over again is a real time waster. If your records and references are complete, you have only to check a standard operating procedures manual, a handbook, a manufacturer's specifications sheet, or your record of how the problem was solved before to find a quick, reliable solution.

c. *A basis for finding new solutions.* When new and different situations are encountered, it is wasteful to approach them hit-or-miss. Your files should provide—or lead you to—background material and basic data about a new process or product, a different material, a new customer, or an unusual request. You may not find any pat answers, but you will probably find a starting point from which to build possible solutions.

Speed of Delivery

Practically speaking, knowledge, intelligence, data, facts, and figures do not become useful information until they have been placed in the hands of the people who need them. The faster the information gets into their hands, the better. Traditionally, there were formidable delays in making information available. A month was not unusual. Today, there are few technical excuses for such delays. This area, nevertheless, is one to watch carefully, keeping in mind that three kinds of time-related information are encountered:

Delayed Information. When low priority is placed upon availability, delays occur. Collection, processing, and transmission are allowed to follow traditional accounting periods. The information arrives at a work station or a manager's office a week or a month after the fact—usually too late to do anything but plan ahead for the next operating interval.

Right-Now, Nonrecorded Information. Information that is merely observed or passed on by word of mouth is *nonrecorded*. When this information is received as the event happens or the condition occurs, it is also "right now," or *real time*. If, additionally, the observation is signaled or transmitted by the operation itself, it is on-line. This triple play occurs, for example, when a sensing device, attached to a machine, signals the completion of a finished part (or the temperature of the process) to a computer system that transmits the data immediately and directly to a cathode-ray tube (CRT) display screen. Real-time information is often the best kind, since it is timely and not subject to errors accumulated as it passes through a complex collecting and reporting network. In principle, therefore, the goal of obtaining real-time information, if only by word of mouth from operator to manager, is to be sought in every situation. If a sale is about to be canceled because of a shipping delay, an immediate telephone call from a salesperson in the field to the marketing manager is far more valuable—and less time-consuming—than is a complete and detailed report that won't be available for a responsive action until it's delivered in the mail three or four days later.

Right-Now, Recorded Information. In situations in which accumulation, processing, and recording of information are useful, most on-line systems today—whether real-time or not—also can be programmed to record the information. The information may be recorded instantly by a printer at the operator's work station or in the supervisor's office, or it may be stored in the tapes and disks of a computer system. The decision about whether to record or not is essentially an economic one, and two factors are involved: (1) the needs of the information users and (2) the cost of collecting and processing the information and making it available for retrieval.

Classification by Source

Such an abundance of information is available today that it must be assembled and reviewed selectively. Experts in the field are able to simplify the process slightly by establishing two major categories of information (internal and external) and two subordinate ones (primary and secondary).

Data From Internal Sources.   All data generated within an organization in the course of its activities are considered internal. The mass of such internal information is very large indeed. Each of an organization's major and minor functions spews out data. Production and operations, marketing and sales, accounting and finance, engineering and design, inventory control, purchasing, inspection, maintenance, advertising, and credit and collections are only some of an organization's sources of internal data. The catch is that not all this information finds its way into central files. In many cases, you'll have to do some time-consuming bird-dogging to track down internal data that you want.

Data From External Sources.   The amount of readily available information "out there," away from an organization's own files, is simply staggering. It is available from an infinite number of public and private sources. Some of the most extensive information—and least expensive to obtain, but often cumbersome to retrieve—can be found in various agencies of the U.S. government and of the United Nations. Guidelines for exploring external sources will be set forth under "Speeding the Search," below.

Primary Data.   Usually the most expensive and time-consuming data to accumulate, *primary data* are gathered to meet particular needs and are not available from published sources. Some companies (almost all marketers of consumer goods—soaps or cereals, for example) have sufficient need and resources to collect primary data for their own use. They may survey customers to find out their product preferences or their reactions to a new credit plan. They may observe buyers' behavior in supermarkets to gather information about the effects of a certain package design or point-of-purchase display. They may gather highway traffic counts to help select a location for a new store. Despite the obvious expense, in many situations, collecting primary data is the only way to go because relevant and essential information is unavailable any other way. In most instances, nevertheless, collection of primary data should be the course of last resort.

Secondary Data.   Usually the least expensive, quickest data to gather, *secondary data* have been collected and published by others. While such information may have the seeming disadvantage of being available to everyone, including a company's competitors, its advantages are (1) immediate availability and (2) low cost. The major drawback is that selecting exactly what you need can be difficult, because secondary data tend to be all-inclusive. After all, they have not been compiled specifically to solve your organization's problem.

Databases.   The trend today is to assemble interrelated data, from whatever source or of whatever kind, into computer files for easy access, retrieval, and updating. Such a file is called a *database*. It is, in effect, an electronic library. The database may be developed and maintained internally by a company for its own use, or the database may be jointly developed by companies with a mutual interest (such as a hotel or trade association) from which all parties draw information. Some of the largest databases are compiled and maintained by quasi-public agencies. Hundreds of databases are put together by proprietary organizations, which offer access to their files to anyone who will pay the fee. Looking ahead 10 years, the probability is that databases will become the quickest, most selective, and least expensive sources of information.

Speeding the Search

When you are faced with the need to find information, you will get the best results, fastest, by using a systematic approach. What *fastest* means in this context, you should be warned, is "in the long run." Like so many other activities, a productive information search needs heavy front-end time. Start-up can be slow. There is a gap between you and what you are searching for, and if you try to close the gap too soon, you're more likely to encounter frustrations and delays than real substance. In most cases, you would be wiser to work through the systematic procedure outlined below.

The Seven-Step Information Search

This procedure is one that many market researchers have found useful. You may not wish to explore each step in detail—or even in sequence—but you should at least give consideration to the potential offered by each step.

1. *Be specific about what you are looking for.* Begin by describing the result you expect to get from the information. Here is an example involving internal information: "It will tell us whether or not the presently excessive work load in our billing department is normal for this time of year." And here is an example involving an external search: "It will provide data that will help us to make a decision about whether we should change the market focus for product A from teenage girls to women over 35."

Next, working from your clearly stated goal, make a list of the kind of data you think will help. For the internal example above, your list might be as follows: "By month for the last 10 years: (a) number of employees in the billing department, (b) total dollar amount billed, (c) number of invoices prepared." For the external example, the list might read: "Year-by-year over the last decade: (a) demographic figures for the female population; (b) industry sales dollars for similar products, by age groups if possible; (c) discretionary income for single women and married women."

2. *Check the availability of (a) print or recorded and (b) database information.* Print is easier to examine and review; you can riffle and mark the pages for reference. Databases, when available, are quicker to call up; also, they often allow for data manipulation on a personal computer. In either event, at this point you may have to make a preliminary choice between a print search and a database search.

3. *Explore the library—corporate, college, or community.* The list prepared in step 1 will help you to communicate with library specialists. They may, in fact, be able to advise you about step 2—whether the print or the database route will be cheaper or more productive. If the library does not have the references you need on hand, it may be able to obtain them on loan from a state or university library. At the very least, the library specialists will be able to point you to the various directories available in the library.

4. *Consult print directories to identify possible sources.* Traditional directories list organizations, agencies, business firms, people, products, services, etc., that have a single focus or common interest. Your starting point should be a search of basic directories, such as the *Guide to American Directories, The Directory of Directories*, the *Encyclopedia of Associations, The National Directory of Addresses and Telephone Numbers,*

Thomas Register of American Manufacturers, Moody's Industrial Manual, Standard and Poor's Standard Corporation Descriptions, and the *Encyclopedia of Business Information Sources.*

5. *Consult indexes of books, periodicals, and newspapers.* The major starting points for these sources are as follows:

Books—*Subject Guide to Books in Print*

Periodicals—*Ulrich's International Periodicals Directory* and its companion, *Irregular Series and Annuals; Business Periodical Index;* and *Ayer Directory of Publications*

Newspapers—*The New York Times Index* and *The Wall Street Journal Index*

6. *Consult indexes of government publications.* The starting points for particular sources are as follows:

United Nations—*United Nations Document Index* and "United Nations Publications in Print" (yearly)

U.S. federal agencies—*Monthly Catalog of United States Government Publications;* a microfiche index titled *Publications Reference File;* periodically the *Index of U.S. Government Periodicals;* and the *United States Government Manual* that lists information about legislative, judicial, and executive branches, federal agencies, and quasi-official and international agencies in which the United States participates

State agencies—*Monthly Checklist of State Publications;* local "blue books"; and information from local chambers of commerce and industrial development commissions

7. *Consult the directories of on-line, computerized databases.* As databases proliferate, it is increasingly important that you select from among them only the most useful electronic sources. Currently, among commonly available directories are: *Directory of On-Line Information Resources* (Rockville, Maryland), *Database Catalog* (Palo Alto, California), and for specialized federal databases, *Information USA* (Chevy Chase, Maryland, and *Information Sources* (of electronic news services). The largest of databases include *COMSEARCH* (mainly for the scientific field), *DIALOG* (for the technologies, engineering, business, economics, and medicine), and *NEXIS* (which gives access to the full texts and abstracts of hundreds of major newspapers and periodicals).

Your Own Information System

Since the "whiz kids" of the Kennedy era introduced the concept to the Pentagon in the 1960s, the management information systems (MIS) has become the popular approach to getting control of information in large, complex organizations. The basic principle of MIS is so simple, however, that it can form a basis for an individual's own information system.

TIME BYTE 4-2
Rocky Mountain Keg Mail

Adolph Coors, the Rocky Mountain brewer, operates a bells-and-whistles kind of MIS between its Elkton, Virginia, plant and its headquarters in Golden, Colorado. Called the KEG system, it logs information back and forth between its 350 managers and employees at Elkton and 30 interested parties in Golden, reporting data for manufacturing processes, quality, maintenance, engineering, and accounting. It also serves as an electronic bulletin board at Elkton, announcing schedule changes, job postings, and other activities. Its electronic mail feature reduces telephone usage and eliminates bothersome "telephone tag." The system also schedules meetings, allowing attendees to confirm, reject, or delay, and when there are conflicts, it will continue to seek a convenient time. *Sounds like a great MIS into which to plug an individual information system.*

"Know-It-All: Coors' 'Kegs' Computer Shows Its Range," by Betty Skeens, *Daily News-Record*, Harrisonburg, Virginia, Dec. 23, 1989, p. 11.

MISs

MISs in large organizations are almost always computer-driven. The amount of information handled can be managed only by computers that can accept, classify, sort, compute, update, and otherwise process millions of bits of information a second and then make them instantly available in processed form for retrieval, for transmission to other information networks, and—most important—in response to inquiries from hundreds of participants in the system. The integrative nature of MISs and their ability to respond to inquiries is what differentiates them from databases. Managers can use an MIS not only to retrieve information from up, down, and across an organization, but they can also ask "what if" questions of it—and get answers. For example: "What if we added another billing clerk? How much would it speed up our billing process?" or "What if we dropped our prices by 10 percent? What would that do to our breakeven point?" The number of such questions that can be put to an MIS is limitless.

The inner workings of an MIS are not what's important to you. What it can do for you is what's important. Broadly speaking, a *management information system* can be defined as a system that (1) makes information from all important functions and activities of an organization available so as (2) to serve the information needs of managers at different levels by (3) providing information in a useful format on (4) a timely basis (5) to support planning and control decisions.

If your employer has an MIS, to which you have access, you can get the most out of it while reducing its demands upon your time by doing the following:

1. *Ask for only as much data as you need.* Little extra conveniences in terms of breakouts and details can add enormously to the costs of designing and operating the system. Since computer printouts are so voluminous, such details can easily overload your own capacity to assimilate the information when it is delivered to you.

2. *Shut off the information you don't need and don't use.* Ask the MIS managers to discontinue excess information, duplicate copies, and overlapping reports.

An Individual Information System

If you were to strip an MIS down to its fundamentals and remove the computer processor from it, you'd have a system that looks like the one in Figure 4-1. Note that its information is gathered from internal and external sources in order to provide primary and secondary data. Decision making is aimed at preparing plans, goals, and actions in order to get results. The results are compared with standards or other criteria. If corrective action is indicated, the decision process is repeated. If additional information is needed, this, too, can be relayed to the data sources, which will then seek to retrieve or reformat the relevant material.

To see how a manager might develop an individual MIS based upon the chart above, look at Figure 4-2. The manager in this case uses as her primary data the information generated each day in her own department. Her secondary data—information available from outside her own department—are industry figures she has found on file in the company's central office.

The manager has set performance standards (right-hand block) at 500 units per day, labor costs at $6000 per week, and reject (or defect) rate at 1.5 percent. She has also made a basic decision to staff the department with 20 employees and to operate 8 hours per day.

To put her information system into operation, the manager requested the following: daily output figures from the shop clerk; weekly labor costs gathered from time cards, processed by the payroll section, and recorded by the accounting department; and the weekly reject rate from the quality-control department.

For the week displayed in Figure 4-2, the department's daily output has been only 480 units, or 20 below standard. Labor costs were $5700, or $300 less than budgeted. The weekly reject rate was up to 2.0 percent, or 0.5 percent over standard.

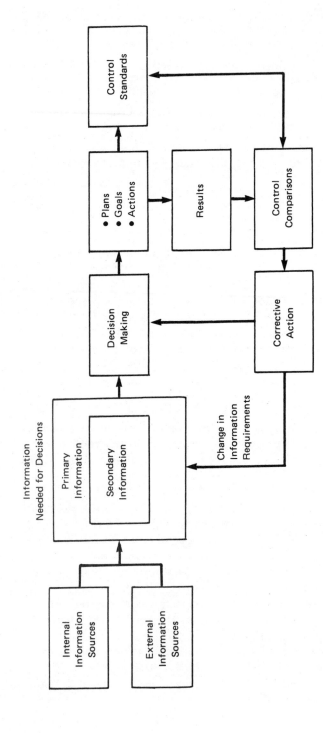

Figure 4-1. Components of an MIS.

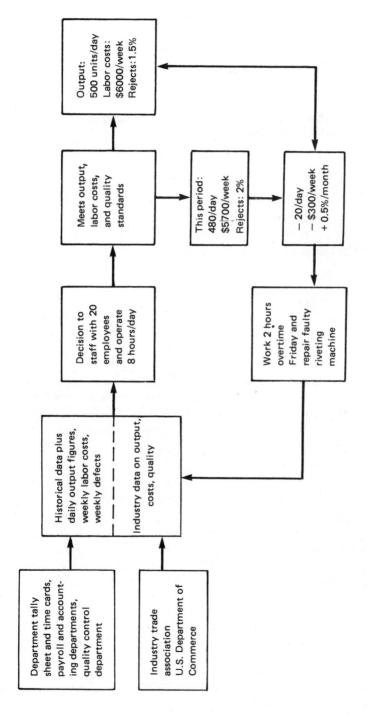

Figure 4-2. An individual or departmental information system.

On the basis of this information, the manager decided to take the corrective action shown in the lower-center block: The entire staff will work overtime for 2 hours on Friday to raise output to the desired level for the week. The supervisor will also place a maintenance request to fix a faulty riveting machine, to which the higher reject rate is attributed.

Shortening Your Information-Handling Time

The big picture in information handling is technology, classification, speed searching, and application—mainly by means of a formal or personal MIS. Another aspect of information handling, however, that is equally important is the way you approach its more commonplace manifestations—paperwork and everything associated with it. Below are some tips on how to speed up the handling of information, not as an abstraction but in the pragmatic world of work.

Stemming the Paperwork Flow

Paperwork is just another name for information in printed form. From a personal point of view, paperwork comes across your desk from three sources:

Operating data—interoffice memos, daily operating printouts, quality-control records, payroll sheets, purchase orders, sales-call reports, expense vouchers, and the like. You need these to run the shop and to keep informed about the progress of your performance.

General reading material—business magazines, technical journals, catalogs, advertising data, reference books, and pamphlets. You'll want to read most of these in hopes of learning something new about your job and keeping abreast of developments that may affect it.

Extraneous matter—any of the two previous kinds of materials coming across your desk *that you don't need*. These may be things that you once requested but that are no longer germane. Such extraneous matter, of trivial worth, can account for as much as two-thirds of what hits your in-basket.

What to do about it? Let's begin by admitting that much of the paperwork that snows you under originates from sources beyond your control. Consider, nevertheless, these simple rules for making you the boss of your desk:

1. *Use the wastebasket.* Free yourself from clutter by disposing of extraneous material immediately—in the circular file.

2. *Cancel everything that you don't need.* As mentioned earlier, you may have to request that the MIS center discontinue unwanted material. Also take time to ask that your name be dropped from the mail lists of irrelevant publishers and advertisers (most of whom will be happy to save the distribution expense) and from internal circulation lists.

3. *Set aside the material that can wait until later.* For reading that appears to be interesting but not urgent, keep a table or bookshelf nearby. Glance through magazines, for example, as they arrive, insert gummed slips at articles you want to read further, then put the magazine on your table or bookshelf—off your desk—to be read in spare moments or at home. If the set-aside pile accumulates, riffle through it once a week and discard what no longer seems of interest.

4. *Act fast on important paperwork.* You probably don't have to be told not to sit on a request from your boss. But it's dangerous—and inconsiderate, too—to defer action or a response on essential paperwork that affects other internal operations, to say nothing of a matter involving a customer.

5. *Don't let paperwork pile up.* It will pile up, of course, if you do not act on it promptly. At the very least, dispose of small matters quickly. Then block out larger periods of time for handling paperwork that requires investigation and reflection.

6. *Leave a clean desk at night.* Try not to leave without having answered all routine mail and cleaned up normal paperwork. Few things will give you a slower start in the morning than to be greeted by a desktop piled with unfinished business—or a desk drawer crammed with deferred responses.

7. *Try desktop sorting.* Some people find it helpful to maintain a number of auxiliary in-baskets on their desks. They use a variety of classification systems, with A ("urgent"), B ("must do soon"), and C ("no time limit") the most popular. Others use "daily," "weekly," and "end-of-month." Still others like to pigeonhole paperwork requests according to their purpose, such as "payroll," "purchase orders," "expense vouchers," and "call reports." Generally speaking, a simple system will work best—mainly because it will force you to either act on or discard each item that crosses your desk.

8. *Avoid needless acknowledgments and confirmations.* In many routine cases, you can follow the "No news is good news" rule. As cynical as that attitude may be, you will save yourself time if you proceed on the basis that if the sender is worried about your receipt of a document, the sender can provide the follow-up. If this approach appears too negative to you, see the next item.

9. *Handwrite responses on the original document.* Especially for internal communications, a handwritten note on the memo or document itself disposes of the paperwork quickly. Of course, sometimes you may want to make a copy for your files.

10. *Guard against carrying precision too far.* Most transactions—even those involving dollars and cents—need not be carried out to the minutest detail. After all, a good many records are expressed as percentages or in broad, summary figures. Try in each case to find out what degree of accuracy is really needed by the people who use the information requested. Then compute and process the information accordingly. Or, if you wish to verify accuracy, try spot-checking for errors rather than inspecting line by line.

TIME BYTE 4-3
Newfangled Filing Cabinets

"Your department staff may spend 16 hours per week looking for missing information.... Wasted time is your company's most costly problem. Managers and clerical staffs often spend 25–40% of their time searching for information that is misfiled or missing." That's the claim, according to a manufacturer of filing equipment. And the solution, according to the manufacturer, is "color-coded systems with special filing, tracking, and retrieval software...which not only save time, but also reduce space requirements by up to 60% compared with conventional filing methods." *Einstein said it first: time and space are inextricably connected.*

Advertisement in *Today's Office*, Wright Line Inc., Worcester, Massachusetts, January 1990.

Unjamming the Files

A corollary of time-consuming paperwork is its storage—and its retrieval. There is always an immediate and persistent problem of filing forms and records—your own and those of the department you may serve or manage. Luckily, there are ways to simplify files and filing and to speed up retrieval.

1. *Establish beforehand what is important enough to be filed and what may be discarded.* This decision should not be delegated, and it must be clearly communicated to whoever maintains the files.

2. *Base retention on long-term usefulness.* Although it is necessary to follow legal guidelines for records retention, one of the most time- and space-wasting of practices is to keep everything. People who keep everything are usually following the course of least resistance, but they also

want to avoid risk of criticism when a record has not been saved—the CYA (cover your anatomy) principle. The sad fact is that, even in the best-designed and best-maintained filing systems, an occasional important document will be tossed away or misplaced. When that happens, the wrath will descend upon you anyway. Consider adopting the cynical viewpoint: It's quicker to be able to say, "We don't keep that sort of record," than to be so much of an archivist that you are a continual target of requests for information.

3. *Set as your goal the slimmest file possible.* In order to attain that objective, answer each of the following questions before relegating anything to your filing cabinet:

- How useful is this information in carrying out your responsibilities?
- How often is this information needed?
- Can you discard other records now if you hold onto just this record?
- Can this information be duplicated easily from other sources if needed?
- Is it necessary to retain this document for legal purposes? Might it be needed later as evidence to avoid or settle lawsuits about employment, accidents, product liabilities, deliveries, contracts, etc.?
- How important is this material to people outside your department? Is your file the main source of this information? Do others rely upon you to maintain this record?

Reading Faster and Better

A decade ago, great emphasis was placed upon speed reading—and the concept of saving valuable time by assimilating written material more quickly still prevails, although the term *speed reading* is less often heard now. Perhaps the problem with speed-reading courses was that they were too complex or too dependent upon mechanical pacing devices. Or they may have concentrated upon reading in the classical sense, rather than upon what is important in work situations—assimilation of content.

As a matter of practical fact, the guidelines that will help you to read faster and better are relatively simple and easy to follow:

1. *Have your eyesight checked.* If you need reading glasses, get them and use them.

2. *Recognize the mechanics.* The eye does not move smoothly across the printed page, but in a series of jerks and stops. When your eye moves, it sees only a blur. When it stops (or fixes), it sees. Fortunately, your eye can see (or span) several words at a time. For example, you

ought to be able to read "units of production," in one span. Most slow readers have narrow span and need six fixes to read a line of print. With practice, you can read a line in three or four fixes.

3. *Read with a purpose.* Don't just stare blankly at a page. Try to form a partnership with it. Ask yourself, *"Why* am I reading this?" *"What* do I expect to gain from it?" Answers to these questions will help to focus your perceptions. If you are reading a technical article, for instance, in order to find ways for retail clerks to avoid errors while entering sales, you'll pay greatest attention to *key words*, sentences, and ideas that suggest "entering procedures," "reduced errors," "keyboarding," "typical entry mistakes," and the like. You'll want to skim over fringe material such as locale, personalities, or anything else not directly relevant to your purpose. If you read an article to find ways to induce a customer to make additional purchases, you'll establish an entirely different mindset and different key words. The point is that when you read for information, you must read very selectively. There is no time to enjoy the luxury of admiring the writer's style or of absorbing everything that the article may include.

4. *Search for the main ideas.* Most fast readers look deliberately for the main ideas that can be skimmed off. Once having found the main ideas, such readers retrace their steps and read about the main points more slowly.

In skimming, you read vertically, running your eyes down the center of the column or page, zigzagging from left to right, picking up key words and phrases. Many key words are, in fact, boldfaced or italicized to help you pick them up. Another way to spot meaningful words is to look for nouns and verbs. Writers use them to tell the main part of the story. They use descriptive words (adjectives and adverbs) mainly to embellish. As a consequence, adjectives and adverbs aren't too important to the main point.

Specifically, here's how to read in such a way as to find the main ideas in a variety of written formats:

In a business letter, the first paragraph usually tells the story.

In a newspaper article, read headlines, then subheads, then the first paragraph. Read further only if you want details.

In a technical journal or business periodical, read the title of the article, the blurb, and the first paragraph. Then check subheads, boldfaced and italicized type, and set-off material.

In a reference book or text, start with the preface, introduction, and table of contents. This will tell you a lot about the book without your having to read further. Then read the first paragraphs and chapter-ending summaries of the first and last chapters, while only skimming the rest of the text. Treat other chapters in which you are interested in the same manner.

5. *Avoid bad habits.*   Faster reading comes from practice—and from breaking, or avoiding bad habits. In particular, avoid:

Narrow spans.   Make a conscious effort to extend your "eye photograph" so that you need only four or five fixes per line of book-width text.

Long fixations.   Don't allow your eyes to hold a fix too long. Keep forcing your eyes ahead.

Lack of concentration.   Don't daydream or reflect. Reading means hard work. If you pay strict attention, assimilation will come much more quickly.

Regression.   Rereading phrases or sentences is one of the worst things you can do. In most cases, what you've missed isn't important. Keep moving forward.

Inward speech.   Saying words to yourself—using your lips or any part of the vocal apparatus—puts brakes on your speed.

Improving Your Deskmanship

Popular advice has it that people should "go with the flow" of their environment rather than contrary to it. When it comes to managing the flood of paperwork across your desk, however, a better admonition is, "Control the flow." A good starting point is to treat your desk—at home or in your professional life—as the vital work station on which you will implement your plans for mastering time. An especially effective desk layout was conceived by Robert C. Lowery.* An updated version is shown in Figure 4-3.

Equipment.   The work station is furnished with: an in-basket, an "urgent now" basket, and an out-basket—for receiving, staging, and returning documents; a desk-drawer file to hold materials and documents awaiting processing; a desk tray to which are taped a list of your most frequently called telephone numbers and a "data bank" of essential, frequently referred to facts (addresses, dimensions, sizes, capacities, social security numbers, credit card numbers, etc.); a telephone; a calendar; a clock with a timing component; a typewriter or word processor, or a PC (with keyboard, display screen, printer, modem, and interconnect input/output devices); a comfortable chair; and a very large wastebasket.

Arrangement.   Your tools and equipment should be arranged for your own convenience. The layout in Figure 4-3 is convenient for many right-handed people. Left-handed people and some right-handed people may not find it comfortable and should adapt it to suit themselves.

---

*Robert C. Lowery, "The Organized Workplace," in *Supervisory Management: Guidelines for Application,* Prentice-Hall, Englewood Cliffs, N.J., 1985, p. 477.

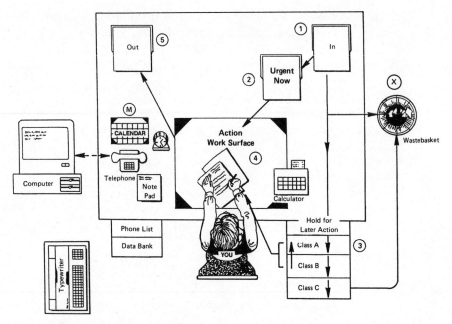

Figure 4-3. A master desk or workplace layout.

Paperwork flow should be roughly U-shaped. That is, incoming mail or requests, received by telephone or in person, should be placed in (1) the in-basket in the upper right-hand corner. Incoming documents should be sorted as soon as possible and routed toward you for (2) immediate action in your "urgent now" basket or (3) filing in the holding file of your desk drawer. Urgent items should move as soon as possible to (4) your work surface for action. When you have completed an item, it goes to (5) the out-basket on the left-hand corner.

Many items should be diverted quickly to (X) your wastebasket before they get into your holding file.

Holding Files.   Incoming items that you judge not to be so urgent as to require your immediate action (2) can go to your file drawer (3). In that drawer, it is a good idea to have three manila envelopes marked:

Class A items.   These need action, review, or response within a week.

Class B items.   These require action, review, or response within a month, but not necessarily within a week.

Class C items.   These (magazines, brochures, historical reports) can be deferred for review at your convenience before being relegated to your wastebasket or placed in a permanent file, magazine rack, or bookshelf.

Action Plan. It is important to review your class A file daily so as to arrange items in order of urgency for work-surface action. Keep this file very slim, since it should contain no more than 5 days of work. You should review class B items weekly and move those requiring action within a week forward into your class A file.

If you have a computer screen (or electronic mail), this is another source of incoming items, and its output device can serve as an out-basket if it is connected to other work stations.

In general, a well-controlled paperwork flow will (1) place only one item on your action work surface at a time and (2) keep only a very few items in your class A file.

PRACTICE TIME 4-1: A Self-Directed Exercise
"When You Have Nothing Else to Do..."

It's a typical workday for you. A dozen items will require your attention and action. These items will arrive at your desk by mail or messenger, through a telephone call, or on your computer screen. Your feeling is that everyone wants a piece of your time. Nevertheless, you have to sort it all out and handle it in some sort of systematic fashion. Your desk is arranged very much like the one in Figure 4-3, and you can use the code letters and numbers from that figure in doing this exercise.

Assignment. Each of the dozen items that reaches your desk is described below. Your job is to decide how you will dispose of them. In the space to the right of each statement, write the code letter or number of the place where you decide to put that item. You may use the same place for more than one item. If you wish, you may also assign a second step in a disposal route for an item.

Item description	Disposition
A. Your boss just called and wants an answer to a question within the next 15 minutes.	_____
B. A brochure arrives in the mail describing a conference that you are sure you will never attend.	_____
C. A form comes from the personnel department that must be completed and returned by next Monday.	_____
D. You are invited to a reception for a retiring employee in a couple of weeks. You are asked to let the company know today whether you will attend.	_____

E. The production control department sends
    you an agenda for a meeting you already
    know about that is to be held a week and
    a half from today.   _____

F. You are notified that there will be a
    telephone-conference call from a branch
    office in which you must participate next
    Friday at 3:30 p.m.   _____

G. An associate sends you a work-related
    book, with the notation, "There is some
    really good stuff in this that you ought to
    read when you get a chance."   _____

H. The safety committee, of which you are a
    member, sends you a memo advising you
    that, though the report the committee is
    working on need not be completed for 3
    weeks, the committee needs a couple of
    figures from you this afternoon in order
    to get the project rolling.   _____

I. You receive a form to fill out from the
    payroll department. It is due a couple of
    weeks from now.   _____

J. Your favorite trade magazine arrives in
    the mail; you are glad to see it because it
    usually gives you some good ideas.   _____

K. You open a third-class mail envelope
    containing a sales pitch for a product for
    which you can see no practical use in your
    work.   _____

L. The call signal on your computer display
    screen lights up. You respond
    immediately. It directs you to activate the
    printer, which prints two pages of last
    month's sales figures.   _____

Commentary. Not everyone agrees about how these items should be
handled with the most dispatch. One manager's solutions, however, are as
follows:

Item		Disposition
A	2	Urgent—now basket.
B	X	Wastebasket.
C	3A	Class A holding file.
D	2	Urgent—now basket; but if you accept, enter date on your calendar, M.

E	3B	Class B holding file.
F	3A	Class A holding file; but also check your calendar, M, to make sure the date has been entered and flagged.
G	3C	Class C holding file.
H	2	Urgent—now basket; then move memo to class B holding file, 3B.
I	3B	Class B holding file.
J	3C	Class C holding file.
K	X	Wastebasket.
L	1	In-basket for segregation decision; then probably move to class C holding file, 3C.

TIME CHECK

Use this action-plan checklist to verify your understanding of the various concepts, ideas, and techniques presented in this chapter and to indicate any need for further action on your part.

	Applies to your situation		Schedule for action	
	Yes	No	Yes	No
1. Identification and classification of the information at your disposal as (a) current operating information or (b) problem-solving and resource information.	____	____	____	____
2. A premium placed on right-now, real-time information.	____	____	____	____
3. Identification and classification of potential sources of information as either *internal* or *external*.	____	____	____	____
4. Identification of data as either *primary* (gathered to meet a particular need and not available elsewhere) or *secondary* (collected and published by others).	____	____	____	____
5. Knowledge of the availability of relevant *databases*, which are, essentially, electronic libraries.	____	____	____	____

6. Ability to mount a seven-step information search, emphasizing the specification of information needed, consideration of print versus electronic sources, library search as a start, and consulting of directories and indexes.   ____ ____ ____ ____

7. Preparation of your own information system as a guide to simplifying your own problem solving and decision making.   ____ ____ ____ ____

8. Shortening of paperwork handling time by eliminating extraneous matter, using the wastebasket, and shutting off information you don't need.   ____ ____ ____ ____

9. Simplification of filing and retrieval by making clear decisions about what should be retained, basing retention decisions on careful estimates of usefulness, and keeping your files as slim as possible.   ____ ____ ____ ____

10. Improvement of your reading speed.   ____ ____ ____ ____

11. Acceleration of information flow across your desk or work station by having the right equipment, properly arranged, and by following an action plan that emphasizes (a) having only one item on your action-surface at a time and (b) retaining a minimum number of items in your class A holding file.   ____ ____ ____ ____

5
Managing Your Problem-Solving Time

How to save time when solving problems, and how to avoid procrastination when making decisions

As a strategic weapon, time is the equivalent of money, productivity, quality, even innovation. GEORGE STALK, JR.
Harvard Business Review

Today, you have to be fast on your feet. You've also got to be flexible.
ROSABETH MOSS KANTOR
When Giants Learn to Dance

Dr. Rosabeth Moss Kantor, noted Harvard University professor, is a leading spokesperson for a faster-moving, more flexible style of business leadership. She warns of the need to keep up with the dynamics of today's world when she says, "Bureaucracies of all kinds are too slow moving, too hierarchical, too tied up in red tape to be effective in a competitive global environment." The implications are broad. Managers and professionals who wish to survive and succeed must be fast on their feet—especially in spotting problems and taking decisive action to solve them.

TIME SIGHT: A Self-Appraisal

How Quickly Do You Solve Problems?

In solving problems and making decisions, how many of the following statements represent your practices or line of thought? Place a check mark opposite each statement in the column that best represents your opinion.

	Agree	Neither agree nor disagree	Disagree
1. When a variance appears between expected and actual performance, you know that you've got a problem.	____	____	____
2. Problems occur spontaneously without any rhyme or reason.	____	____	____
3. There have been lots of changes in your department recently: you can expect fewer problems from now on.	____	____	____
4. A problem is solved by removing its causes.	____	____	____
5. Reggie states his production problem this way: "We're having trouble with our output these days." This will lead him quickly to the heart of the matter.	____	____	____
6. If you know the cause of a problem, it's a waste of time to consider more than one alternate solution.	____	____	____
7. It's a good idea to delegate as many problems as possible to subordinates for solving.	____	____	____
8. You remain calm when faced with a critical decision.	____	____	____
9. If you have a difficult problem, it makes sense to postpone it until you have the time and information to solve it properly.	____	____	____

10. When it comes to problems and
    decisions, it's realistic to assume that
    you won't be right all the time.   ____   ____   ____

Scoring. Give yourself 1 point for each of these items you *agreed* with: 1,
4, 7, 8, 10. Give yourself 1 point for each of these items you *disagreed*
with: 2, 3, 5, 6, 9. You get no points for items checked as *Neither agree
nor disagree.*

Interpretation. If you scored 9 or 10 points, you seem well prepared to
handle problems quickly and effectively. If you scored 8 or under, you're
likely to leave too many problems unsolved and to arrive at faulty
decisions.

Problem-Solving Time

Paradoxically, lower-level managers must solve many more problems
each day than do upper-level managers. Problems at the lower level are
smaller, of course, but they strike with machine-gun frequency. Ten an
hour is not unusual. First-level managers, then, cannot afford to delay
in finding solutions and rendering decisions. If they do not respond
quickly, chaos will reign on the shop floor as the problems queue up
waiting for action. Because problems at middle and upper levels of
management are more complex and often have far-reaching implications, there is a natural tendency for managers at those levels to procrastinate. While hasty, haphazard decisions are always risky, problems
that remain unattended rarely grow smaller. In most instances, they become larger. The antidote for delay and procrastination at all levels
seems to lie in faster problem recognition and a more focused search
for solutions.

 TIME BYTE 5-1

Problem-Solving Personalities

Can you believe a test that helps to pick basketball players for the
Phoenix Suns and managers for Honeywell, Inc? There is one that seems
to do just that. Developed by Kathy Kolbe, a management consultant, this
test identifies four particularly interesting types of personalities, each with
its own set of desirable characteristics:

   The *fact finder*, who evaluates, probes, and deliberates
   The *follow-through*, who coordinates, plans, and schedules

The *quick start*, who originates, experiments, and improvises

The *implementer*, who crafts, constructs, repairs, and demonstrates

The test points up the fact that people tend to develop specialized personalities, that few people are suited for every kind of situation. Fact finders make good problem solvers, and follow-throughs make good planners. Implementers are just right for carrying out decisions. And quick starts are handy to have around when an organization has to play fast-break ball. *To make the "time savers" team, you may need a little of each kind of personality.*

"New Test Quantifies the Way We Work," by Earl C. Gottschalk, Jr., *The Wall Street Journal*, Feb. 7, 1990, p. B1.

Faster Problem Recognition

Problems that are detected in their earliest stages are the easiest to deal with, as most people would agree. Why, then, do problems remain hidden for so long? It is usually because people don't recognize what a problem is in the first place. *A problem exists when there is a difference between an expected condition (such as a goal or standard) and the actual condition.* There is a problem, for example, when a customer wants 100 dozen cases shipped today and there are only 90 dozen cases in your warehouse. To take another example, there is a problem if your budget is based upon raw materials costing only $1.25 a pound and your supplier announces an increase to $1.30 a pound. Another sort of problem arises when you expect a subordinate to greet an announced change with enthusiasm and the response is distinctly negative. Based upon the definition above, the presence of a problem can be spotted more quickly if you are alert to:

- A *difference* between what *should* have occurred and what *is* occurring, or has occurred. The differences can be size, appearance, timing, attitude, performance, or any other condition that has been established as important.

- An *unplanned change* in the way things are being done. The change can occur in a process or procedure, the reporting system, or any other ongoing activity.

Speeding Up the Solution

Problem solving takes place when a conscious effort is made to reduce or eliminate the difference between the actual and the expected condition. It is important, however, not to jump to conclusions. The problem-solving process, as illustrated in Figure 5-1, consists of seven steps. Each

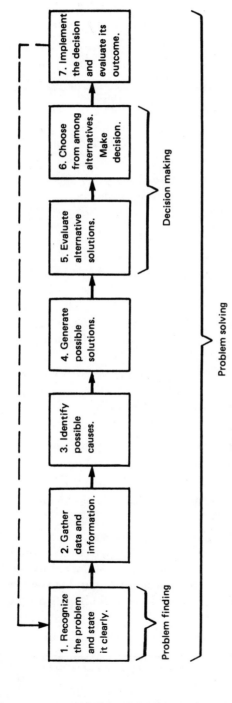

Figure 5-1. The problem-solving process, incorporating decision making and implementation.

97

step is part of a rational analysis and depends upon completion of the previous step; thus, the steps should be taken in sequence. That may seem like the long way, but in terms of effective use of your time, it is the short way.

Step 1. *Recognize the problem and state it clearly.*   Vagueness and generalization will slow down the search for a solution. Don't say, for example, "There's a problem with the cost of raw materials." Instead, say, "The problem is that the cost of raw materials will be 5 cents a pound higher beginning the first of next month than the cost estimates that were projected originally." Note that there is no implication in the statement of either a cause or a solution. To include either is to invite wild-goose chases.

Step 2. *Gather data and information that further specify the problem and conditions related to it.*   Ask questions such as:

When did it, or will it, happen?

Will it affect other raw material prices?

Are price reductions anticipated elsewhere?

Is this price increase being made across the industry or only to selected customers?

Step 3. *Identify possible causes of the problem.*   The list of possible causes should be as long as possible. Unlikely ones can be weeded out later. Questioning should focus on identification of changes that might have occurred. Ask, for instance:

Have we changed our specifications for quality, packaging, or delivery times?

Has the supplier changed instructions to us?

Has there been any change in our relationships with the supplier?

Has the market for these raw materials grown larger?

Are there more or fewer suppliers now than before?

Each question implies the possibility of a change. When the investigation shows no change in the suspect condition, it can be eliminated as a cause.

Step 4. *Develop alternate solutions.*   Remember, it is a waste of time to try to draw solutions from the thin air. The path to solutions is found by removing the possible causes that were not eliminated in step 3. The target is always removal of causes—closing the gap between "what is" and "what should be." Four popular search techniques are especially helpful at this stage:

- *Policy and procedure reviews,* which often lead quickly to proven solutions.
- *Networking,* in which the problem solver seeks ideas from qual-

ified people with whom a relationship has previously been established. This approach has the special virtue of identifying proven solutions without first having to evaluate their effectiveness.

- *Brainstorming*, by which ideas are sought through group ideation. This technique is fully explored in Chapter 8.
- *Nominal group technique (NGT)*, which is a variation of brainstorming. NGT solicits ideas written on slips of paper from groups gathered to solve a problem. The ideas are posted on a chart and discussed, and their appropriateness is voted upon. This time-consuming approach is suitable mainly for problems that affect many people and/or are of great importance.

As indicated in Figure 5-1, it is at the next step that problem solving switches to decision making.

Decision-Making Time

Decision making encompasses steps 5 and 6 of the problem-solving process: evaluation of alternatives and choice of a solution. Step 7—implementation of the solution—requires action, which may or may not be the responsibility of the decision maker.

Step 5. *Evaluate alternate solutions.*   This step relies on an objective, often mathematical, assessment of the pros and cons of each alternative. Assessments are made more quickly, and more reliably, when the following exists or can be obtained:

- *Criteria for judgment.*   These criteria should specify the various parameters the solution must satisfy, such as cost, space, capacities, timing, and delivery modes.
- *Relevant information for each alternative.*   Data gathered in defining the problem are helpful here, as are data obtainable through the various information sources listed in Chapter 4.

Step 6. *Make a decision.*   This is, essentially, a process of choosing from among the alternatives. The process can be pursued rationally and systematically, or it can be approached intuitively. Most often, both a little rationality and a little intuition are needed. A number of mathematical techniques can also help to demonstrate and/or quantify the relative value of, and risks associated with, each alternative. Such analysis should not be overly prolonged. Otherwise, it leads to equivocation and, often, to procrastination.

Step 7. *Act on the decision.*   Once the decision has been made, implementation should proceed without delay. If there is a solution, it should be implemented. After all, action is the bottom line of the problem-solving process. Without implementation of the solution, the problem would remain unsolved.

TIME BYTE 5-2
Momentum, Even in Politics

Just when we thought momentum was a phenomenon observed only in physics and sports, a New Zealand politician now writes of its significance in political reforms. Apparently, political decisions, like those at ordinary levels of a business firm, are easier to carry out while the blood is still racing high. Roger Douglas, who at various times held the titles minister of police, minister of immigration, and minister of finance "down under," says this of political reforms:

> Speed is essential. Move too slowly, and the consensus that supports [the decision] can collapse before the results are evident.
> Once you build momentum, don't lose it until you have completed the total program.
> Let the dog see the rabbit. People cannot cooperate with the process unless they know where they are going....Spell out your objectives and intentions in advance. If programs are to be implemented in stages, start by publishing a timetable.

This is pretty good advice for implementing any kind of decision.

"The Politics of Successful Structural Reform," by Roger Douglas, *The Wall Street Journal*, Jan. 17, 1990, p. A20.

Problem Screening and Selection

Problem-solving challenges can threaten to overload you on the one hand, while offering unique opportunities on the other. The overload can be avoided by proper screening of the problems that face you. The opportunities lie in delegating to others the problems that are not of vital importance.

Problem Screening

Two techniques, in particular, have proved useful for identifying problems that are vital and urgent, and for separating them from problems of lesser importance. A third technique provides guidelines for screening problems according to their suitability for assistance from one or more employees. Each technique screens a different kind of problem:

1. *Problems arising out of regularly recurring activities.* These are best screened by an activities-time analysis, explained in Chapter 2 and illustrated in Figure 2-2. It helps you to set priorities based upon combined rankings of intrinsic importance, urgency, potential for delegation, and communications. Lower-priority items can be deferred. Many of these are the items identified in the analysis as being suitable for delegation.

2. *Problems of a nonrecurring nature.* These are best screened by ABC analysis—a refinement of what you may already know as Pareto's law, or the 80-20 rule, which predicts that:

> *80 percent of the total value of all the items in any "economic array," such as an inventory, will be accounted for by only 20 percent of the items in that array.*

The obverse also holds true: 20 percent of the total value of all the items in an array will be accounted for by 80 percent of all the items.

In choosing problems to solve, therefore, it is wiser to devote your efforts to the 20 percent of problems that account for most of your difficulties—*the vital few*—than to the 80 percent—*the trival many.* The trivial problems may be annoying, but they don't really add up to much in the way of contributions to profit or loss, success or failure.

ABC analysis carries the 80-20 rule one step further. It recognizes a *gray zone* between the extremes of the vital few problems and the trivial many, and then provides a new set of labels for each class of problem:

> *Class A problems*—the most troublesome and time-consuming, yet the most rewarding when solved
>
> *Class B problems*—the problems that fall somewhere between the most and the least rewarding
>
> *Class C problems*—the least troublesome and time-consuming, and the least rewarding when solved

The class B area helps to make your problem-screening process realistic, since some problems will be hard to assign to either A or C. The ABC classifications are widely accepted, and as a result, communications about them are readily understood.

If you also classify your personal time as A time (most valuable) and C time (least valuable), with B time somewhere in between, then, when faced with a choice of problems to work on, you may be able to match your time against the problems at hand. You accomplish this by asking the following questions and taking whatever actions your answers imply:

- Am I spending my A time on my most vital, goal-related class A problems and activities? If not, what can I do to redirect the distribution of my personal time?
- Am I devoting too much of my A time to class C problems and

activities? If I am, what can I do to change that distribution, such as assigning or delegating the trivial problems to others?

If all goes well, you'll soon be devoting 80 percent of your time to the important 20 percent of your problems—the class A problems! For a further demonstration of ABC analysis, see Practice Time 5-1 at the end of this chapter.

3. *Problems for which employee assistance is especially appropriate.* These problems are best sorted out using the guidelines for seeking help in problem solving shown in Table 5-1. The degree of assistance recommended ranges from "none" to "considerable" and "essential."

Table 5-1. Guidelines for Seeking Help in Problem Solving

Factors to consider	Choice 1: You decide alone.	Choice 2: You consult with one of your employees.	Choice 3: You consult with a group of your employees.
Whose problem is it?	Yours alone.	His or hers.	The group's (ours).
Amount of time.	Not available.	Have some time available.	Plenty of time available.
Expertise.	Fully expert.	Expert advice is needed to fill in gaps in your own knowledge.	Yes, as for choice 2.
Can others add to decision?	No.	Yes.	Yes.
Will you accept suggestions?	Not likely.	Yes, from someone you respect.	Yes, from an effective unit.
Will it help others to carry out the project if they are involved in the decision?	No; you will carry out the project.	Yes; helpful and essential.	Yes; necessary and essential.
Coordination of effort.	Not needed: you will handle it yourself.	Vertical; necessary with your superior or your employees.	Horizontal; needed and necessary among your employees.
Learning value.	No value to anyone else.	Potential value to one employee.	Potential value to group.

Decision Making and Procrastination

Most people agree: decision time is crunch time. For some people, it generates the heat that drives them out of the kitchen. Other people simply procrastinate when faced with a decision, or try to pass the buck to someone else. This is too bad. Why? Because in most circumstances, you've got at least a 50-50 chance of doing the right thing. Extensive deliberation rarely improves the odds. Accordingly, on average, the best approach is to make up your mind fast and commit yourself before you're troubled with self-doubts.

TIME BYTE 5-3
Avoiding Panic at Decision Time

Professional tennis players are notorious for feeling the pressure as they try to close out an important match. Dr. Jim Loehr, a sports educator, says it needn't be that way. To begin with, he identifies four types of panic reactions: the *tank*, in which the player gives up, the *choke*, in which nervousness takes over, *anger*, in which the player loses control and self-destructs, and *challenge*, in which the player picks up confidence and determination and plays his or her best game.

Loehr suggests that to reach the challenge way of coping with stress, a player adopt one or all of the following responses between points:

- *Physical response.* Pumping up, acknowledging a great shot, smiling.
- *Relaxation response.* Stretching, moving, taking deep breaths, taking more time.
- *Preparation response.* Assuming a strong, confident position, focusing eyes on the opponent's court, rehearsing your intended shot.
- *Ritual response.* Moving to a predetermined position, swaying back and forth from a crouched position, pausing as you await the next play.

Tennis or business, these four techniques seem better than nail biting when faced by your next decision.

"Choking," by Jim Loehr, Ed.D., *World Tennis*, February 1990, p. 24.

Choke Time

It would be unrealistic, of course, to dwell too long on the wisdom of making decisions quickly. Many of us simply don't like the responsibility for handling situations in which risks are high. Accordingly, our reactions may take any of three paths: (1) we may do anything we can to avoid the responsibility, (2) we may panic, or (3) we may procrastinate. The first reaction is self-defeating. Managers and similar professionals cannot avoid decision-making situations for long if they are to enjoy successful careers. When panic sets in, however, we're all likely to "choke," much as professional athletes do when they're trying to close out a match. Successful athletes use several techniques, such as those reported in Time Byte 5-3, to relieve the pressure. Many of these techniques can help you, too, at decision time.

Procrastination Time

We all procrastinate at one time or other. We put off doing things we could—and should—do now. Of course, we put off not only decisions but anything that is difficult, tiresome, or unpleasantly time-consuming. When we do it only occasionally, procrastination is harmless. But when procrastination becomes a persistent habit, it is a serious threat to professional and personal success.

Why do people procrastinate? Many causes have been suggested. Acknowledging the causes that affect you most can give you a basis for overcoming the habit.

Fear of Failure.   You may put off difficult work because you are not sure you can do it acceptably. If you are a perfectionist—if you want absolutely excellent results from any effort—you are probably especially prone to fear of failure. In fact, there is probably no human task that can be done perfectly. Most management theorists argue that "good enough" is the proper goal when efforts are directed toward priority goals.

Protective Self-Image.   You may have a view of yourself that prevents you from making a strong and immediate effort. You may be protecting your feelings of mastery by declining to try very hard for anything. Since you never really try, you are not threatened with discovering that your inflated self-image is vulnerable.

Waiting for the Right Time.   You may be placing disproportionate stress on outside events and conditions. You may say you'll start straightening out your bookkeeping after this month is over; then everything will be clear to make a new start. In fact, however, such ideal conditions never materialize.

Preperformance Rewards.   You may find that the rewards you give yourself for performing well—relaxing with a cup of coffee or doing something else enjoyable—are so enticing that you can't wait until you've actually performed. It is easy to say, "There! Now I know what I'm going to do; I'm ready to start right away. I think I'll take a break first." Rewards for performance are excellent ideas, but be sure to give yourself the reward after the accomplishment, not before.

Have You Recognized Yourself Here?   Quite possibly not. Many people find that procrastination doesn't stem from any identifiable cause. It is simply a bad habit. A natural tendency to put off things that require effort has become engrained in behavior patterns. This can be good news. It is easier to break a bad habit than it is to change your personality, for example, from being a perfectionist to not being a perfectionist.

Breaking the Procrastination Habit

Changing entrenched habits, whether time-related or not, is a difficult but not unattainable goal. The essential approach is to block old habits with new and better ones. Several tactics are usually employed:

1. *Make a definite, even radical change in your routine.*   Eliminate behavior that is associated with the habit you want to extinguish. If you procrastinate by drinking coffee and chatting with your coworkers, stop doing this completely for a while. Give up coffee, and tell others that you have given it up. Give yourself mental or physical rewards for any period during which you have stuck to your new habit. Write down a list of the reasons you want to change your behavior and keep it with you; refer to it often.

2. *Allow no exceptions to your new habit early in your campaign.*   If you decide to put your work in priority order and always complete the highest-priority item before tackling the next task, *always* do it.

3. *Begin immediately.*   Making resolutions about a change that will become effective "next week" won't work except in unusual circumstances. If you have time-wasting habits that need to be eliminated, start right now. The rudiments of a successful habit-breaking campaign can be worked out in only a few minutes. You can refine your approach after you have hours or days of success under your belt.

4. *Set up barriers to procrastination.*   Experts suggest these ways for breaking the logjam on your put-off projects:

- *Set a starting time for each planned task.*   Not everything can be done immediately, but establish a definite time for starting each of your planned actions.

- *Generate momentum.* If necessary, start working on an easy, routine matter. Set a definite limit, however, of say 15 minutes or a half-hour, on how long you will perform the easy work before tackling the project you feel like putting off. Use an alarm clock to alert you to when the getting-started period is over.
- *Break major tasks down into subtasks.* Reward yourself for completing each of these smaller units of effort. A break for a soda is fair enough for work taking a few hours. An afternoon off playing tennis or hiking might be justified for a lengthy, difficult project. The idea of subtasks is critical. These are the activities that should appear on your daily agenda, not the major task. Suppose you are preparing the annual budget. Don't write "Annual budget" on your schedule. That will take you weeks. Instead, write "Complete table on projected materials costs." That task can be done in a reasonable amount of time, and it will contribute significantly to preparation of the annual budget.

5. *Try some tricks.* Reformed procrastinators advise that the following techniques really work:

- *Do nothing for 15 minutes.* One busy executive, for instance, just stares at the papers on her desk until the urge to get something done overtakes her.
- *Down-size your goal.* Instead of attempting to make a dozen telephone calls today, for example, settle for a half-dozen. That way, you'll get a sense of accomplishment sooner.
- *Adopt the "so long as I'm here" attitude.* If you've got the file drawer open, perhaps—so long as you're here—you might as well reorganize it as you've planned for months.
- *Try the "spinach method."* If a certain task is unpleasant, as vegetables often are to children, try "eating" it first to get it out of the way so that you can enjoy the more attractive aspects of your job.
- *Play the "penalty game."* Assign a minor penalty—such as missing your favorite TV show—whenever you put off a task that you want to complete.

PRACTICE TIME 5-1: A Self-Directed Exercise
Counting Your ABCs

Charlie Jones, department manager in a cookie factory, made a detailed analysis of his activities and found that his own work time in an 8-hour day was distributed as follows:

Activity	Hours and hundredths of an hour
1. Assigning work	1.50
2. Training employees	0.05
3. Inspecting work	1.60
4. Expediting orders and supplies	2.90
5. Time cards and routine paperwork	0.30
6. Preparing schedules	0.15
7. Safety and health	0.05
8. Employee grievances	0.15
9. Employee counseling	0.05
10. Customer complaints	0.50
11. Reporting to boss	0.70
12. Creative and self-improvement activities	0.05
Total	8.00 hours

Instructions. Using the format provided in Table PT 5-1 on page 108:

A. Rearrange Charlie's activities according to their times in descending order, with the longest time at the top of the list.

B. Complete all the calculations indicated in the table.

C. Divide the activities into A, B, and C classes.

D. Comment on the appropriateness of Charlie's distribution of his time. Do you think he is placing his A time on activities of major importance? Does he appear to be working on the right problems? What changes would you make?

Commentary. A times (activities 4, 3, and 1) totaled 6.00 hours; 25 percent of the activities (3 ÷ 12) accounted for 75 percent of the hours (6.00 ÷ 8.00) for a ratio of 25:75. B time (activities 11, 10, and 5) totaled 1.50 hours; 25 percent of these activities (3 ÷ 12) accounted for 18.75 percent of the hours (1.50 ÷ 8.00) for a ratio of 25:18.75. C time (activities 6, 8, 2, 7, 9, and 12) accounted for 0.50 hours; 50 percent of these activities (6 ÷ 12) accounted for 6.25 percent of the hours (0.50 ÷ 8.00) for a ratio of 50:6.25.

It would appear that Charlie is devoting far too much time to expediting, inspecting, and assigning work—and perhaps is spending too much time with his boss and handling customer complaints. As a consequence, schedule preparation and training of employees suffer, as do safety and health and creative work. Long-term, at least, Charlie will have to stop fighting fires in order to solve problems related to schedules

Table PT 5-1. Calculations for an ABC Analysis

Ranked activities	(1) Cumulative percentage of activities	(2) Ranked times, hours	(3) Cumulative time, hours	(4) Cumulative percentage of time
4	8	2.90	2.90	36
3	17	1.60	4.50	56
1	25	_____	_____	_____
11	33	_____	_____	_____
10	42	_____	_____	_____
5	50	_____	_____	_____
6	58	_____	_____	_____
8	67	_____	_____	_____
2	75	_____	_____	_____
7	83	_____	_____	_____
9	92	_____	_____	_____
12	100	_____	8.00	100

Explanation and directions for calculations:
Column 1: Each activity, regardless of time, accounts for one-twelfth of the total items.
Column 2: Enter the time provided by Charlie's study for the particular activity.
Column 3: Add the time in column 2 to the previous time in column 3.
Column 4: Divide the time in column 3 by the total time for the day (8.00 hours).

and training. This should make his assignments more ordered and reduce his need to spend so much time on inspection.

 TIME CHECK

Use this action-plan checklist to verify your understanding of the various concepts, ideas, and techniques presented in this chapter and to indicate any need for further action on your part.

	Applies to your situation		Schedule for action	
	Yes	No	Yes	No
1. Recognition that a problem exists when there is a difference between an expected condition and the actual condition.	_____	_____	_____	_____
2. Problems approached systematically, using the time-saving seven-step process, beginning with a clear and specific statement of the problem that implies neither causes nor solutions.	_____	_____	_____	_____

3. Causes identified that can be related to changes that may have taken place.   ____ ____ ____ ____

4. Solutions generated to remove causes and/or to close gaps between actual and expected conditions, using as sources (a) policy and procedure reviews, (b) networking, and (c) brainstorming and/or NGT.   ____ ____ ____ ____

5. Recognition of decision making as incorporating the evaluation and choice stages of problem solving.   ____ ____ ____ ____

6. Evaluation of alternatives based upon criteria to be satisfied by the decision and by obtaining information relevant to each alternative.   ____ ____ ____ ____

7. Decisions made either by rational analysis or by hunch or by a combination of both, but always without undue delay.   ____ ____ ____ ____

8. Action taken as soon as possible after a decision has been made, in order to sustain momentum.   ____ ____ ____ ____

9. Problems screened for delegation and assistance, using an activities-time analysis, ABC analysis, or the guidelines for seeking help in problem solving (Table 5-1).   ____ ____ ____ ____

10. Acceptance of the nature of decisions (they are often difficult and troublesome) and realization that procrastination rarely makes them any easier.   ____ ____ ____ ____

11. The habit of procrastination diminished by radically changing your routines; sticking to a new regimen; setting a starting time for every task, no matter how small; generating momentum based upon small accomplishments; and breaking formidable tasks into smaller ones with more readily attained deadlines.   ____ ____ ____ ____

PART 2
Managing the Time of Others

6
Time Sampling for Assignments

How to find out where—and why—time has gone, so that you can make more effective work assignments

Work is the scythe of time.
NAPOLEON BONAPARTE
On board H.M.S. Bellerophon

Work for the night is coming.
Biblical hymn

A fair day's wages for a fair day's work: it is as just a demand as governed men ever made of governing. THOMAS CARLYLE
Past and Present

Work can be assigned equitably to subordinates only if the manager in charge has a reliable knowledge of (1) the skills required of a job and (2) the time needed to perform the job. There are many ways to measure this time accurately, and these are explored in depth in Chapter 9. Unhappily, most of these techniques require the attention of a specialist.

There is, however, a time-measurement technique—time sampling—that pretty nearly everyone can use. It is especially suitable, too, for lining up job assignments.

In addition, a number of supporting techniques have evolved, not only for making job assignments more equitable but also to relieve managers of some of their own time-consuming assignments. These techniques include the work-distribution chart, short-interval scheduling, management by exception (MBE), and delegation. All of these will be explained in this chapter.

Time Sampling

Time sampling is a technique for finding out how time is distributed within an organization according to a number of classifications of work. This technique was originally called *ratio-delay study* by statisticians. The reason for this nomenclature is that these studies are aimed at finding the ratio of (1) the amount of work performed during a given period as compared with (2) the extent of delays that occurred during that time. The technique relies, not upon continuous observation of time use, but upon observations made at random intervals. In effect, the use of time within a work group or by an individual is sampled. Sampling studies are infinitely less expensive than continuous measurements. And, if the sample is drawn correctly, the time-use measurements will be statistically reliable.

TIME BYTE 6-1

Sampling the Social Workers

Simi, a social worker in Baltimore, viewed the form she had just been handed as a welcome break in her routine. Called "Random Movement Survey," it directed her to write down the letter code that best described her activity at the time stated on the sheet, 9:25 a.m. At the time, Simi had been talking on the telephone to a foster mother, so she put down "G." G was one of 13 categories under "Service Administration." The activity was defined as "routine contacts, other monitoring and/or communication with natural parents or substitute care providers on the status of the child, the case plan, goals for the child and the family, and administrative procedures of the agency." *Seems to cover a lot of territory!*

"Lives on File: Cases of a Social Worker," by Megan Rosenfeld, *Washington Post*, Dec. 27, 1989, p. D1.

The technique was originally dubbed *work sampling*—a term still commonly used by industrial engineers. Actually, however, the technique focuses as much on time sampling as work sampling, and *time sampling* will be the term used in this text.

Time-Sampling Procedures

The underlying procedure for time sampling goes something like this. Suppose, for example, you wanted to find out how much of the time a lift truck used for stacking goods in a warehouse was actually in—or out—of operation. To get a rough idea, you might visit the truck a predetermined number of times a day, say 10. If in 10 days you made 100 observations, and if during 23 of them the truck was idle, it could be statistically sound to conclude that the truck was idle 23 percent of the time. You can use the same approach to make a study of any sort of activity or inactivity. The important caveats are, however:

1. *Make your observations at random intervals.* If, for example, you made your observations every day at the same time, you would not be getting a representative idea of what was actually going on. Your study would be biased. It takes random observations (*random sampling*) to make sure that the results are valid. Tables of random numbers, for use in choosing observation intervals, are available in books of statistics. Another way to choose random intervals, however—a simple, fairly reliable way—is to take them from a telephone book. If you wanted to make one observation every hour, you would use only the last two digits of the numbers listed on any page of a telephone book. For example, if the first number on the page were 869-2402, you'd make the first observation at 8:02 a.m. If the next number were 869-1029, you'd make the next observation at 9:29 a.m. And so on, in sequence down the page. You'd just skip over any numbers with the last two digits between 60 and 99.

2. *Make enough observations.* For statistical reliability, you should make a minimum of 100 observations; 200 is preferable. Observations should ordinarily be made for at least a full week from Monday through Friday.

An Example of Time Sampling of One Individual

The situation recorded on the worksheet in Figure 6-1 is a study of the work-time activities of one employee, Jones, in a mailroom. Jones's supervisor, Nancy, wanted to find out whether Jones had work time avail-

Time-Sampling Work Sheet

Department: _Mail_ Subject: _Mail Handling_

Operator(s): _Mail Clerk (Jones)_ Date _9/27_

Work Activity	Observations	Totals	Percent of All Observations
1. Opening incoming mail bundles	THL THL THL THL	20	10
2. Sorting mail for distribution	THL THL THL THL THL THL THL THL THL THL THL THL THL THL	70	35
3. Sorting outgoing mail for postage	THL THL THL THL THL THL	30	15
4. Bundling outgoing mail	THL THL THL THL THL THL	30	15
5. Idle	THL THL THL THL THL THL THL THL THL THL	50	25
Totals		200	100%

Figure 6-1. Example of a time-sampling study of an individual.

able, because she wanted to assign additional duties to Jones. Before making the study, the supervisor listed Jones's principal duties, as follows:

1. Opening incoming mail bundles
2. Sorting mail for distribution
3. Sorting outgoing mail for postage
4. Bundling outgoing mail

In this case, the supervisor asked her secretary to drop in on the clerk at random intervals each day and to record what the clerk was doing—on a sheet like the one shown in Figure 6-1. The sample was taken over a 2-week period and included 200 observations. Analysis of the record showed that the clerk's time was distributed as shown:

Number of observations	Percentage of time	Duty being performed
20	10	Opening incoming mail bundles
70	35	Sorting incoming mail
30	15	Sorting outgoing mail for postage
30	15	Bundling outgoing mail
50	25	Idle

Based upon the indications that Jones spent only 75 percent of his time on productive work, Nancy concluded that it would be reasonable to expect him to handle other assignments, within the scope of the 25 percent of his time that was idle.

An Example of Time Sampling of a Group of People

Time sampling can also be used for judging how busy a whole department is. In Table 6-1, a supervisor has recorded the activities of several people at each observation interval. (The number of people who can be observed at one time depends upon the number of categories of activities that are being classified. Usually, no more than 10 people can be observed accurately. If more are in the group, the categories are best limited to "working" and "not working.") The supervisor chose to place the observations in eight categories and to make 990 observations, which strengthened the reliability of the findings.

TIME BYTE 6-2
Slower, Not Faster

When H. J. Heinz moved its StarKist tuna packing operations overseas, it speeded up its production lines to cut costs. The company saved labor, all right, by 5 percent—but the fish cleaners were so overworked that they were leaving tons of edible fish on the bones each day. After StarKist's managers studied the work times, they slowed down the production lines and hired 400 additional workers. Labor costs rose $5 million, but fish yield rose by $15 million, a neat savings of $10 million a year. *Knowledge of the time needed to do a job helps point to the best way, whether it's faster or slower.*

"Cost Cutting: How to Do It Right," by Ronald Henkoff, *Fortune*, Apr. 9, 1990, p. 40.

Table 6-1. Example of a Time-Sampling Study of a Group of Employees

Time-Sampling Study of Clerical Employees

Observation Sheet

Name	Random Observation Times								
	9:09	9:57	11:18	1:15	2:43	3:11	3:52	4:21	4:39
Chavez	7	8	1	1	3	5	6	3	1
Yost	2	1	6	4	1	3	7	6	2
Albers	7	4	5	1	8	1	1	3	8
Dowdy	7	8	7	4	1	1	2	1	8
Calabrese	4	1	2	5	7	5	1	4	1

Activity Category Code Numbers

1. Keyboarding
2. Taking dictation
3. Transcribing from machine
4. Clerical activity at desk

5. Away from desk but in office
6. Talking, telephoning
7. Personal
8. Not in office

Date: __7/21/__   Supervisor (Observer): __Z. Diell__

Summary of 990 Observations

Category	Number of Observations	Percentage of Observations
1. Keyboarding	487	49.2
2. Taking dictation	23	2.3
3. Transcribing from machine	86	8.7
4. Clerical activity at desk	71	7.2
5. Away from desk but in office	36	3.6
6. Talking,telephoning	68	6.9
7. Personal	113	11.4
8. Not in office	106	10.7

Applications

Time sampling can be used in many ways to tighten up your work assignments and to provide valuable information about the distribution of time, your own as well as that of others in your organization. Some uses are listed below.

1. In its simplest application, time sampling will quickly give you a rough-and-ready estimate of how much idle time is actually occurring in any work activity. Experiment with this usage by observing such things as (a) how many salesclerks in a retail store are actually with customers at any one time, (b) what percentage of bank tellers are actually at the

counter, and (c) what proportion of people in an office are away from their desks.

2. The technique is especially useful in assessing the extent of non-productive time in clerical groups. Most such studies will show from 40 to 60 percent nonproductive time, depending upon daily or seasonal peak loads.

3. Time sampling provides helpful measurements of the activities of maintenance gangs and road-construction crews. Studies of maintenance gangs are likely to show large amounts of time spent on travel, whereas delays for traffic and waiting for equipment or materials can be quite time-consuming for road-construction crews.

4. You can also use time sampling advantageously to learn about the distribution of time among your own work activities. In so doing, you will probably need to have an assistant or colleague make the observations so that you will not, by anticipating their occurrence, be influenced (perhaps subconsciously) to do something that you would not ordinarily be doing. *Possible classifications of your own work activities include the following*:

- At desk alone:
  Using telephone
  Using computer terminal
  Doing paperwork
  Not occupied
- At desk with:
  Subordinate(s)
  Colleague(s)
  Boss
- On shop floor:
  Alone
  With employee(s)
- Attending a meeting
- Conducting a meeting
- Out of office:
  In the building
  Out of the building
- Personal time

For another list of work-related activities suitable for sampling of individual work time, see the table in Practice Time 6-1.

5. Data gathered from time sampling also help to make job assignments that distribute work effectively, as shown in the next section.

Work-Distribution Chart

Regardless of the particular scheduling technique an organization uses, work should be distributed among employees on the basis of (1) the number of tasks to be done, (2) the time it takes to do each task, (3) the number and qualifications of people available to do the work, and—where machinery or equipment plays a part—(4) the capacity and availability of the proper machines and equipment. A good way to put all this together for office and clerical work, especially, is to use a *work-distribution chart*—a device that shows visually how tasks and activities, and the times needed to perform them, are distributed among the workers in a department so that equitable work loads may be planned and assigned.

Table 6-2 shows how repetitive, routine work in an office might be balanced among eight employees by means of a work-distribution chart. (Machine capacity and availability are not considered as factors in this example.) Note that the manager has grouped together activities of roughly the same skill levels into job assignments for each person. For example, Apgar handles all the mail and part of the copying—fairly simple work. Bond and Crisi handle the balance of the copying, along with filing—slightly more difficult work. Dalt and Eigo have more highly skilled work, whereas Finch's job is mainly word processing. Grey is a keypunch operator who also handles the check-writing machine, and Hruska is the posting clerk.

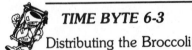

TIME BYTE 6-3

Distributing the Broccoli

After the Mann Packing Company of Salinas, California, installed an automatic bagging machine for bagging its broccoli, it faced a work-distribution problem. When the broccoli bagging was done manually, the maximum rate was 22 bags per minute. The automatic machine could run as high as 40 bags per minute and easily averaged 30 per minute. The question the company faced was what to do with the 12 hand-baggers who were replaced by the machine. The solution was to place the 12 workers on a similarly low-level task. The baggers now pitch in on "prep" work, where the broccoli is hand-cut into florets before packing. And, of course, these baggers are still on board in case the machine breaks down or is being cleaned. *As automation continues to offer time-saving advantages over hand labor, flexibility in assigning work becomes increasingly important.*

"Automated Bagging Lets the Florets Fly," *Packaging Digest*, January 1990, p. 32.

Table 6-2. Example of a Work-Distribution Chart

Tasks or Activities to Be Done Each Week	Total Time (in Hours) for Each Task, Each Week	Weekly Time Distribution in Hours per Employee							
		Apgar	Bond	Crisi	Dait	Eigo	Finch	Grey	Hruska
Mail in	15	15							
Mail out	15	15							
Dictation	20				10	10			
Transcription	30				10	10	10		
Typing	80			10	20	20	30		
Copying	30	10	10	10					
Filing in	35		20	15					
Filing out	15		10	5					
Keypunching	30							30	
Check writing	10							10	
Posting	40								40
Total hours	320	40	40	40	40	40	40	40	40

Short-Interval Assignments

Short-interval assignments, a scheduling technique, is another application in which time-sampling data are useful. The techniques can also be used with any other reliable time data, whether based upon specialized experience or upon time studies such as those described in Chapter 9. The success of short-interval assignments is predicated on the assumption that—especially in unstructured work environments—few people are capable of planning their own work in advance. Their estimates of the time needed to complete a task are generally faulty. Furthermore, many people do not like to take responsibility for estimating. A great many people, in fact, prefer to know exactly how much work is expected of them in the immediate time span (1 to 4 hours) ahead, rather than being left to their own devices. Given an assignment and its deadline, most people will work effectively to meet it.

Application Procedure

In applying short-interval assignments, a manager doles out work assignments in relatively small time bits, rather than lining up work for a whole day or a whole week in advance. For example, an office manager may hand a clerk a pile of 10 forms, saying that they should be completed in the next 55 minutes. Similarly, a maintenance supervisor may give a work order to a mechanic with the instruction that it is to be completed in an hour and a half, at which time the next assignment will be issued. A hospital housekeeper may tell a window cleaner that the windows in six rooms are to be washed in the next hour; when finished, the cleaner is to return to the housekeeper to find out what the next job will be and how long it should take.

Assignments can also be handed out in standard lots that can be expected to be completed in uniform blocks of time of 15, 30, 45, or 60 minutes.

Advantages and Disadvantages

A key advantage of short-interval assignments is that they enable you to find out very quickly whether an employee is keeping up or falling behind in output. The system also forces you to estimate and enforce time standards, and it calls to your attention expectations that may be wishful thinking on your, or management's, part. For example, suppose that you have been assuming that a clerk should be able to record 140 catalog-order telephone calls a day. When you break this assignment up into 20 calls per hour, however, you may discover that unexpected peculiarities in your kind of work make it impossible to record more than 15 orders an hour—and consequently only 100 or so a day.

There are many proprietary programs for formal installation of short-interval assignments. Most of these are cumbersome to manage and control. *It is the principle of short-interval assignments, however, that has the greatest application.* This is the idea of (1) assigning tasks of relatively short duration (2) along with a reasonable deadline and (3) repeating the process throughout the day. It's a good technique to apply informally or even sporadically, and you can often get unusually good results in terms of time saved and goals met.

MBE

An important benefit of knowing how time is distributed within your organization is that it points the way toward assignment of some of your lesser tasks and decisions to your subordinates. Such tasks may be either assigned permanently if your subordinates have the necessary time and skills or delegated temporarily as circumstances arise and permit. One technique—*management by exception*—also enables you to delegate problem solving and decision making to subordinates according to the degree of difficulty in a particular set of circumstances. In principle, MBE is a form of delegation in which a manager allows an activity to continue without supervision so long as performance is within prescribed limits. Here's how it works:

1. The MBE manager determines beforehand what kinds of conditions, or performance, will require his or her attention and what ones will not. In effect, the manager says to a subordinate, "So long as things

are running according to plan, don't bother me. But when they exceed such and such established limits, let me know and I'll take over."

2. Surveillance is maintained over the activity or process, either by personal observation or by some kind of reporting system, perhaps on-line with a computer or perhaps by means of status and budgetary reports. If a budget is used to establish the control limits, a periodic *variation report* marks conditions that fall outside the prescribed limits.

3. As long as performance and progress are within prescribed limits, the manager pays no further attention to the activity. However, when the variation exceeds the prescribed limits—when *an exception* occurs—the manager steps in and takes corrective action.

The MBE system can be broken down further, as shown in Figure 6-2. In zone 1, where conditions are as expected, the subordinate re-

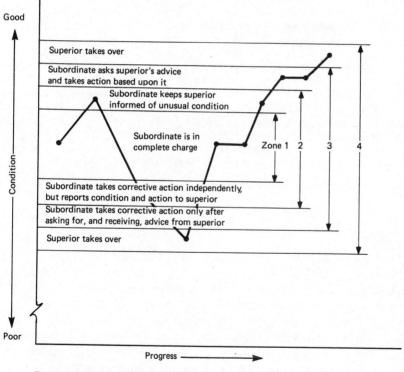

Zone 1: Expected, or planned, conditions
Zone 2: Unusual, but acceptable, conditions
Zone 3: Undesirable conditions
Zone 4: Vitally disturbed, or unacceptable, conditions

Figure 6-2. Chart of an MBE system.

mains in complete control. In zone 2, where conditions are unusual but acceptable, the subordinate takes action independently but reports the condition to the superior. In zone 3, where conditions are truly undesirable, the subordinate takes action only after consulting with the superior. In zone 4, where conditions are vitally disturbed and unacceptable, the superior takes over.

Willingness to delegate both responsibility and authority is at the heart of MBE. By delegating nonexceptional decisions to subordinates, a superior gains considerable time to devote to important matters and to major exceptions when they arise.

TIME BYTE 6-4
Counting the Accountants

In 1988 Gary Ames, chairman of U.S. West Communications, looked at his payroll with awe. It totaled over 58,000 people. "What in the world do they do with their time?" he asked. He found out enough to cut 5000 people from that payroll by 1990. Among the interesting facts turned up by a time survey of West's 7000 middle managers was that 350 people were engaged in drawing up the corporation's annual budget. In Ames's mind, this was 250 too many, and the number of professionals actively employed in this activity was reduced to 100. *The indirect labor needed to support a modern control system is sometimes more costly than the time and money it saves. Only by surveying the time involved and by counting noses can you get an accurate fix on these costs.*

"Cost Cutting: How to Do It Right," by Ronald Henkoff, *Fortune*, Apr. 9, 1990, p. 40.

Delegation

By delegating to others tasks and problems of lesser priority or importance, you gain valuable time needed for working on activities and problems of larger importance. *Delegation* means farming out a portion of your work to a subordinate who is capable of performing it. Along with responsibility, the subordinate must also be given authority to obtain the tools, information, and other resources needed to do the job. While the subordinate should be allowed to carry out the assignment with minimal supervision, you must be available for counsel when it is sought. An essential aspect of delegation, however, is that, while responsibility and authority can be delegated, accountability for proper accomplishment of the task cannot. If something goes wrong, it will be your fault.

Many managers hesitate to assume the risks entailed in delegating. These risks can be minimized by incorporating the following safeguards into your delegation practices:

- Understand that most employees will readily accept a fairly delegated task when it provides a chance to learn, a special challenge, or an extra measure of variety in their work.

- Provide subordinates with a clear statement of what must be accomplished, the extent of their authority, and how far they can go without checking back with you.

- Delegate whole tasks rather than pieces of tasks. To ask an individual to clean up the loose ends of another person's work can be demeaning.

- Don't promise rewards for performing delegated tasks unless you can fulfill them. Generally speaking, delegated tasks should either fall within an employee's expected job skills or be offered only as a learning experience.

- Don't overload one willing worker. Delegated tasks should be spread around, so that they will raise the general level of skills and knowledge in your department.

- Be ready to give up tasks that you enjoy. If a task is trivial, a subordinate should be performing it.

- Retain for your own attention critical, class A tasks and activities, especially those for which only you have the information and/or technical competence required. Confidential matters also should not be delegated.

- Consider your delegating options as ranging from tasks that *you must do* to those that *others could, should,* or *must do,* as illustrated in Figure 6-3. By all means, don't waste time doing what others should do.

PRACTICE TIME 6-1: A Self-Directed Exercise

Who's Wasting Time? The Employee or Management?

Background. Complaints were being voiced by the keyboard-entry clerk in the sales-order department of a distributor of industrial supplies in a small town in the Midwest. The clerk's argument was that she wasn't given enough time to keep up with the orders that were being relayed to her. The supervisor, however, thought that the clerk was idle too often of her own account. Nevertheless, in order to determine the validity of the clerk's complaint, the supervisor conducted a work-sampling study of the

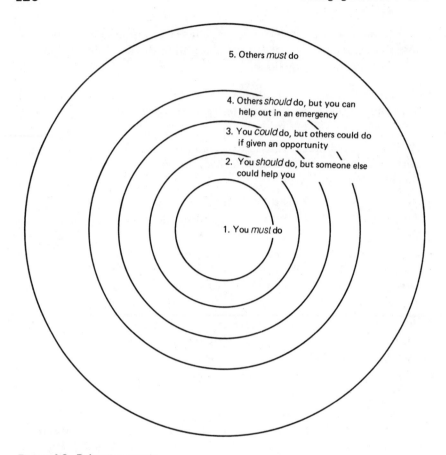

Figure 6-3. Delegation targets.

clerk's activities over a 2-week period. The observations made in that
study are recorded below:

Work activity	Observations	Total	Percentages of all observations
1. Preparing to work	xxxxx xxxxx xxxxx		
2. Working	xxxxx xxxxx xxxxx		
	xxxxx xxxxx xxxxx		
	xxxxx xxxxx xxxxx		
	xxxxx xxxxx xxxxx		
	xxxxx xxxxx xxxxx		
	xxxxx xxxxx xxxxx		
	xxxxx xxxxx xxxxx		
	xxxxx xxxxx		

3. Traveling for supplies, etc.	xxxxx xxxxx xxxxx xxxxx xxxxx xxxxx xxxxx		

4. Uncontrollable delays	xxxxx xxxxx xxxxx xxxxx xxxxx xxxxx		

5. Idle	xxxxx		
Total		200	100

Assignment. Complete the last two columns of the sampling sheet: totals and percentages of all observations. Then answer these questions:

1. What percentage of the clerk's time was spent working? _____%
2. What percentage of the clerk's time spent not working can be attributed to the way her job is arranged? _____%
3. Do you think the clerk is at fault for taking too much time at her work? _____yes _____no
4. What can you suggest to improve the amount of time the clerk can spend actually working?_____

Commentary. The clerk spent only 57.5 percent of her time working. It would appear that 40 percent of the time she spends on her job can be attributed to: preparing to work, 7.5 percent (activity 1); traveling for supplies, etc., 17.5 percent (activity 3); and uncontrollable delays, 15.0 percent (activity 4). From this sampling, it would seem as if the clerk is not at fault for taking too much time on this job.

Typical improvements might come from: (1) rearranging the workplace for greater convenience so that the setup would remain constant for each order, thus reducing the clerk's preparation time, (2) having supplies delivered to the work station or placed within arm's reach, thus reducing travel time, and (3) improving job schedules and departmental coordination to minimize uncontrollable delays.

PRACTICE TIME 6-2: A Self-Directed Exercise

Don't Bother Me, Except When It's Important

Jane Burro, marketing director for Abacus Computers, is very upset because she just learned today about bad news in a sales-call report that was filed 3 months ago. The call report from a sales representative in Kansas had been meant to alert the home office that a major customer was about to switch from Abacus to another brand. When Jane asked her sales manager, Sam Watson, why she hadn't seen the report when it was received, the sales manager said, "You told me you were operating on an MBE system. You said that all you wanted to know about sales calls was how many were made. If one of our reps failed to make the specified quota, you'd get on the phone and put heat on that rep. 'Otherwise,' you said, 'don't bother me with them. I really don't have time to read them all.' "

' "That's true," said Jane, "but I *did* expect you to bring to my attention anything that was exceptional in a call report."

"In other words," said Sam, "you want a system that alerts you not only to exceptions in the quotas but also to exceptions to what's in the reports?"

"Yes!" said Jane.

The sales manager went back to his office and reviewed the last 100 or so call reports. Most of them seemed pretty routine. They reported the customer called on, products of major interest, potential for a sale, etc. Admittedly, there was an occasional notation that seemed significant enough to warrant more than routine review. Sam pondered several ways to sift out the exceptional material for Jane's attention. Among his approaches were the following:

A. Ask each sales representative to send a copy of reports containing exceptional information directly to Jane.

B. Assign a clerk to review each report and pull out the ones containing exceptional information for review by Jane.

C. Send Jane a random sampling of reports to give her a feel for what was happening in the field.

D. Review each report himself in order to select exceptional ones to be sent to Jane.

E. Add to the call-report form a box marked "Worth special attention," along with a brief designation of the kinds of things that sales representatives might include in the box. Send to Jane only those reports which had entries in that box.

Assignment. Consider the suitability of each of the above approaches in terms of saving time for Jane, the sales manager, the sales representatives, and the organization as a whole. Then rank the approaches on a scale from 1 (greatest potential for saving time) to 5 (least potential for saving time).

Commentary. A group of experts who looked at the above approaches assigned the following rankings:

A. 5. This would be an invitation for the sales representatives to dump all their ideas and complaints into Jane's lap, with no assurance that the information would be genuinely significant.

B. 3. This would add to the cost and might still require the sales manager to spend time screening the reports before sending them on to Jane.

C. 4. This idea has merit, but it is not relevant to Jane's request that exceptional information be brought to her attention.

D. 2. Since the sales manager should be reading the reports anyway, it would take only a little more time for him to mark the exceptions and send them on to Jane.

E. 1. While not perfect, this approach systematizes and simplifies the reporting of exceptions and avoids possible delays that might occur while the sales manager reads and screens the call reports.

TIME CHECK

Use this action-plan checklist to verify your understanding of the various concepts, ideas, and techniques presented in this chapter and to indicate any need for further action on your part.

	Applies to your situation		Schedule for action	
	Yes	No	Yes	No
1. Knowledge of the time sampling procedure whereby random observations are made of work activities in order to find out how time is distributed within a work force.	___	___	___	___
2. Time-sampling studies conducted of your own personal time and that of a work group.	___	___	___	___
3. Use of a work-distribution chart to create equitable task assignments within a work group.	___	___	___	___
4. Use of the short-interval technique to make assignments of relatively brief duration.	___	___	___	___
5. Use of the MBE principle as a guide to delegating problem solving and decision making.	___	___	___	___
6. Delegation to subordinates of as many of your activities of lesser importance as they have the time and qualifications to carry out.	___	___	___	___

7

Time as a Motivator

How to take time into account when you are motivating and directing the work of others

Time is the element in which we exist....We
are either borne along by it or drowned by it.
                    JOYCE CAROL OATES
                    Marya: A Life

When you hear on every side the lament, "If only I had enough time," you'd think that the granting of free time would be a powerful motivator. But more often than not, it isn't. It can sometimes be made more powerful, however, when you fully understand the part that time plays in a person's motivational pattern.

Time Aspects of Motivational Theories

The two concepts of motivation that are most relevant to time as a motivator are (1) expectancy theory and (2) the belief that the greatest motivating power can be generated by the nature of the work itself. Both theories are usually addressed to managers in regard to their subordinates; nevertheless, you can easily see how the theories apply to your own personal behavior at work or elsewhere.

Expectancy Theory

The logic of expectancy theory is that individuals will (1) exert extra effort at work (2) to achieve performance (3) that will result in outcomes that they prefer. Bob, for example, will make this extra effort only if, *first*, he believes that he is capable of achieving the stipulated performance and, *second*, the reward he expects to receive for this achievement is something that he values enough to make the extra effort.

If the performance can be achieved only by Bob's putting in extra time—on the job or preparing for it—that may, in itself, be a deterrent if Bob feels that he has no time available for the extra effort. In effect, Bob will fall out of the equation at stage 2 simply because he feels that he cannot achieve the desired performance. In a great many instances, employees will feel just as Bob does—that they are being asked to squeeze the impossible into their work-time or leisure-time budgets. Hence, they will balk at the request for extra effort, even though they may value the outcome that is promised.

Now consider time off as the reward for the stipulated achievement. Time off as a reward for performance can take many forms, of course. It can be a Friday or Monday off so as to make a long weekend, or it can be leaving a half-hour before quitting time to miss the rush-hour traffic, or it can be an afternoon off for shopping during the holiday season. For professional employees, time off may simply be "free time" on the job for exploring a project of their own choosing. Here again, however, the expectancy equation will not be completed if the individual does not value time off sufficiently to be willing to make the extra effort required. Many people do not.

In summary, when the availability of time is a negative factor at the performance stage of expectancy theory, motivation will not take place—no matter how strongly the reward may be valued. Similarly, if time as a reward at stage 3 of expectancy theory is not valued strongly enough, motivation will not take place—whether or not the individual believes that the stipulated performance might otherwise be achieved.

Remember this about expectancy theory: It predicts that motivation will not occur unless the conditions (or expectancies) at both stage 2 and stage 3 are satisfied. Dissatisfaction at either stage will nullify motivation.

Motivation in the Work Itself

A truism supported by reams of research is that the secret of motivation is hidden in the nature of the work itself. Work that is viewed as boring and purposeless provides no motivation. In fact, such work has just the opposite effect upon the persons performing it. They will do almost anything to escape it. On the other hand, work that challenges skills and intellect and seems meaningful in content is a powerful motivator.

To understand the significance of motivation as a factor in performance, you should be aware that until the middle of the twentieth century two beliefs about work-related motivation prevailed: (1) pressure from management was required to make people work hard and (2) money was the most powerful motivator of all. More affluent times and an enlightened work force showed those two beliefs to be severely flawed. People could be pushed only so far; then they'd devise ways to deflect management's pressures—or they'd simply walk away from a bad situation to find a better one. Money, too, lost much of its power as a motivator. Increasingly, employees came to expect equity in pay as an entitlement rather than an incentive for harder work.

Almost all students of human and organizational behavior today subscribe to a more enlightened theory. *This theory predicts that people will make an extra effort—be motivated—by work that*:

1. Brings them respect and raises their self-esteem, usually because the work is challenging, *often because it places demands upon their time* and is well-regarded by others, *and often because of the flexibility of the time schedules it accommodates*

2. Enables them to participate in setting the goals and standards for that work, *including its time standards and deadlines*

3. Allows them to establish to some degree the way that work will be done, *including the pace of the effort to be extended*

Time, then, can play a significant role in motivation, either as an aid or as a detractor.

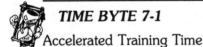

TIME BYTE 7-1
Accelerated Training Time

With so many part-time employees, quits and hires, and process changes in the work environment, training (and retraining) time has become a limiting factor in productivity improvement. Professional trainers, however, have come up with an approach, originally called *accelerated training*, that seems to speed up the process. The currently popular term for this technique is *competency-based training*. Its essence is that, unlike old-fashioned apprenticeship, which aimed to create a well-rounded craftsperson, competency-based training focuses on identifying and training workers for only the skills that are directly related to a particular job. Job functions are described, and three classes of competencies are prescribed: administrative, technical, and personal. Critical behavior traits are also described. Finally, training is provided according to the level of expertise the job requires. *Employee training, while time-consuming and costly, is still one of the most effective motivators of all.*

"Job Competencies: Can They Help You Design Better Training?" by Ron Zemke, *Training/HRD*, May 1982, p. 28.

Employee Empowerment

The contemporary view is that motivation at work is generated from empowerment of the work force. The term *empowerment* is popularly used to describe a human condition in which people are in control of their own destinies, and in which they are also responsible for their destinies and have the means to fulfill them. You might suppose that this would be a radical notion for most hierarchical organizations to consider, and it is, in theory at least. In practice, however, empowerment-related programs have made great inroads under a number of guises. For example, there are such bottom-up approaches as Quality Circles and work teams.

Quality Circles. Lower-level employees, by working together in groups called *Quality Circles*, become empowered to investigate operational problems and to make recommendations for their solutions. The solutions formulated by Quality Circles are typically highly regarded by upper-level management.

Work Teams. *Autonomous work groups* (also known as *employee involvement (EI) programs* in some industries) have evolved from groups of volunteers working together on problem solving into self-managing work teams of from 5 to 15 members. Such teams produce an entire product instead of subunits, and members learn all tasks and rotate from job to job. Teams assume many managerial duties, including ordering materials and scheduling of work and vacations. It is not unusual for firms to report a 30 percent increase in productivity as a result of placing time controls in the hands of these teams.

At General Electric Company, for instance, nearly 20 percent of its 120,000 employees now work under some variation of the team concept. The company claims an increase of productivity of better than 40 percent when these teams are combined with automation.

As another example, work teams at AT&T Credit Corporation were given "ownership and accountability" over processing of lease applications. Not only did these teams double the output from 400 to 800 per day with the same labor input, they also cut applicants' waiting time for a "yes" or "no" from several days to 1 or 2 days.

Benefits and Drawbacks

Empowerment of employees, in Quality Circles, autonomous work teams, and other similar groups can, and does, contribute greatly to an organization's effectiveness. There are, however, drawbacks to this approach as well.

1. *Work teams can save time because they:*
   - Anticipate and solve problems, especially ones that require intragroup coordination.
   - Iron out personality conflicts without management intervention.
   - Assume responsibility for allocating scarce resources within the group.
   - Find ways to get things done more quickly.

2. *Work groups may not save time because they:*
   - Have a long start-up time when faced with new situations. There is heavy front-end loading on new projects.
   - Have a tendency to become bureaucratic. Once a group has established a routine, that routine will tend to persist regardless of evidence of a better way of doing things.
   - May reject management intervention, even when it can be proved to be justified.

Guidelines

When applying employee involvement approaches in hopes of saving time, here are three guidelines that you should keep in mind:

1. Employee empowerment is a form of delegation. It is probably the most permissive form, and it certainly places the most demands on the organization that initiates it. When genuinely proferred, however, employee empowerment is likely to be the most effective form of delegation ever conceived.

2. Genuine empowerment treats subordinates as equals, not necessarily socially or in terms of status, but in terms of their ability to contribute and their commitment. Most firms that have employee involvement programs avoid referring to their people as employees or subordi-

nates. Instead, they use the term *members, partners, stakeholders, staffers,* or *associates.*

3. Empowerment signals the trend away from hierarchical views of authority. As John Naisbitt says in *Megatrends,* "Hierarchies remain; our belief in their efficiency does not."*

"Inhuman" Time

Time has become so fast-paced that it is often a sensitive issue for any kind of discussion, let alone discussion that involves performance. Even when time is presented positively, as a reward, employees are likely to interpret the presentation as an implied criticism. In light of a number of facts, this is not surprising. In Chapter 1, for example, you were asked to make an assessment of your quickness. The intent was to see how well you are prepared to handle today's fast-paced living. This only scratched the surface.

A respected psychologist, Robert Levine, devised a simpler but more demanding test.† In 35 cities in the United States he asked a sample of the population these questions:

How fast do you walk?

How fast do you talk?

How fast do you work?

Do you wear a watch?

The fastest-paced cities were Boston, Buffalo, and New York, all in the Northeast. The slowest-paced cities were Shreveport, Louisiana, and Sacramento and Los Angeles, all in the South or the Far West. Middle-paced cities were Detroit, Chicago, and Indianapolis. Incidentally, scores obtained in a similar study of an urban population in Japan went off the high side of the chart!

For comparison's sake, you may want to check your own pace against these observations of U.S. populations:

The fastest pedestrians covered 60 feet in about 11 seconds, which is 3.6 seconds faster than the slowest walkers. This means that the fastest walkers would travel 100 yards while the slowest were walking only 75.

The fastest talkers could read aloud the text of a broadcast of *The Six O'Clock News* by seven o'clock, whereas the slowest wouldn't finish until 7:25. That's 3.9 syllables a second as compared with 2.8.

*John Naisbitt, *Megatrends: Ten New Directions Transforming Our Lives,* Warner Books, New York, 1984, p. 213.

†Robert Levine, "The Pace of Life," *Psychology Today,* October 1989, p. 42.

The fastest clerical work was performed in Chattanooga, Tennessee; Rochester, New York; New York City; and Kansas City, Missouri. The slowest performers were clerks in San Diego, San Francisco, and Los Angeles.

The most watches were worn in New York, the fewest in Atlanta.

In addition, Levine observed that type A cities attract type A individuals, whereas type B cities tend to attract type B personalities—a finding that implies that time pressure in itself is not necessarily stressful and damaging. Accordingly, you might ask yourself what sort of city you prefer to live in—one that you would be likely to find in the Northeast, or one more typical of the South or the West.

Levine drew two especially important conclusions from this study:

1. The time pressures in some environments are demonstrably higher than in others.

2. Fast-paced environments are likely to be stressful to slow-paced (type B) individuals, while slower-paced surroundings are just as likely to cause distress among impatient, fast-paced (type A) individuals.

TIME BYTE 7-2
Faster! Faster! Faster!

Jobs that are most skilled often require the fastest reading skills, too. A study conducted by the Hudson Institute found that the gap between reading skills of workers entering the labor force (ages 21 to 25) and those required by the available jobs increases markedly from the lowest job-skill levels to the highest. For example, for the three lowest skill levels measured, reading requirements rise from a vocabulary of 2500 words and a reading rate of 100 words per minute to 6000 words and 200 words a minute. The reading skills of people entering the labor force match up pretty well at those levels. A dramatic shift in match-ups takes place at the fourth level, however, where reading manuals and writing business letters and reports are required. Only about one of six entering workers has these skills. People who can read scientific and technical journals and financial reports (required at the fifth and sixth levels) are in even shorter supply. *Time (and skill) pressures in the work environment are increasing, rather than subsiding.*

"Where the Jobs Are Is Where the Skills Aren't," by Aaron Bernstein, *Business Week*, Sept. 19, 1988, p. 104.

Relaxation

When time pressures become extreme, they act as deterrents to motivation. The wise thing to do under those circumstances is to back off a little. For example, psychologists advise the following techniques:

- In intense situations, take a 10-minute break instead of pressing on.

- If time pressures have been prolonged, try a day off for relief, or a long weekend, or leaving for a vacation now rather than later at the planned time.

- If change has been turbulent in the organization, stabilize work schedules so as to reestablish a degree of normality.

- Temporarily, at least, relax time standards to relieve what may have become unbearable pressure.

- Try alternating deep and shallow breathing, a performance-enhancement technique commonly used to psych up or calm down athletes. Another useful technique is to engage in vigorous exercise to relax your body and clear your mind, after leaving a pressured situation.

- Consider seeking psychotherapy for help with stress management. Relaxation techniques, biofeedback, cognitive coping strategies, or group therapy can also help you to put time in perspective and to reduce a tendency to seek perfection.

Quality of Work Life

If you are a manager, you are responsible for trying to maintain or improve the quality of work life (QWL) in your organization. Even if you do not have this responsibility in a formal sense, it is important to do what you can to influence QWL conditions for the better. QWL means different things to different people, of course. The Michigan Quality of Work Life Council, Inc., however, offers this generally accepted view of the goals of QWL: ·

1. Enhancing the quality of life at work in terms of dignity, learning, participation, fulfillment, and engagement

2. Improving organizational effectiveness in the areas of productivity, quality, cost-effectiveness, creativity, and adaptability

Employee involvement programs, work teams, and Quality Circles are concrete examples of the practical application of QWL philosophy.

Since time is so large a factor in all work, it follows that use or abuse of time has the power to add to or subtract greatly from the QWL. As a consequence, neither managers nor individuals should allow time to get out of hand. When time dictates every decision, time not only loses its motivating power, it also becomes a major source of job dissatisfaction. And such situations will not be remedied by a "1-minute manager."

Accommodation Time

As you've already deduced, rigid 5-day work weeks on an 8-to-5 schedule are fast becoming an anachronism. The new trends are seen everywhere. Because of a worldwide labor shortage, especially of skilled people, employers now offer a wide variety of time schedules.

 TIME BYTE 7-3

Flexible Hours, and More

"If you want unpaid time off, take it." That's the stated policy of Harbor Sweets Company. In fact, the company's 114 employees can set any schedule that suits them, as long as it includes at least 20 hours of work per week. Part-time work is the norm, and the factory works four 4-hour shifts a day instead of the more usual two 8-hour shifts.

Most of the employees at Harbor Sweets are neighborhood women from nearby, affluent Marblehead, Massachusetts. They are paid only a little above the minimum wage, but they are attracted by these privileges:

- *No assembly line.* Production is clustered in work stations; at each work station, a group of employees work together on a task.
- *Cross-training.* Employees work on a variety of jobs, each with unique skills.
- *"Come when you please."* Employees who intend to be absent are asked only to notify their supervisors in advance. In customer-service jobs, however, employees must arrange for someone to cover their shifts.

Flexible work hours are attractive from an employee's viewpoint, but they put a scheduling burden on management.

"Managing the New Work Force," by M. E. Mangelsdorf, *Inc.*, January 1990, p. 82.

A Time-Pressed Work Force

These less rigorous time schedules are initiated to accommodate the needs of a number of different kinds of working people, some of whom are discussed below.

Working Parents, Especially Working Mothers.   For example, 60 percent of all school-age children have mothers in the work force. Women with children under 6 are the fastest-growing segment of the work force. These working parents seek jobs with flexible and/or part-time working hours as well as other time-related accommodations.

Workers Who Care for Aged Parents. About 40 percent of all workers provide some care for their parents. About 12 percent of women who care for an aged parent have had to quit their full-time jobs to do so. These workers, too, are attracted to part-time employment and to flexible work schedules.

Retired Persons. Increasingly, retired people are looking for part-time work that will allow them to pursue leisure-time activities and for earnings that are not so high as to cancel out social security benefits.

High School and College Students. Working students have become commonplace, especially in fast-food establishments where part-time work is the major way of life.

Accommodating Programs

In response to the needs of the new work force, a great many firms offer one or more of the following accommodations:

Flextime Schedules. Especially prevalent in government and in office work for smaller firms, flextime schedules (flexible working hours) permit employees to choose their own working hours to some extent, provided that they work the normal number of hours. As illustrated in Figure 7-1, flextime schedules generally include several (often 6) hours of core time during which all employees must be on the job. An employee may choose to come to work an hour late and make up the hour after normal closing time, or the reverse. This kind of schedule satisfies the needs of many of the workers described above, as well as people who are by nature early or late starters. Flextime has its drawbacks in situations in which continuous interaction between employees is needed, and in which it is difficult to get employees to share early and late options.

Telescoped Workweeks. A few organizations have recently introduced 4-day weeks made up of 10-hour days. This appeals to employees who commute from faraway homes and to those who value long week-

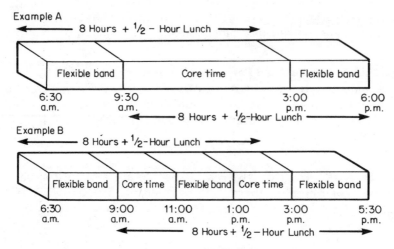

Figure 7-1. Two ways to design flextime schedules.

ends. There is a widespread belief, however, that productivity will suffer under this system.

TIME BYTE 7-4

Interviewing Timetable

Since it often takes 10 interviews of job applicants to find one good employee, Tom Melohn of North American Tool & Die Company sets a 30-minute time limit on his interviews. His interviewing timetable is as follows:

> 2 minutes for small talk
>
> 2 minutes for "housekeeping," during which the ground rules of the employment procedure are stated
>
> 7 to 15 minutes for answering questions posed by the applicant
>
> 10 to 12 minutes for either (1) selling the job to the applicant or (2) cutting off the interview.

To stick with this timetable, the interviewer must focus on the applicant's interests and encourage the applicant to do most of the talking.

"How to Hire Employees," by Joshua Hyatt, *Inc.*, March 1990, p. 106.

Part-Time Employment. Offering something for just about everyone with a time problem, part-time employment can be based upon: (1) a weekly schedule, usually of fewer than 19 hours in order to meet tax and wage laws; (2) seasonal employment to replace vacationing employees or to meet peak work loads; or (3) fill-ins for weekends, holidays, and night shifts.

Time Off for Home Care.   Only a few companies now offer this accommodation which allows employees to care for dependents with prolonged illnesses—although there is increasing political pressure for this accommodation. Leaves are usually granted without pay and for only a limited number of weeks.

Job Sharing.   This occasionally encountered approach allows two employees to share responsibility for one job, usually on a skilled or professional level. This approach must be handled carefully since its administration invites wage and tax problems.

Use of Temporary Services.   This popular approach to handling peak loads and emergencies enables a firm to hold its permanent employment level to a minimum. Drawbacks include the premium paid for the service (about 20 percent of the hours billed), time needed to lay out work for and instruct the temporary person, and potential dissatisfaction of the permanent staff due to the perceived higher rates of pay for the temporaries. Some companies have found it convenient to rehire—through a temporary-help vendor—their own experienced employees who had been let go because of a work shortage or who had left because they could no longer meet a full-time schedule.

PRACTICE TIME 7-1: A Self-Directed Exercise

Expectations

Background. Grace has been a salesperson in a branch store of a home-furnishings retail chain for several years. She is divorced and has two young children at home. When working the day shift, Grace leaves the children with her aunt; when on the evening shift, she leaves them with a baby sitter—often difficult to find and always expensive to pay. As to finances, Grace struggles to make ends meet. Grace, nevertheless, considers her work a career and hopes that her excellent performance will lead to the position of store manager.

Assignment. A week ago, Grace approached the chain's regional manager about her chances of becoming a store manager. Yesterday, the regional manager offered Grace a number of options. Expectancy theory assumes that the degree of motivation depends upon both (1) the individual's belief that the required performance can be obtained and (2) the value placed by that individual on the outcome, or reward, for that achievement. On the basis of expectancy theory, which of the options listed below do you think Grace will accept? Rank the options in order of preference, with 1 the highest and 3 the lowest.

Option A.	Promotion to day-shift manager at the local store, with a 15 percent pay increase. Her hours would remain essentially the same as they are now.	_____
Option B.	Promotion to full-time manager of a store in a town 100 miles away. This job would require Grace to work from 10 a.m. to 5 p.m. most weekdays and from noon to 6 p.m. on Saturdays. Her pay would be doubled, however, and the chain would pay her moving expenses.	_____
Option C.	Promotion to full-time manager at the local store. Her hours would be the same as in option B, but she would receive only a 50 percent raise.	_____

Commentary. Grace would probably take option A, since she can meet the hours, and the reward will help her finances, if only slightly, and keep her on her career track. Her second choice would probably be option C: Under the circumstances, however, Grace can't really meet the hourly requirements, even if the rewards are in line with her expectations. Option B would be her third choice: The rewards are great, but they are not strong enough to overcome the difficulty she would encounter with the hourly requirements, removed as she would be from her aunt's baby-sitting services.

PRACTICE TIME 7-2: A Self-Directed Exercise
The Time-Powered Carrot

Though time can be used to motivate the behavior of others, it may also act as a deterrent, depending upon its place in a particular situation. This is an opportunity to see how well you can read a situation and determine whether or not the time element in it will be a motivator.

Assignment. In each situation given on pages 143–144, an action that has taken place, or will take place, is described. For each situation place a check mark in the column to the right that best represents your opinion of the probable effect of the action described upon the motivation of the individual involved.

	Effect upon motivation		
	None or negative	Some-what positive	Strongly positive
1. Ella is satisfied with her pay, but she greatly values her leisure time. Her boss asks her to take on an assignment that will require her to work on an occasional weekend, for which she will be rewarded with a small bonus.	____	____	____
2. Ella's boss makes her a similar proposition, only this time she will be repaid by receiving two long weekends off for each weekend she must work.	____	____	____
3. Ted's boss promises him a chance to make a little extra money by working overtime for a couple of hours every night for the next 6 weeks. Ted's family life is such that he must get home each night immediately after work to take care of his aging father.	____	____	____
4. Glenda is an upwardly mobile individual. Her supervisor asks her to take on a difficult new assignment that will add to her status but will leave her little leisure time.	____	____	____
5. Bill tells his work crew that he wants them to put in extra effort next week, but they can decide how and when the work will be accomplished.	____	____	____
6. Charlene tells one of her most self-motivated engineers that he'll be asked to take charge of a big, new project. Details are lacking, but the engineer will be allowed to set the deadline for the project's completion.	____	____	____
7. There is a shortage of powered trucks for use by the warehouse crew. Typically, this has caused delays in stacking shelves. The crew's boss tells the crew that they should devise the best way to share the trucks.	____	____	____
8. Betsy is a high-powered professional. Her boss asks her to accept a yearlong assignment in a sleepy country town. "This is your big chance," she is told.	____	____	____

9. You've pushed your best employee
hard for the last 3 weeks. He seems
about to collapse under the pressure.
You need him, but you decide that in
the long run it's better if you say,
"Why don't you take a couple of days
off now, before you tackle the next big
job?"   _____   _____   _____

10. A well-qualified job applicant, mother
of three children, says she can only
work a part-time schedule. You offer
her a higher-than-average starting
salary if she'll take the job on a
full-time basis.   _____   _____   _____

Scoring. Give yourself 1 point for each of the following situations that
you checked as having no effect upon motivation or a negative effect: 1,
3, 8, 10. Give yourself 1 point for each of the following situations that
you checked as having a somewhat positive or strongly positive effect
upon motivation: 2, 4, 5, 6, 7, 9.

Commentary. A score of 9 or 10 indicates that you're pretty good at
assessing time-powered motivation. A score of 7 or 8 indicates that you're
a little behind time in your motivational sense. A score of under 6
suggests that you may place too great or too little a value on time as a
motivator.

TIME CHECK

Use this action-plan checklist to verify your understanding of the various
concepts, ideas, and techniques presented in this chapter and to indicate
any need for further action on your part.

	Applies to your situation		Schedule for action	
	Yes	No	Yes	No
1. Awareness of expectancy theory, which assumes that a person will be motivated only if he or she believes that the required performance can be attained and values the outcome of that achievement highly enough to make the extra effort worthwhile.	_____	_____	_____	_____

2. Understanding that time needed to achieve the required performance may be a deterrent in expectancy theory, and that people will place different values on time off as a reward for achievement. ____ ____ ____ ____

3. Awareness that the most powerful motivation of all can be created by the design of the work itself. ____ ____ ____ ____

4. Alertness to opportunities to enhance the work itself by inviting others to participate in setting their own time standards and deadlines and in deciding upon the pace of the effort to be expended. ____ ____ ____ ____

5. Consideration of using employee-empowerment approaches, such as Quality Circles and work teams (autonomous work groups and employee involvement programs) to save time in solving problems, ironing out personality conflicts, allocating scarce resources, and finding ways to get things done more quickly. ____ ____ ____ ____

6. Recognition that the pace of some work environments is faster and more pressing than others and that individuals vary in the degree to which they can cope with either fast-paced or slow-paced situations. ____ ____ ____ ____

7. Use of relaxation techniques to diffuse or cope with extraordinary time pressures: taking a short break or time off from the job, stabilizing work schedules, and relaxing time standards temporarily. ____ ____ ____ ____

8. Guarding against allowing time to dictate decisions so much that they destroy the Quality of Work Life. ____ ____ ____ ____

9. Recognition of the special time-related needs of various groups in the work force, such as working parents, retired persons, and high school and college students. ____ ____ ____ ____

10. Time-related accommodations for people with special needs; flextime schedules, 4-day workweeks, part-time employment, time off for dependent care, job sharing, and use of temporary employee services. ____ ____ ____ ____

8
Time for Creativity and Innovation

How to make better use of time by tapping individual and organizational creativity

Let me exhort everyone to do their utmost to think outside and beyond our present circle of ideas. For every idea gained is a hundred years of slavery remitted.   RICHARD JEFFERIES
The Story of My Heart

According to George Stalk, writing in the *Harvard Business Review*, one of the most important of the Japanese competitive advantages is derived from flexible factories with time-based strategies. These factories have rapid product-development cycles, capable of introducing a great variety of products in a shorter time and with shorter life cycles. This capability is largely attributed to Japan's encouragement of innovation and creativity. It is ironic, of course, that a nation once notorious for copycatting is now so successful at innovating. Japan's success, however, is instructive to all of us, since the implication is that creativity can be learned and is not necessarily the sole province of geniuses. It is worth noting, too, that the Japanese have applied their creativity not only to new products, but also to ways and means for compressing time.

Innovation and creativity, when directed toward time-saving results, bloom only with careful nurturing. Such nurturing includes time for creative thinking, a focus on time-related goals, knowledge of how ideas are generated, and suggestions for creating ideas more quickly.

Time for Creativity

People are innovative and creative in organizations that encourage it. Conversely, they are unlikely to be creative in environments that discourage it. Consider the differences between the two environments.

A Supportive Climate

Creative environments provide the working conditions and the cultural climate that nurture and support creative thinking. This support is expressed in several ways:

1. *Time to think.*   Many companies make "thinking time" a matter of written policy. At 3M, for example, technical employees are encouraged to make 15 percent of their time discretionary, for use on projects of their own choosing. Whether the time is made available formally or informally, it is an essential factor in stimulating new ideas.

2. *Genuine involvement.*   Studies show that employees of innovative, "fast-cycle" companies think of themselves as important parts of an integrated system. They know that their ideas will be taken seriously.

3. *Tolerance of failure.*   Innovative companies—and their managers—understand that when a stigma is placed upon failure, people will hesitate before exploring opportunities.

Inhibiting Environments

Despite their claims to the contrary, many organizations and individuals are guilty of actively discouraging creativity. This mostly occurs unwittingly, because of either a persistent demand for conformity or an adherence to a tradition of linear, sequential thinking. These conditions manifest themselves in a number of ways:

1. *"Pass-along" processing.*   This is the term that W. Edwards Deming, an international authority on quality control, uses to describe the time-honored practice of passing along ideas in sequence. Designers at Ford, for example, used to put their design for a new car on paper and send it to the engineers, who figured out how to make the car.

Their plans were passed along to the production and purchasing people, and in turn to the marketing, legal, and dealer-service departments. The pass-along system locked in the designers' original ideas—regardless of their faults—and greatly discouraged innovation by the people downstream.

2. *Territorial barricades.*   Overzealous protection of a department's turf from encroachment by others induces a "not-invented-here" syndrome. Ideas from other departments are, when not rejected outright, allowed to wither and die.

3. *Independent fiefdoms.*   Entrenched individuals and departments are allowed to become overly focused on doing their own thing. Typically, they are unaware of developments and changes taking place elsewhere in the organization to which they could make significant contributions.

4. *Tolerance of delays.*   Not only are traditional ways of doing things defended, there is also an acceptance of process delays as inherent and normal. Innovators have to sell their ideas very hard in order for change to occur. This is a persuasive argument for eliminating delays in product introductions, for example. A McKinsey and Company study showed that products that go to market 6 months late, but within their expense budgets, earn 33 percent less than expected. Products that go to market on time, however, even if 50 percent over budget, will still earn only 4 percent less than expected. The implication is that a premium can be paid for ideas that accelerate the attainment of objectives.

5. *Unrealistic time frames.*   Paradoxically, many companies that are tolerant of delays can be unrealistic in their demands for the amount of work required within a particular time frame. This is especially inhibiting to creativity. In a study of 129 scientists conducted by the Center for Creative Leadership at Brandeis University, for example, one-third of respondents mentioned either insufficient time or too great a work load as a hindrance to creativity. Said one person, "When you are pressed with a problem and told to come up with a new X within a short period of time, you start looking at what has been done before. Really new things aren't going to come from pressure."*

---

*T. M. Amabile and S. S. Gryskiewicz, "Creative Human Resources in the R&D Laboratory: How Environment and Personality Affect Innovation," chapter 56 in *Handbook for Creative and Innovative Managers*, Robert L. Kuhn, editor in chief, McGraw-Hill, New York, 1988, p. 513.

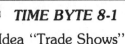

TIME BYTE 8-1
Idea "Trade Shows"

At 3M, where researchers and other selected creative people are encouraged to spend 15 percent of their time on projects of their own choice, the company also holds an annual idea show. These shows are likened to trade shows, although they are private, since each of the company's more than 115 research laboratories sets up a booth displaying its latest technologies. For 3 days, 3M scientists, like hucksters at a fair, try to sell their developments to other labs and departments within the corporation. The only catch in this enlightened environment is that the company president insists that 25 percent of each division's annual sales come from products developed in the prior 5 years. *An idea trade show could be an annual event in any organization, even if arranged on a greatly modified basis.*

"Leader's of the Most Admired," by Brian O'Reilly, *Fortune,* Jan. 29, 1990, p. 29.

Cross-Functional Ideas

Organizations that actively seek new ideas use three important ways to encourage their development:

Design for Manufacturability and Assembly. A widely accepted strategy for managing idea-to-market product-development processes, *design for manufacturability and assembly (DFMA)* tries to get as many informed people as possible into the act as soon as possible. *Fortune* magazine reports that this approach has reduced product introduction time from 50 to 75 percent.

Early-Involvement Manufacturing. Used at IBM, *early-involvement manufacturing (EIM)* is a less formal approach than DFMA but has the same objective—simultaneous development of product and process.

Cross-Functional Teams. A generic term for a concept similar to both DFMA and EIM, *cross-functional teams* are teams formed in the beginning stage of product or project development. These teams are made up of representatives from many functions, such as design, engineering, marketing, manufacturing, purchasing, safety, and product liability; even customers are included on some teams. Use of cross-functional teams offers significant advantages in that ideas are not only communicated across functions but also greatly stimulated by the interaction of many perspectives.

Creative Goals

Almost all research on creativity concludes that more ideas, and better ones at that, are generated when goals are set for their creation. The goals may be expressed in many ways, but the following are of special import to time-saving and time-use goals:

Number of Ideas.   Without question, more ideas will be generated when people are given a figure to strive for. Accordingly, when setting a target number, it is better to err on the high side than the low. Many people are inclined to think that coming up with one or two ideas is an accomplishment. Instead, they should be confronted with the goal of creating a dozen ideas. Ultimately, the really good ideas will be derived from, or will evolve from, one or two of the original ideas.

Time Frame.   Contrary to the thought expressed above that people often find it difficult to generate ideas under pressure, it is always a good idea to set a specific time for the delivery of the ideas. If you say to a person, "Let me have your ideas on that," the chances are slim that you'll get any ideas at all. If, however, you say, "Submit 10 ideas for handling this situation by 8 a.m. tomorrow," you will almost certainly get 10 ideas—and by the designated deadline. And among the 10 ideas, 1 or 2 will be worth following up.

Time Span.   In this book, *time span* is used to specify either (1) the time scope of an idea once it is in place (i.e., a 5-minute task, a 30-day trial, a six-month plan) and/or (2) the expected time needed to go from acceptance of the idea to its effective implementation (i.e., in 2 days, within a month, by the peak season, up to a year).

Potential Impact.   People who are asked for ideas often need to know just how big an idea is being sought. Generally speaking, ideas can be bracketed between two extremes:

1. *Conservative ideas* are those that will have an immediate but relatively small impact, usually of short-term benefit, and can be quickly and economically implemented. These are sometimes denigrated as "suggestion-box" ideas. This is unjustified. Conservative ideas far outnumber all others, and they make a significant contribution to innovation everywhere.

2. *Radical ideas* are the ones with the big payoff. Their drawback is that they are often, but not always, costly to undertake and time-consuming to implement. Such "big-bang" ideas usually arise in response to major changes in technology and markets, or in the economic,

physical, or political environment. Their impact has long-term benefits. These are also the ideas that meet with the greatest resistance, since they almost always are disruptive to the traditions and culture of the organization.

The Creative Process

Behind the planned creation of new ideas is the basic principle that they are triggered subconsciously by the *free association of ideas.* To illustrate, suppose you—as a designer—were seeking a solution to the problem of keeping an idle television screen from gathering dust or from intruding unpleasantly upon the visual design of a living space. While driving home from your office, you see a sports car with a retractable shield over its headlamps. This suggests that a similar shield might be used over the TV screen when it's not in use. You enter your garage using an automatic door opener. It occurs to you that a similar device could be used to open and close the door of a cabinet into which the TV set has been placed. You draw the drapes over a window in your room, and this suggests that the TV screen could be hidden in a like manner. Next day, at the airport, you see a venetian-blind advertising display in which the rotation of the blinds produces a picture. Perhaps, you think, this technique could be used to conceal your silent TV screen with a decorative picture. On and on, your mind will keep searching for an association of one idea with another to create a new one.

Green-Light Time

Your mind doesn't have to be instructed in its search for an association of ideas. It performs this activity naturally. Your part is (1) to alert your mind to the need to solve a particular problem and then (2) to stand aside and allow your mind to roam around unfettered, without interference from you. This search phase of creative thinking has been dubbed *green-light thinking.* The implication is that while the mind is searching for ideas, nothing should be done to stop it. Ideas should be allowed to flow without criticism or evaluation.

Red-Light Time

Later on, you can stop the action to examine the ideas that your mind has evolved. This is the time for evaluation and *red-light thinking.* Like undersized fish caught in a net, unsuitable ideas can then be cast aside. Or they can be tossed back into your mind; they may resurface at a later date, when they are more appropriate.

TIME BYTE 8-2
Corporate Idea Screening

John F. Welch, dynamic CEO of General Electric Company, emphasizes *speed, simplicity,* and *self-confidence* as the company's watchwords. He also seeks to transfer the company's best ideas and practices across all its businesses "with lightning speed." To accomplish this, the GE corporate executive council (CEC) meets 2 days each quarter. Every meeting deals with a vital corporate issue. Each division is free at that time to propose its own plan or program. But, says Welch, "We put it through a central screen at (the CEC meeting) strictly to make sure it's within bounds of good sense." *Even the best ideas must face a red-light screening eventually. If they're good, they will pass muster. Otherwise, it's "back to the drawing board."*

"Speed, Simplicity, and Self-Confidence: An Interview with Jack Welch," by Noel Tichy and Ram Charan, *Harvard Business Review,* September-October 1989, p. 111.

Rational and Irrational Ideas

The ideas suggested for the TV screen in the example above were all fairly logical. In each instance, there was a reasonable similarity between ideas. This need not be the case. The best innovations often come from associations that appear at first to be illogical. That's one reason it's so important to put off red-light thinking as long as you can. Otherwise, the rational part of your mind (the left brain, if you like) will inhibit the flow of ideas. A raindrop sliding down a window pane, for example, might illogically suggest a way to use an assembly line for the packing of parts for shipment. *The connections?* The raindrop is carried by gravity. It moves continuously. Because of surface tension, the drop moves under a degree of control. Small drops merge, and together become large ones. *The mind puts it all together*: Completed parts can be fed from an overhead hopper onto a rubber-coated chute, where they slide down at a controlled rate onto a belt that carries them to empty cartons for packing.

Go-It-Alone Time

There are really no rules, regulations, or procedures for getting good ideas on your own. Successful innovators, however, seem to employ the seven principles described below.

1. *Narrow down the search.* This is somewhat akin to making a clear statement of a problem. If, for example, you were searching for ideas to

reduce absenteeism, your search might be targeted like this: ideas for solving the problem of second-shift workers who are absent more than five times a year. Being specific helps to focus your subconscious mind.

2. *Concentrate on one search at a time.* While it's fine to let your subconscious mind wander, you should search for solutions to only one problem at a time. If you try to think about many things, your mind loses its focus.

3. *Be persistent.* Good ideas rarely come in the first try. If your mind is a blank today, try again tomorrow—and the next day, too. If you have assigned the innovation to someone else, you may have to extend the time frame.

4. *Believe in yourself.* Self-confidence has always played a big part in the search for ideas. Build up your faith in your ability by practicing getting ideas—first with things that don't matter much. Then when you face a rough situation, you'll know that your mind has the capacity to produce.

5. *Let your subconscious take over.* When you're tired of thinking, stop for a while. Move around. Work on something else. Forget the problem for a day or two. Surprisingly, a good idea will then flash out of the blue.

6. *Keep ideas flowing.* Momentum plays a big role in idea generation. One idea quickly begets another, and another. Don't be too easily satisfied. When your mind is on a roll, don't stop until you've piled up a dozen ideas or more.

7. *Take action.* Idea creation may begin with inspiration. Nothing much comes of a good idea, however, until it is put into action. Crude preparations of penicillin, for example, were described in 1929, but nobody followed through on the discovery for a dozen years. Don't let your good idea become just another dust gatherer.

Collective Brainstorming

Brainstorming is the group approach to creative thinking. It is more limited in scope, however, and usually applies only to the green-light phase.

A typical brainstorming session involves a group of from 8 to 12 people. Sessions last no more than an hour; often 15 minutes is sufficient. Mornings are better than afternoons. *Sessions work this way:* A leader is put in charge; a problem is stated; possible solutions are asked for; concentration and participation are intense. A successful session will produce 50 or more ideas. Of these, 6 to 10 percent may be fruitful.

Four rules govern a brainstorming session:

1. *Don't criticize ideas.* There will be time later for judicial thinking, but it is not appropriate during brainstorming. Anyone who "puts down" an idea during the session may be penalized—may be required to pay for a round of coffee or put a dollar in the kitty, for example.

2. *Welcome freewheeling.* The wilder the idea, the better. It is easier to tame down an idea than to think up one. Accordingly, a "Can you top this?" attitude is encouraged. Participants are to be applauded when they use others' ideas as jumping-off places for their own.

3. *Strive for quantity.* As with go-it-alone creativity, the more ideas there are, the better some of them will be. Seemingly stupid suggestions and screwball ideas sow the seed for more fruitful thoughts. Typically, impulsive, top-of-the-head thinkers will offer ideas that break the ground for participants who are more reflective and slower to add their contributions.

4. *Combine and improve.* Since ideas are like building blocks, session members are encouraged to suggest how others' ideas can be made better, or how two or more ideas can be turned into one idea that is better than either alone.

TIME BYTE 8-3
A Five-into-One Combination

Combine Quaker Oats Company, CBS, direct mail, grocery redemption coupons, and electronic scanners at the checkout counter and what do they add up to? A unique form of market research. Quaker Oats sponsors the direct mail of the coupons to householders. CBS rides piggyback, for a fee, since the network's audience is so large that direct-mail surveys for it as a sole sponsor are not economic. When the coupons (which are coded with the householder's address) are redeemed at the grocery counters, detailed data about the purchase is automatically dispatched to Quaker Oats. With that data, the company can determine who has a dog, say, or a child, and can then target its next round of mailings to that particular household. CBS gains access to the information, too, so that it can get a better idea of the products its audience buys. *The process shows how combining ideas can help to kill two birds with one stone. Electronic scanning surely saves time at the tabulating end, too.*

"For You, Sally Smith, Coupons and Comedies," by Thomas R. King, *The Wall Street Journal*, Jan. 22, 1990, p. B-1.

Making Good Ideas Come Faster

When seeking to innovate, you could wait until lightning strikes. That's the slow way, however. It's better to take advantage of a number of idea-stimulating techniques of proven worth. Most of them are useful any time. A few also add a unique time dimension.

Anytime Idea Stimulators

The following techniques for making good ideas come easily have been used by amateurs and professionals with great success. These techniques are helpful any time:

- *Build up your idea sources.* Freshen your mind by exploring new territories. Take a walk in a different part of town, for example. Talk with people with whom you don't ordinarily associate. Drop by the library and scan magazines you didn't know existed. The goal is to expose yourself to idea sources outside your normal routines.

- *Keep your eye peeled for the unexpected.* Chance favors the idea seeker. Be alert to unusual variations in the way things are done. Look for an unexpected turn of events, a surprising result. These often furnish the clues to a sparkling idea.

- *Split your search into pieces.* When big problems are broken into smaller ones, the search for solutions is simplified. For example, in the design of the first typesetting machine, the problem was broken down into three steps: (1) composing a line, (2) adjusting line length, and (3) redistributing type. Taken as a whole, the problem seemed overwhelming. When it was segmented, solutions came readily.

- *Use the X method.* Suppose, as with the typesetting machine, you are faced with several problems to be solved, and you have no idea for solving one segment. Instead of waiting for a solution to surface, call the solution X, then go on to the next step. After you find the other solutions, the X solution may occur to you. This is the method that General MacArthur used in his island-hopping campaign in the South Pacific during World War II. When he couldn't conquer an island, he bypassed it to take another. The ones he didn't conquer were left to wither on the vine.

- *Sharpen your ability to spot problems.* Listen to complaints. They will tell you plenty about problems that need new solutions. Jot down your own complaints, too, about the way things are run in your own work. Or ask customers or clients, for instance, what they see wrong with your services. They may tell you things that will open your mind to innovations.

- *Develop a honeybee mind.* Gather your ideas everywhere. Don't be afraid to associate your ideas freely. Let your mind buzz from one idea source to another, just as a honeybee buzzes from a rose to a clover to a hollyhock.

- *Prepare yourself for the hot flash.* Relax your mind from time to time. After a hard day's work, let it wander. Daydream as you walk home from work or ride on your commuter train. Try a hot shower or restful music. After a good night's sleep, get up an hour early, take a long walk, meditate. While you're relaxing, your subconscious will be working, getting ready to release the hot idea you've been looking for.

- *Use idea banks, traps, and museums.* That's what Charles Clark, a noted creativity consultant, calls them. He suggests that you keep an *idea bank* in a file folder of clippings, notes, pamphlets, etc., even if you're not seeking an idea at the moment. An *idea trap* is a notebook in which you jot down ideas as they occur to you; that way they are not lost or forgotten. An *idea museum* is the shelf behind your desk that holds catalogs for equipment and supplies—catalogs that you can peruse when you're looking for ideas.

Time-Related Idea Stimulators

Time seems always to be a distracting concern. Accordingly, when you become impatient with the creative process, consider the perspective offered by the following advice:

- *Find the right time of day.* The time when you feel most creative, when your energy is at its peak, is when you can build your store of ideas. Later, when your energy is somewhat drained, is the time for red-light thinking.

- *Schedule practice sessions.* You can build important self-confidence by scheduling regular practice sessions, once a week, for instance, for 15 minutes before your work begins. During each session, seek and develop ideas that apply to minor matters. Skills and confidence developed in these practice sessions will make ideas come faster when you are working on an urgent problem.

- *Use the two-day formula.* When stymied for ideas, set the problem aside for a full day. Then hit it hard on the second day.

- *Expect time to appear to be wasted.* In seeking ideas, you must accept two facts: (1) ideas will not always flow readily, and (2) many ideas will be useless. Hunting for inspiration may seem to be a waste of time. In the long run, however, the time used in searching for ideas is well-invested. You'll reap only about two good ideas for every fifteen you think up. But two ideas are a lot better than none.

Idea-Selling Time

No matter how much an idea may be needed by an organization, it will rarely be accepted at first sight. More often, the idea will have to be sold persuasively up the line, and across the line. In such instances, these three dictums will help advance your cause:

1. *Anticipate a negative reaction.* Be prepared to hear objections like "It's impractical," "It's been tried before," and "It won't work here." Also be prepared to hear that your idea comes too early, or too late. In advance, figure out rebuttals to these arguments. Be ready to try a new tack, a detour, or a compromise in order to gain a toehold for your idea.

2. *Emphasize the benefits.* Your boss and others will ask, "What is in this idea for us?" Try to win support for your idea by showing how its implementation will benefit other individuals and departments as well as the organization as a whole.

3. *Make it easy to say "yes."* Think through every problem likely to arise in carrying out your proposal. Then provide an acceptable answer to show that you've planned for every such circumstance. Busy executives have problems of their own. If, in order to approve your proposal, they would have to stop and solve a problem relating to your idea, the easiest and quickest answer would be "no." You need to give them a proposal that inspires a "yes."

PRACTICE TIME 8-1: A Self-Directed Exercise
Coat-Hanger Time

Good ideas come in bunches—and under pressure. In this exercise you'll have an opportunity to demonstrate your talent for creativity and innovation under pressures of time.

Assignment. Obtain, or think of, a typical wire coat hanger—that ubiquitous device used by the dry cleaner to hang your coat or jacket on. Coat hangers accumulate in your closet—appearing to be too good to discard, but with a potential usefulness that often escapes you. Your assignment will be to think of as many ways as you can for using these wire coat hangers—in a very brief time period.

Instructions. Be ready to time yourself, preferably with a kitchen timer or similar device. Also, have paper and pencil handy for writing down your ideas. Your record doesn't have to be beautifully or precisely written; you may use any kind of shorthand or jotting-down procedure that you find convenient, as long as it will be clear to you later.

1. Set the timer for 5 minutes. Start jotting down your ideas. When the 5 minutes are over, draw a line under the last idea you have recorded.
2. Set the timer again, for 3 minutes. Jot down your ideas. When the 3 minutes are over, draw a line under your last idea.
3. Set the timer once again, for 2 minutes. Again jot down your ideas.
4. Stop. Add up your ideas.

Scoring. A total of 15 ideas makes you a master of creativity. A total of 10 or more ideas indicates that you have an excellent capacity to generate ideas. A total of under 10 ideas is below normal for this exercise.

If you thought of more ideas during the last 5 minutes than you did during the first 5, you've demonstrated the value of persistence in seeking ideas.

Commentary. The number of ideas created says nothing, of course, about their quality. Many deliberate thinkers are very creative, and low scorers here may be among them.

Typical uses suggested. Opener for a locked car, garden fence, back scratcher, paint-can holder, paint stirrer, mobile, flowerpot holder, tie rack, belt, concrete reinforcer, door latch, retriever for items on high shelves, hooks for many purposes (closet items, garden tools, etc.), binding newspapers, cleaning mud from boots, fishhooks, bookends, baling wire for hay, cut up into nails, and—inevitably—coat hanger.

TIME CHECK

Use this action-plan checklist to verify your understanding of the various concepts, ideas, and techniques presented in this chapter and to indicate any need for further action on your part.

	Applies to your situation		Schedule for action	
	Yes	No	Yes	No
1. A supportive climate for innovation: time to think, genuine involvement, and a tolerance for failure.	____	____	____	____
2. Recognizing and minimizing environments that inhibit innovation: pass-along processing, organizational barricades, independent fiefdoms, tolerance of delays, and unrealistic time frames.	____	____	____	____

3. Applications of cross-functional ideas such as DFMA, EIM, and cross-functional teams.   ____ ____ ____ ____

4. Establishment of creative goals that specify: (a) number of ideas to be generated, (b) time frame, (c) time span, and (4) potential impact, according to either the conservative or the radical scope of the ideas.   ____ ____ ____ ____

5. Understanding the nature of free association and of green-light and red-light thinking.   ____ ____ ____ ____

6. Knowing how to search for ideas on your own, by (a) narrowing the search, (b) concentrating, (c) persisting, (d) having self-confidence, (e) using your subconscious, (f) keeping ideas flowing, and (g) taking action.   ____ ____ ____ ____

7. Application of group creativity using brainstorming, for which the rules are: (a) don't criticize, (b) welcome freewheeling, (c) strive for quantity, and (d) combine and improve.   ____ ____ ____ ____

8. Understanding techniques used to stimulate creativity, such as: building idea sources; keeping alert for the unexpected; splitting the search into pieces; using the X method; sharpening your ability to spot problems; developing a honeybee mind; preparing for the hot flash; and using idea banks, traps, and museums.   ____ ____ ____ ____

9. Application of time-related stimulators, including: finding the right time of day, scheduling practice sessions, using the two-day formula, and expecting time to appear to be wasted.   ____ ____ ____ ____

10. Selling your ideas by (a) anticipating a negative reaction, (b) emphasizing benefits, and (c) making it easy to say "yes."   ____ ____ ____ ____

PART 3
Managing Organizational Time

9
Time Measurement for Management

How to find out exactly how much time it takes to get a job done, and why this is so important to you

When you can measure what you are speaking about, and express it in numbers, you know something about it. But when you cannot measure it, cannot express it in numbers, your knowledge is a meagre and unsatisfactory kind. LORD KELVIN, PHYSICIST

Time is the yardstick by which we measure our lives and accomplishments. That's pretty heady philosophy, but it is also enormously practical. The principle of time as a measuring stick slowly dawned on the minds of the earth's earliest societies, and gradually became one of the guiding forces of civilization. Early people measured time by the movement of the stars and planets, by the shadows cast by the sun, and by the rising and setting of the moon. Today, we measure time by clocks and calendars and by vibrations in tiny crystals that cycle millions of times a second. The principle of time as a yardstick for our actions and progress, however, remains a very practical matter. That is because time measurement enables you:

■ To know in advance how long it will take to complete a job

- To set realistic performance standards for employees and yourself
- To establish reliable plans and schedules

The secrets of time measurement, unfortunately, have always been concealed within the realm of specialists. In ancient times, the specialists were temple priests. Later on, astronomers and scientists became the keepers of the calendar. Today, there is a small—and obscure—cadre of engineers who practice time study. Their expertise is badly needed and underutilized, however. Understanding the evolution of time measurement and the way it is practiced by time-study specialists today will be of great practical value for you. This chapter offers you that understanding, along with some useful insights into how you can judge the reliability of time measurements and time standards that the experts are likely to impose upon you.

Ancient Time Keepers

The people whom we like to characterize as "primitive" were really not so naive when it came to keeping time. Early on, they learned to distinguish daytime from nighttime, mark the phases of the moon, and observe the regular succession of the seasons. For the hunting, grazing, and gathering societies, these were important designators of the passage of time. More significant, these observations led early societies to assume that time was periodic and would repeat itself, if not exactly, at least with some degree of certainty. This knowledge encouraged these people to make plans in much the same fashion as we do today. They rose early in the morning when the trek ahead was known to be long; they laid traps in the daytime for the night-prowling animals; they learned to plant in the spring in anticipation of harvesting in the fall; they put away food for the winter, knowing that hunting and gathering would be sparse during that season; and they looked ahead to the moon that signaled the new year with its promise of renewal of the earth.

Progression From Macro to Micro Measures

The ancients' general awareness of the absolute nature of time and its cycles led to their attempts at more precise measurements. This progression from very broad—*macro*—measurements to very small—*micro*—measurements is illustrated in Figure 9-1. For example, the following developments were especially significant:

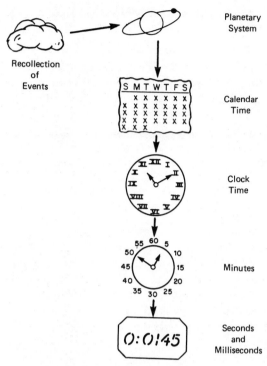

Figure 9-1. Progression from macro to micro time measures.

1. *Measurement by event.* If ancient people did not count the years, although many did, they nevertheless marked them with remembrances of past events. They spoke of the year of the flood, or the drought, or the pestilence, and of the time of human landmarks, such as the bitter battle, or the great rulers, or the exodus.

2. *Measurement by the planetary system.* You are probably aware of how precise some of the ancient civilizations became in timing their days, months, and years by careful observation of the sun, moon, and stars. Even such a primitive society as existed at Stonehenge on the Salisbury Plain in England marked the summer and winter solstices and the equinoxes by sighting the rising sun above a "heelstone" set 100 feet outside its mysterious circle of standing stones.

3. *Measurement by calendar.* The Babylonians of Mesopotamia perfected the first calendar, as is common knowledge, but it is instructive to learn also that prehistoric American Indians in dozens of locations throughout the midwestern United States and Canada (Medicine Mountain in Wyoming is an example) erected crude horizon-calendars.

These Indians counted the days by using a circle of stones for sighting the sun and stars with reference to stationary landmarks in the Rockies.

4. *Measurement by clock.* Early civilizations also had their own devices for counting the hours and its fractions. The sundial, in one form or another, appeared more than 3500 years ago. The water clock, which counted the hours according to water leaking through a hole in a calibrated vessel, appeared at about the same time. By about 400 B.C., Plato had invented a hydraulic version that not only indicated the hours with a pointer, but also played an organ on the hour. Almost certainly, the water clock was the immediate predecessor of the mechanical clock.

Origin of the Fiscal Year

The Egyptians, better than most people of their day, fashioned a remarkably useful system for observing and recording time. They knew, for instance, that the year contained about 365 days, but they considered this an awkward figure to deal with. Accordingly, the daily income for the temples was accounted for as $\frac{1}{360}$ year. To adjust this figure for dating purposes, the extra 5 days were just "added on" at the end of the year. There is some indication that these extra days became a time of holiday, somewhat like Mardi Gras.

A census of cattle was taken biannually, and these times marked the fiscal years, usually referred to sequentially through a dynasty as the sixth, seventh, etc., "year of the numbering."

The Egyptians also divided their calendar into 12 months of 30 days each (based upon phases of the moon)—hence the 360 days.

The Egyptian approach to hourly timekeeping was also pragmatic. These early scientists were the first to divide the day into 24 hours, with 12 for day and 12 for night. But for accounting convenience, the hours of the day were made longer in summer than in winter. That is, in summer there might be 12 units of daylight, each lasting 1¼ hours, and 12 units of night, each ¾ hour in length.

Measurement by Minutes and Seconds

The designation of the minute and second evolved from the measurement of space. The ancient civilizations, Egypt among them, found it convenient to divide a circle into 360 degrees, perhaps to match the notion of the 360-day yearly cycle. The Babylonians, however, figured everything in 6s and 60s, which led to a further subdivision of each degree of a circle into 60 parts. When the Romans divided a circle into 360 degrees, they called each degree the "first minutae part," or "minute." When they split this degree into 60 parts, they called each such segment the "second minutae part," or "second." Later, because the thinking was that the study of astronomy was close to the study of time, hours were divided the same way. Hence, an hour has 60 minutes, and a minute has 60 seconds.

TIME BYTE 9-1
Split-Second Clock-Watching

When the decade of the 1980s passed into 1990, an adjustment was made in all the official clocks of the world. One second was added so that atomic clocks could stay in synchronization with the earth's rotation. This is the fifteenth second that has been added to clocks since 1972. The adjustments are necessary because atomic clocks keep more accurate time than the earth. Our planet's rotation has been slowing, while atomic clocks keep on ticking precisely. Adding the "leap second" at 23:59:60 Coordinated Universal Time (formerly Greenwich Mean Time) on December 31, 1989, enabled the earth to catch up.

Similarly, computer-aided time measurements of employee performance offer incredible precision.

Modern Time Studies

Most people today are concerned mainly with microtime—months, days, hours, minutes, and perhaps seconds. After all, you can't make much of a daily or weekly time plan for yourself—or for others—without having a clear idea of how long it takes to get things done. Happily, you can find out by borrowing from modern time study.

An End of Guesswork

As the individualized craft system of Europe evolved into a managed factory system, especially in the United States, the need to anticipate how long a task should take increased. Otherwise, managers could use only the roughest rules of thumb to distribute work equitably among their employees. Most of these early time estimates were pure guesswork and were patently unfair. Plans and schedules based upon them were often useless.

It wasn't until the turn of the twentieth century, however, that serious attempts were made to find out systematically exactly how long it should take to perform a specified job effectively. Studies were conducted then by Frederick W. Taylor, noted—or notorious—industrial engineer (or "efficiency expert"), the first of the time-study men and women. Taylor made these studies at the Midvale Iron Works outside Philadelphia, by observing employees at work. Taylor's technique was to watch a reasonably skilled worker performing a repetitive task in a prescribed manner. As the worker developed a rhythm, Taylor would record the times taken for a dozen or so repetitions and then strike an average of these times. This average time then became the time allowed to perform the task, or the *time standard.*

Time and Efficiency

Until Taylor's time, few people were concerned with how much time it took to do anything. Labor was cheap, and employers simply sweated work out of their employees. Wages for manual labor were paid by the day or week, not by the hour. Taylor observed, however, that when work was performed under these conditions, it was rarely done efficiently. He became obsessed with finding the "one best way" to perform a task, regardless of how much the laborer was paid. Taylor introduced the use of the stopwatch to measure the time it took to perform even the tiniest portions of a job. The work studied was mainly repetitive jobs, like those on an assembly line. Taylor discovered that by breaking a job down into its smallest segments, often taking only a few seconds, he could, in some instances, eliminate waste motions and, in others, use time-saving devices. The importance of this discovery led to the general application of *work measurement,* the term applied to any system for establishing a reasonable time for performing a job efficiently. Taylor and his followers tied these systems to wage incentive plans, by which workers were paid in proportion to how well they performed against the time standard. *What was important, however, was establishment of the principle that in order to know whether time is utilized efficiently or wastefully, it is necessary to know how long it should take to perform a given task under existing or stipulated conditions.*

Time Study Today: Much More Than "How Long?"

Variations, modifications, and improvements on Taylor's technique have been introduced, and a number of associated problems have been discovered. These problems have mainly to do with a shortsighted focus on how long it should take to do a job, without taking into account the often unnoted, or unspecified, variables that can influence how much can be accomplished in the observed time period. As illustrated in Figure 9-2, these factors include the following:

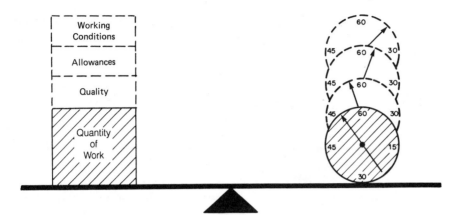

Figure 9-2. Factors that affect time standards.

1. *The quality factor.* All acceptable time studies are based upon the operator's performing the task up to a specified standard of quality. It is obvious that the more stringent the quality requirement, the greater the time needed to perform the task. For example, a time study might show that it takes 2.05 minutes to grind an aircraft gear accurately to 1/1000th inch or 2.85 minutes to grind one to 1/10,000 inch. Similarly, a file clerk might take a certain time to file 1000 documents with 25 misfiles or a longer time to file the same number of documents with only 5 misfiles.

2. *Allowances.* To the average time, most studies add an allowance, usually a standard percentage, for unavoidable delays caused by factors such as shortages of materials. For example, measurements might indicate an average time of 1.50 minutes. To this figure an allowance time of, say, 10 percent might be added, to create the time standard. Thus, the final standard would be calculated as 1.50 minutes + (0.10 × 1.50) minutes, or 1.50 + 0.15 = 1.65 minutes.

3. *Conditions.* A good time study preserves a record of the methods and conditions under which the performance was observed. That is, the technician should record the machine with which the work was done, the materials used, the methods employed, and their sequence. This helps to sustain the value of the time standard derived from the study over a long period of time. If methods and conditions are changed later on, a new study must be made.

Insights Into the Time Specialist's World

Time-study engineers are well aware of the requirements and difficulties described above, and they have taken a number of steps to minimize problems. So that you can use your time measurements wisely and keep your time-study experts honest, you should be aware of the following techniques and practices:

1. *Rating and leveling.* Much controversy surrounds the process of rating and leveling. You might well ask whether the time observed for a very fast operator should be used as the standard for other employees. It can be used, but only after it has been rated. *Rating* is gauging the operator's pace as he or she performs the job while observed by the time-study technician. This pace is compared with a judgment of what is felt to be a normal pace. This *normal pace* is, in effect, the time it would take an average employee to do the job. An employee, further, must be able to keep up the pace all day long. Technicians are trained to judge paces through the use of generally accepted training films. Surprisingly, the rating procedure is held by most labor unions to be a valid technique. Here's the way it works.

When an employee is working, he or she may, consciously or otherwise, work as far below normal as 40 percent or as far above as 200 percent. The time-study technician can't wait until the operator performs at exactly 100 percent: it wouldn't be practical. Instead, the technician rates the operator's pace, and then adjusts the time measured by an estimate of the operator's pace.

Take, for example, John, who is soldering wire ends to a television chassis. Mary, the time-study technician, times John while he makes 10 connections. The actual times measured are 0.13, 0.12, 0.15, 0.11, 0.12, 0.23, 0.12, 0.12, 0.13, and 0.11. Mary looks at the times and throws out the 0.23 reading as abnormal. Then she totals the remaining readings and divides by 9 to get an average time of 0.12 minutes. Now comes the critical phase of time study. Mary must apply her rating factor—the process of *leveling*.

While she observed John making the connections, Mary mentally compared his pace with what she estimated was normal pace for an operation using similar skills. Her estimate was that John was working at 110 percent of normal, or 10 percent faster than would be normally expected. Therefore, the leveled time for the standard is not the actual time observed. It is modified by the rated time, or in this case, 0.12 minutes × 110 percent = 0.132 minutes. Had the operator been rated at 80 percent, the leveled time would be 0.12 minutes × 80 percent = 0.096 minutes. You can readily see that no matter how conscientiously the rating is made, it is always a matter of opinion. Consequently, it is also a matter of debate. Many of management's disputes with labor unions over time studies arise over the rating factor. It should be noted that times observed by operators rated below 80 percent or over 125 percent are not generally accepted as a good basis for setting time standards.

2. *Standard data.* Many large organizations rely upon an accumulation of standard times rather than making a time study for each new job as it arises. For example, take the case of a machinist turning down a spindle. Over the years, this kind of operation has been studied thousands of times. The time standards for the separate steps—or elements—in the operation are recorded in tables (either held by the company itself or available from proprietary firms). These tables cover practically every possible variation. The tables will show standard times for a variety of machines and chucks, for carbon and stainless steel, for short spindles and long, for deep cuts and shallow, for wide tolerances and narrow.

The time-study technician need only analyze the elements in the job in hand, the order in which they are performed, and the number of times they are repeated. The next step is to look up in the tables the standard data for each element, and to add them up for a time standard for that job.

3. *Predetermined elemental time standards.* Similar to standard data, but with one big difference, are predetermined standards. The data for these standards are based upon times that have been established, not for elements of specific tasks, like machining a spindle, but for basic hand, arm, and body movements as well as for movements of a wide variety of machinery and equipment. The time-study specialist examines the specifications of the job to be done and determines the series of movements to be performed. Then, without observing the job actually being performed or timing it, the technician consults a catalog of elemental time data and builds the total time needed for the job from the standards in that catalog.

This concept was first advanced by H. B. Maynard, an industrial engineer with Westinghouse Electric Corporation and was based upon previous work by Frank and Lillian Gilbreth. This famous couple pioneered the study of human motions as they affected time use and devised a shorthand system of 18 symbols that can be used to describe any human motion. They called these symbols *therbligs* (a "therblig" is "Gilbreth" spelled backward). Maynard called his data *methods-time measurement (MTM)*. Other popular proprietary approaches are Work Factors, Basic-Motion Times (BMTs), elemental time standards (ETSs), and Dimensional-Motion Times (DMTs). *Because predetermined elemental time standards are so cost-effective, especially in this age of rapidly changing products and methods for making them, they have all but replaced the practice of studying every job with a stopwatch.*

Beware the Seduction of Historic-Data Times

Time study is an essentially systematic, if not wholly scientific, way to establish the time needed to perform a job. You should understand, however, that it is not the only way. Work (or time) sampling, as described in Chapter 6, is a simple technique that is commonly used to gather data. Perhaps the commonest method of all, however, is examination of past performance as represented by production and accounting records. Using this approach, historic data are studied and approximations derived from them. For example, if the records showed that five employees in the word processing department produced 2500 order-entry documents in a week a year ago, they ought to be able to repeat that performance next week. To carry the method further, the word processing supervisor might calculate that one employee could produce 100 order-entry documents a day.

$$\frac{2500 \text{ documents}}{5 \text{ employees} \times 5 \text{ days}} = 100 \text{ documents per employee per day}$$

The supervisor might go one step further and derive a rule-of-thumb time per document per employee of 5 minutes.

$$\frac{8 \text{ hours} \times 60 \text{ minutes}}{100 \text{ documents}} = \frac{480 \text{ minutes}}{100 \text{ documents}}$$

$$= 4.8 \text{ minutes per document,}$$
$$\text{rounded to 5 minutes}$$

There's no denying that 5 minutes per document is a pretty useful figure. Even if it is rough and subject to many errors, it is better than nothing when planning a schedule or in assigning work. The danger, of course, is that many unrecorded conditions may have influenced the data and made it unreliable under present conditions. There are many things that might have changed since the data were originally recorded, such as the document itself; the data on the document; the word processing equipment; the office support system; and the pay, skill, and/or training of the operators. If any or all of these changes have occurred, the times derived from the data will be erroneous and misleading—and they very often are. *Generally speaking, the historic-data approach is a very useful technique for estimating, but it is unreliable—and it is also often difficult to justify to employees.*

Time Standards and Their Applications

As you may have already concluded, a body of specialized time-measurement language has been developed, as illustrated in the glossary in Table 9-1. You should be familiar with these terms. Otherwise, you will be at the mercy of time-study specialists and systems analysts and the output standards they issue. For example, the times measured by time studies usually become *time standards*. But, as a typically confusing point of terminology, the time for a *job*, as opposed to the time for an *element* of it, is called *standard time*. Happily, however, most authorities agree on the definitions of time standard and standard time (see Table 9-1). Standard time is computed by multiplying the number of good pieces to be finished by the time standard for the particular operation.

For instance, the standard for grinding an aircraft gear accurately to ± %₀₁ inch might be 2.05 minutes. The standard time, however, for a job that requires grinding 10 pieces would be:

10 pieces × 2.05 minutes per piece = 20.5 minutes

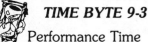

TIME BYTE 9-3

Performance Time

"We have moved from the age of paternalism to the age of performance," says Prof. Robert Kelly at the Carnegie Mellon University Graduate School of Industrial Administration. His observation is triggered by the increasing number of clerical and professional jobs in which pay is tied to some sort of performance incentive. In almost all cases, these incentives bear a close resemblance to classic wage incentive and bonus plans in that financial rewards are based upon increasing output over a specified period of time. Among the jobs now included are bank tellers at Security Pacific, who have drawn bonuses of $50,000 a year. Also targeted are hospital nurses, whose incentive is based upon the number of patients tended; laboratory technicians, whose incentive is penalized by faulty tests; graphic artists; and draftspersons. *Apparently, no kind of work will be immune from the time factor.*

"A Banker's Prescription for Making Retail Pay," by Tim W. Ferguson, *The Wall Street Journal*, Feb. 6, 1990, p. A19. "Tying Professional Pay to Productivity," by Elizabeth Spayd, *Washington Post*, Jan. 28, 1990, p. H3.

Table 9-1. A Glossary of Time Measurement Terms

Allowance: The amount of time added to a time study or time standard to allow for unavoidable delays, personal time, and—sometimes—fatigue.

Historic-data time: A time standard established on the basis of past performance as represented by production and/or accounting records.

Leveling: A technique for adjusting an observed time either upward or downward, based upon an estimate of how fast the person observed is working, as compared with what might be a normal pace.

Measured daywork: The use of time standards to prescribe and control employee performance, but with no wage incentives attached to that performance.

Normal pace: The working speed that an average employee can be expected to maintain all day long while making a reasonable effort.

Predetermined elemental time standard: A time standard derived not from direct observation, but from times previously established for performing the various *elements*—especially fundamental hand, arm, and body movements and/or machine processes—entailed in a particular task.

Rating: Gauging of an operator's pace as a percentage of a normal pace, as he or she performs a task while observed by a time-study technician.

Standard data: Time data and time standards that have been compiled in tables for a great variety of tasks and jobs. New time standards can be calculated, not by making new studies, but from data in the tables.

Standard time: The total time allowed for a job, which may include one or more defined units of work.

Time standard: The base time allowed for a defined unit of work to be finished to a specified quality.

Time study: The process of observing a task while it is being performed and of systematically recording the time it takes.

Wage incentive: An increment of additional pay that can be earned by an employee who completes a task or job in less than the time established for it.

Wage-Incentive Plans

Taylor, and a great many who followed him, believed that the best way to ensure that employees worked up to the established time standards for a job was to provide a wage incentive or bonus for those who did. This led to a variety of piece-rate and/or wage-incentive plans. The principle remains today, mostly in plans that reward employees in direct proportion to how well their output compares with the standard.

Take the example of a stock clerk in a retail store. She is issued a standard time of 50 minutes for placing the contents of a specified number of cartons on the proper shelves. If the clerk takes only 45 minutes to do this, the reward will be 5/50, or a 10 percent incentive. Typically, this is applied to the employee's hourly rate. If the clerk is paid $10 per hour (often called a *base rate* or *guaranteed rate*), and she maintains her performance at 10 percent above standard all day, her pay for that day will be at the rate of 110 percent of $10, or $11 per hour. Typically, under the guaranteed-rate system, employees' pay is not penalized if they fail to meet the standard.

Since keeping track of the performance against standard for every single employee can become complex and very time-consuming, many companies operate *group incentive plans*. These plans (1) establish the total time allowed for all the jobs performed by a department, for instance, in a day, a week, or a month, and (2) compare this figure with the accumulated output of the department, as measured by the standard-time credits for all the jobs completed. A percentage is struck at the end of the period, and each employee in the department is paid this percentage of his or her particular base-pay rate.

Special plans have also been introduced for *machine-paced* jobs. For many of today's industrial and clerical jobs, the speed is controlled not so much by the operator as by the machine tended by the operator. Under such conditions, many companies establish a wage incentive based upon the degree to which the operator keeps the machine running at its scheduled capacity. This places a premium on the operator's keeping the machine supplied with materials, for instance, and properly oiling and otherwise maintaining the equipment. In effect, the incentive is based not upon the operator's productivity but upon the operator's not obstructing the inherent productivity of the machine.

Employee and Union Reactions. Wage incentives of any kind have rarely been popular with labor union leaders. The basis for their objection is that if four employees work at 125 percent above standard, the need for a fifth employee is eliminated. The reaction of individual employees to wage-incentive plans differs widely. As might be expected, high achievers prefer the opportunity to earn more than their guaranteed hourly rate; other employees, however, often resent what they feel is unjustified pressure to speed up their work.

TIME BYTE 9-4

UPS by the Clock

For United Parcel Service driver Richard Kolwicz, it's a trot from truck to customer's door at 3 feet per second. He holds the clipboard under his right arm and package under the left, with only one look at the package to fix the address in his mind. The paperwork is done on the return trip to the truck, where his left foot is programmed to hit the step first. By following these rigidly prescribed time standards, each day Richard will make 145 stops to deliver 246 packages and pick up 70 others. He's paid a handsome wage to stick to the standard, and he likes it very much. However, his union—the Teamsters—would like to cut back on the drivers' tight schedules in order to increase jobs. But, say UPS officials, if just 30 seconds were added to every stop, the driver's day would be longer by an hour and 12 minutes. That's a drop in output of over 8 percent, something the company's price structure couldn't stand. *Are you surprised that UPS, which is an employee-owned company, is largely managed by executives who were trained as clock-watching industrial engineers?*

"Hello, I Must Be Going: On the Road with UPS," by Todd Vogel, *Business Week,* June 4, 1990, p. 82.

Measured Daywork: A Compromise

Management has generally liked the idea of wage-incentive plans for employees but has disliked the extent of paperwork involved. Some managements, however, subscribe to the idea that most employees will work effectively without a wage incentive, so long as they know what is expected of them and so long as the expectation is reasonable. The concept of measured daywork appeals to these managers. This system applies any available form of time standard for planning, scheduling, and assigning work, *but it does not offer any kind of wage incentive to employees in return.* In effective measured daywork plans—and there are many—considerable effort is made (1) to involve employees either in setting or reviewing the time standards and (2) to incorporate the time standards into the company's performance appraisal program.

Be a Doubter

Mention was made earlier in this chapter of the dangers of using historic-time data. The risk in applying time standards doesn't stop there. All time measurements and standards should be regarded with a degree of caution. Before applying time standards to your plans and schedules, give consideration to the following long list of factors and conditions that might affect the accuracy or present worth of your time data:

Seasonal influences

Equipment conditions and capacities

Extent of supporting labor

Operational methods in use

Materials and supplies used

Product or service specifications

Organizational structure

Extent of staff support

General economic conditions

Growth rate of the organization

State of employee morale

Absence or presence of a labor union

Technological developments

Product or service mix

Company, plant, office, or unit size

Caution: Unless the factors and conditions listed above have been examined and their influences incorporated into the time standard, the standard will be flawed—and you should apply it with caution. The least you should do is to assess the current status of the potentially distorting conditions to see if there have been significant changes since the standard was established. If there have been such changes, you are better off not using the standard.

Unintentional Errors

Even with the best of intentions, time data can be infected with any number of errors, such as these:

- Simple mistakes in observation or recording

- Convenience, as when the tallies are closed early in the day and the remainder of the output is transferred to the next day

- The "halo effect," as when the observer is impressed with either extraordinarily high or extraordinarily low times

- Losses in transferring data from one period to another

- Misunderstanding the system, as when "late" deliveries are recorded by a clerk only if they are a week overdue, when the intention is to identify every delivery that is as much as a day late

Caution: Accidental and unintentional errors can be reduced, if not eliminated, by more careful design of the observing, collecting, and reporting system. The measurement process also needs cross checks, just as accounting systems do. And the people in the measurement system need adequate indoctrination and continual training.

Deliberate Falsification

While we don't like to dwell upon it, a great deal of time-related data is deliberately falsified or misrepresented. This takes place for a variety of reasons. For example:

- *To improve individual earnings and bonuses.* This is likely to happen among certain individuals from the bottom to the top of the organization.

- *To conceal poor performance.* All along the line, output or production rates may be reported as higher than they are, and the incidences of waste and errors as lower.

- *To imply progress.* When goals are long-range, progress against project or strategic milestones may be misstated, with the hope that these will be overtaken in the next reporting period.

- *To divert attention.* If there are serious delays in one area of performance, accelerated progress may be "creatively reported" elsewhere in order to divert attention to the shortcomings in the vital zone.

Caution: Curtailment of deliberate falsification is difficult to achieve. It is deeply rooted in motivational causes. The ideal, of course, is to encourage all members of an organization to embrace the concept of self-control—as opposed to the belief by so many that measurement is a punitive device designed to undercut them.

PRACTICE TIME 9-1: A Self-Directed Exercise

Standardizing the Reservation Time

Background. The manager of an airline reservation system wished to establish a reliable time standard for telephone-reservation clerks. Accordingly, the manager chose a well-trained, experienced, competent clerk to time-study. The times observed—in minutes and hundredths of a minute to complete a satisfactory reservation—were as follows: 1.50, 1.35, 1.60, 0.80, 1.55, 1.60, 1.40, 1.40, 2.10, 1.65, 1.45, 1.50. The manager rated the clerk's pace as 110 percent. The company's allowance for personal time, interruptions, and fatigue is 20 percent of the observed and leveled time.

Assignment—Part 1. Find the time standard for completing a satisfactory reservation.

1. Discard any of the observations that seem far enough away from the central value to be nonrepresentative:_____
2. Find the average time taken for the remaining observations:_____
3. Level the average time by applying the rating factor:_____
4. Determine the final time standard by applying the allowance factor to the leveled time:_____

Commentary. Observation times of 0.80 and 2.10 should be discarded as nonrepresentative. The average time for the remaining 10 observations is 1.50 minutes (15.00 ÷ 10). The leveled time is 1.65 minutes (1.50 × 1.10). The final time standard is 1.65 + 1.65 × .20 = 1.65 + 0.33 = 1.98 minutes.

Assignment—Part 2. Calculate the following extensions of the time standard.

1. If the manager were to set up the job assignments so that a clerk could rotate to another station after completing a block of 25 reservations (a "job"), determine the *standard time* for such a job:_____
2. If the clerks work a 7-hour day (after rest periods have been subtracted), determine how many reservations a clerk should be expected to complete in a day:_____

Commentary. The standard time for the designated job is 25 × 1.98 minutes = 49.50 minutes. In a 7-hour day, a clerk could be expected to complete 212 reservations; 7 hours × 60 minutes ÷ 1.98 minutes = 420 ÷ 1.98 = 212.12.

 ## TIME CHECK

Use this action-plan checklist to verify your understanding of the various concepts, ideas, and techniques presented in this chapter and to indicate any need for further action on your part.

	Applies to your situation		Schedule for action	
	Yes	No	Yes	No

1. Lessons learned from the pragmatism of the Egyptian time system, with its 360 civil (or fiscal) days. ____ ____ ____ ____

2. Knowledge of the evolution of time keeping from macro measurements to micro measurements. ____ ____ ____ ____

3. Knowledge of how to make a time study, and the effect of quality and other conditions, allowances, pace rating, and leveling upon the ultimate time standard. ____ ____ ____ ____

4. Understanding the availability and use of standard data, especially predetermined elemental time standards. ____ ____ ____ ____

5. Caution in application of historic-data times. ____ ____ ____ ____

6. Ability to convert time standards for an element of a job into a standard time for a job. ____ ____ ____ ____

7. Knowledge of how a time standard can be used to create a wage incentive. ____ ____ ____ ____

8. Knowledge of how measured daywork (time standards without wage incentives) can be used to control and improve the use of employee time. ____ ____ ____ ____

9. Alertness to the many factors and conditions that can affect the reliability of time data. ____ ____ ____ ____

10. Alertness to the possibility of (a) unintentional errors in time measurements as well as (b) deliberate falsification. ____ ____ ____ ____

10
Improving Productive Time

How to improve the productivity of facilities and other key resources by using time effectively

In 3050 B.C., the first stone masonry had not been laid. Yet, within 150 years the grandest monument ever built by man was raised to stand immutable and eternal in the desert. It took 100,000 men twenty years to lift the monolithic blocks of the Great Pyramid by some combination of levers and planes. Labor might be cheap at a few handfuls of grain a day, but this did not solve the element of time.   STUART CHASE
Men and Machines

Time is a uniquely universal measure that is present both in our personal lives and in the fortunes of an organization. As a result, time has a profound effect upon our productivity—the measure we use to gauge the extent to which our input efforts add value to our output results. Time value can be applied to just about any *input* of an enterprise. The time value of facilities and equipment, for instance, is rent. The time value of an electric bill is measured in kilowatt-hours. The time value of money and materials is interest. The time value of a work force is measured in labor-hours. Similarly, *outputs* are valued by the number of units produced per minute, per hour, per week, per year. We measure our accomplishments by what we've done this week, this month, this year. We tick off the remaining opportunities of our lives as we celebrate our annual birthdays. Even profits are judged by an annual reckoning.

The Productivity Factor

You might quite rightly ask, how—exactly—does the concept of productivity fit into the time picture? The answer is that, in many ways, and especially in popular awareness, productivity measures have overshadowed the importance of time measurements. The fact is, however, that productivity measurements almost always incorporate a time measurement. Let's see how that happens.

Productivity Measurement

Basically, productivity is a measurement of the efficiency of a person, a process, a machine, or an organization. Productivity is determined by comparing (1) the value of the output or result with (2) the cost of the input resource. It is usually expressed as a ratio (or rate):

$$\text{Productivity} = \frac{\text{output}}{\text{input}}$$

For example, the productivity of a hand-assembly department in a furniture factory might be stated as five chairs per labor-hour. *(Note that productivity is immediately related to a time period!)* In this instance, the number of chairs assembled is the output; the labor expended is the input. If the furniture factory wished, it could convert both figures to dollars. The value added to the chairs by the assembly operation might be estimated at $6 each, or a total of $30. If the cabinetmaker were paid $10 an hour, the productivity of the assembly operation would be $30 divided by $10, or a ratio of 3:1.

Ratios can be converted to percentages, and some companies state productivity that way. For instance, the 3:1 ratio is 300 percent. If the ratio were 2:1, it would be stated as 200 percent. Very often, you will hear present productivity compared with previous productivity. This is usually expressed as a percentage increase or decrease. For example, if your department's productivity ratio was 2:1 last year and it improved to 2.2:1 this year, it would be correct to say that your productivity had improved by 10 percent:

$$(2.2 - 2.0) \div 2.0 = 0.10 = 10\%$$

TIME BYTE 10-1

At Ford, Productivity Is Job 1

The Japanese haven't won all the automobile battles. When it comes to productivity, Ford is out in front. The comparable measure is the number of workers needed to assemble a car in 1 day. At Ford, the figure is 3.36 workers. The five Japanese automakers in the United States require 3.48 workers per car. Chrysler comes next, with 4.38 workers, and General Motors is a poor last at 4.99 workers. There is one hitch, however. Workers in the Japanese-owned plants not only assemble cars but also are expected to perform other duties. According to the experts, without those additional operations, the Japanese plants would match Ford's productivity. *Of one thing you can be sure: the productivity race will go to the swiftest.*

"Study: GM Program a Costly Mistake," by Warren Brown, *Washington Post,* Jan. 3, 1990, p. C1.

Productivity Standards

Just as there is no way of saying that a particular time standard is "good" without comparing it to a previous one or to a standard obtained by another organization, it is also impossible to judge the value represented by a particular productivity ratio without comparing it with another. Many organizations, however, including the U.S. Bureau of Labor Statistics (BLS), often select a particular year as a base for their productivity measurements and then make comparisons with that "standard" from year to year. For example, in 1990 the BLS could show that, compared with 1980, productivity (as measured by output per hour) in U.S. manufacturing plants had averaged an improvement of 3.6 percent per year over the decade. *(Note again, the derivation of a productivity ratio from measurements against a time period!)*

Dangers in Productivity Comparisons

By using comparisons between productivity ratios of a particular activity or process, it is relatively easy and useful to determine whether or not there has been an improvement. The comparisons will be valid, of course, *only* if the units of output and input of the ratios being compared remain the same. The BLS, for example, always uses an index of output based upon value added by manufacturing plants and an input based upon total hours worked in those plants. *The factors that contribute to the inputs and outputs may change*—that's the essence of productivity improvement—*but the methods for calculating their value must be consistent from period to period.* Otherwise, there is an ever-present danger that apples will be compared with oranges.

Rising and Falling Productivity Rates

Over time, the productivity of an operation can do any of three things: it can remain constant, or it can rise or fall. The ways in which changes in either input or output can affect productivity, as shown by the charts in Figure 10-1, are:

- If the value of output from a process remains the same but input costs go down, productivity will rise.
- If the value of output from a process goes up and input costs remain the same, productivity will rise.
- If the value of output from a process remains the same but input costs go up, productivity will fall.
- If the value of output from a process goes down and input costs remain the same, productivity will fall.

If output and productivity both change, you will have to use the basic formula *productivity equals output value divided by input costs.*

Length of the Measurement Period

Traditionally, productivity has been measured over extended periods of time, usually a year. With on-line data reporting, there is no reason why the simpler productivity ratios shouldn't be available weekly and monthly, or even daily. While some firms do provide their managers with daily ratios, there is reason to believe that daily fluctuations will be misleading. There are statistical techniques, of course, that can iron out the impression of these fluctuations; nevertheless, there are so many factors that can contribute to a productivity ratio that it is usually better to make judgments based upon longer periods of time—perhaps a month at the shortest.

Targets for Productivity Improvement

While productivity measurement and improvement had its first major use in manufacturing industries, the principles are applicable everywhere. In many clerical and service occupations, productivity measures

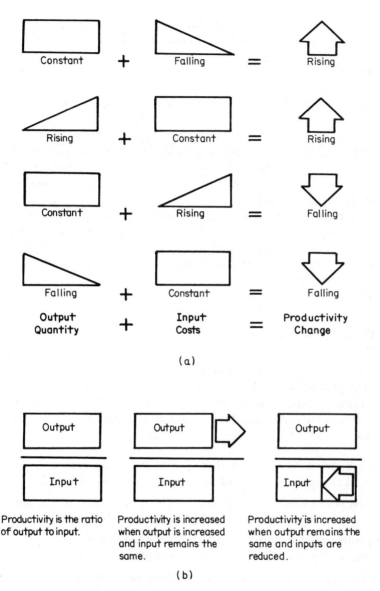

Figure 10-1. (a) How relative changes in output quantities and input costs affect productivity. (b) Two basic ways to increase productivity.

are routinely made exactly as they are in product-related operations. A word processor operator's productivity, for example, might be judged by the number of letters or lines typed per hour worked. A supermarket checkout-counter clerk's productivity might be measured by the number of items checked (or dollars taken in) per day of the clerk's time. Similarly, a bank teller's productivity might be gauged by the number of transactions handled in an hour, day, week, or month of the teller's time.

The only real limit to the application of productivity is the need to obtain reliable measurements of output and input. It is difficult, for example, to measure the value of a nurse's output, although many hospitals use the number of patients handled per shift as a measure of productivity. Here again, for a genuine measure of input, the time value of several contributing factors must be calculated. These include not only the time and wages of the registered nurses, but also the time and wages of licensed practical nurses, nurses' aids, laboratory staff, housekeepers, and food-service personnel.

Another factor to watch is the impact that changes in quality demands can make upon productivity. If quality requirements are raised, output may drop accordingly. Or, if product specifications are loosened, output may rise solely because of this change and not represent a real improvement in productivity.

Consistency in Defining
the Time Period

Finally, careful attention should be given to defining the specifications of the time period over which productivity measurements are made. The following questions, in particular, should be asked to make sure that the consistency needed for meaningful comparisons has been maintained:

Are the hours used this year the same as last year's hours, or is an additional rest period, a longer lunchtime, etc., now included?

Were last year's hours worked at the same time of day as this year's, or did they include night work, overtime hours, etc?

With professional activities (such as with teaching), how long is the actual "contact hour"—45, 55, 60, or 75 minutes?

Is work on holidays included in the computations, or is it discarded?

Did last year's hours include hours worked on split shifts or flextime schedules, as this year's do?

Were the measurements made during the same months this year as last? Are these months rightly comparable?

Do the years consist of 50 or 52 weeks? Of 360 days or 365 days?

If indexing is used for productivity comparisons, was there anything unusual about the base year?

Improving Employees' Use of Time

Earlier in this century, time-study experts fixed the human energy/skill factor as the major target for productivity improvement. Hidden within this target, however, were a number of other manageable conditions that could have a significant influence on the time taken to perform a task, including the following:

- Hand, arm, and body motions employed
- Methods used and/or prescribed
- Physical arrangement of the work station
- Ergonomic aspects of the work station
- Tools and equipment provided
- Organizational support systems

As a consequence of a growing awareness of these factors, management has shifted its emphasis to a continuing search for time-saving techniques that affect a broad scope of human energy and skill inputs. The most important of these improvement techniques include the following:

1. *Methods improvement.* Also called *methods engineering*, this technique involves a systematic examination by managers and specialists of the job as it is being performed now, with a view toward improving procedures and adding mechanical devices to assist and otherwise speed up the job in the future.

2. *Motion economy.* This involves a concerted effort to modify motions of the human body, as it performs work, in such a way that movements are made in the most effective, but also the easiest and least fatiguing, way possible. Motion economy emphasizes these guidelines:

- *Motions should be productive.* That is, every motion should bring the job closer to a finish. Hands, for instance, should not be wasted holding work; they should be released for more productive operations.
- *Motions should be simple.* The fewer the parts of the body used, the better. Use a finger and a thumb, for example, rather than the whole hand. Grasp objects by reaching with the forearm rather than the whole arm. Motions should be along curved paths, rather than in straight lines, since most body parts swing from a joint in a circular motion.
- *Motions should be rhythmic.* Arrange work and prescribe methods so that it is easy to work with smooth motions. It's easier, too, for hands to move in opposite directions and along similar paths.
- *Make workers comfortable.* The workbench, the keyboard, the

chair, the CRT screen should all be arranged so that operators feel comfortable sitting and standing—or walking and lifting, when the work requires it.

- *Limit awkward activities.* A person works more comfortably within the swing of the arms forward and up and down. Reaching, stretching, twisting, bending, and stooping add time to the task and are fatiguing.

TIME BYTE 10-2

What a Difference Some Walls Made!

When Aetna Life & Casualty in Hartford, Connecticut, put up three walls around each of its clerical work stations, productivity went up 53 percent and absenteeism dropped by 14 percent. Privacy was only part of the massive redesign of the company's 1.6 million square feet of work space. Major changes included elimination of the traditional "bullpen" with its crowded sense of clutter and inevitable, nerve-jarring noise level. Other comforts provided were ergonomic chairs, special task lighting, new carpeting along with a sound-masking layout, and glare-filtering window shades.

Still other work improvements included document holders, palm rests, footrests, and "articulating keyboard arms" that enable employees to adjust the position of their computer keyboards.

Active in the redesign was Aetna's environmental psychologist, Carol Sullivan, who observed that, "It's important that your work space say something about you and your company." *It's just as important that the work space say something for productivity.*

"Finding a Fit between Form and Function," by Cindy Skrzycki, *Washington Post*, Dec. 3, 1989, p. H3.

---

3. *Work simplification.* This variation in methods improvement was the first attempt to involve workers themselves in the improvement process. In many ways, it was the precursor of today's Quality Circles concept. Work simplification advises that the status quo should always be challenged. Its guiding principles for saving time are:

- Eliminate unnecessary, nonproductive elements of a task; when possible, eliminate the task itself.
- Combine tasks; doing two or more things at once saves time.
- Change sequence so that elements of a task are performed in the simplest, not necessarily the most logical, order. It may be quicker to stamp all the special notices on a batch of letters at once, for example, than to enter the notices in their logical sequence as each letter is typed.
- Simplify. After focusing on the three principles above, this final step exhorts the supervisor or worker to search for ways to

apply the techniques of methods improvement and motion economy.

4. *Mechanization and automation.* While methods improvement and work simplification tend to focus on small improvements of the human inputs, these highly technological approaches emphasize large-scale improvements, often involving replacement of human effort by computers and machinery.

5. *Systems analysis.* This approach now underlies most techniques for improving the performance of all work. Systems analysis looks for improvements by considering *all* the conditions and components of a task or process as being interdependent, so that a change in one factor will always affect the condition or influence of another. This analysis is greatly aided, perhaps only made possible, by sophisticated analytical techniques such as those offered by quantitative methods, operations research, and computer-aided simulations.

Improving the Time Use of Facilities and Equipment

The space occupied by the facilities of an enterprise can be thought of as its real estate. The time cost of real estate is measured in terms of its rent (per month or year), its mortgage payments (a form of periodic rent on money), or the cost of ownership (loss of possible earnings from interest). The time cost of buildings, equipment, and machinery is measured in much the same way as real estate. These important resources are rented or leased under periodic agreements; they are bought, in part at least, with borrowed money (for which interest must be paid); or they are owned outright (with concurrent loss of interest earnings). Anything that can be done (1) to get more output from these facilities or (2) to reduce their cost is welcomed. Output can often be improved by increasing the operating rate of facilities and equipment, thus obtaining greater time utilization as the equipment approaches its rate capacity. Input costs can also be decreased by improving the facilities utilization rate. A number of techniques are available to serve these purposes.

Budgetary Control Reports

This technique approaches time control from preconceived specifications of what the facility utilization rate should be. As seen in Figure 10-2, a production control department typically issues a budget that first shows (column C) how many hours the machine is expected to be in operation and (column G) a budgeted standard of output per hour of operation. After the operating period has been completed, the budget

Machine (A)	Number of hours		Percent Budgeted Hours Utilized (D)	Number of Units			Percent Effective During Hours Worked (H)
	Worked (B)	Budgeted (C)		Produced This Period (E)	Produced per Machine Hour Worked (F)	Budgeted Standard per Hour Worked (G)	
Lathe	160	200	80	14,400 pieces	90 pieces	100 pieces	90
Press	150	180	83	840 tons	5.6 tons	8 tons	70
Blender	120	240	50	72,000 gallons	600 gallons	1,000 gallons	60

|◄— Extent of Utilization —►|◄————— Effectiveness of Utilization ————►|

$$\text{Column D} = \frac{B}{C} \qquad\qquad \text{Column F} = \frac{E}{B} \qquad \text{Column H} = \frac{F}{G}$$

INTERPRETATION OF THESE MEASURES:

Lathe has good utilization and effectiveness rates.
Press has good utilization rate, but only a fair effectiveness rate.
Blender has poor utilization rate and poor effectiveness rate.

Figure 10-2. Budgetary measures of equipment utilization.

reports (column B) the actual hours of operation and (column D) the percentage of budgeted time utilized. The report then shows (column E) the number of units of output actually produced during the period, and it also (column F) converts this figure to (column G) the number of units of output per machine-hour worked. Finally, in column H, the budget report shows how effective the machine was during the hours it was in operation.

The value of this report is that it gives the manager of the department two important pieces of information:

1. The extent to which the budgeted hours have been actually utilized

2. The effectiveness with which this time has been used to produce units of output

An analysis of the data in columns D and H of Figure 10-2 shows that the lathe displays good utilization and effectiveness. Utilization of the press has been good, but its effectiveness has been poor. For the blender, both utilization and effectiveness are poor.

Equipment Utilization Chart

This kind of study is undertaken—machine by machine, facility by facility—to find out not only (1) how productively each piece of equipment is used, but also (2) the reasons for any underusage. The best way to grasp this technique is to look at Figure 10-3. The chart is con-

Department____________ **Period**____________ **Studied by**____________

Equipment	Monday Day Shift Hours								Tuesday Day Shift Hours								Wednesday Day Shift Hours								Hours possible during 3-day period	Totals						
	8–9 A.M.	9–10 A.M.	10–11 A.M.	11–12 A.M.	12–1 P.M.	1–2 P.M.	2–3 P.M.	3–4 P.M.	8–9 A.M.	9–10 A.M.	10–11 A.M.	11–12 A.M.	12–1 P.M.	1–2 P.M.	2–3 P.M.	3–4 P.M.	8–9 A.M.	9–10 A.M.	10–11 A.M.	11–12 A.M.	12–1 P.M.	1–2 P.M.	2–3 P.M.	3–4 P.M.		[S]	□	○	◒	●	⊗	└
Lathe	○	[S]	□	□	□	[S]	○	[S]	□	□	◒	□	[S]	□	□	□	◒	□	[S]	◒	□	□	□	□	24	5	14	2	3	—	—	—
Press	[S]	□	□	[S]	□	□	[S]	□	●	□	□	[S]	□	⊗	□	□	●	□	[S]	□	□	□	□	●	24	5	15	—	—	3	1	—
Blender	[S]	⊗	⊗	□	⊗	□	□	⊗	□	□	□	[S]	□	⊗	⊗	⊗	□	⊗	⊗	⊗	⊗	□	□	⊗	24	2	10	—	—	—	12	—
Totals																									72	12	39	2	3	3	13	0

Productive Time
[S] Setting up (make ready and tear down)
□ Running

Idle, Nonproductive Time
○ No orders available
◒ Stopped, waiting for materials
● Stopped, no operator available
⊗ Stopped for repairs (mechanical downtime)
└ Scheduled lunch or other breaks

Figure 10-3. Equipment utilization chart.

structed so that only when the machine is running on a productive job (either setting up ⑤ on a job or running ☐ on one) is it considered utilized. All other times represent lost time. These lost times can be classified according to whether there are no orders available for scheduling ◯ ; whether the machine is held up by lack of materials ◒ ; or whether the machine is down for lack of an operator ● or for repairs ⊗ . Some observers also indicate when the machine is idle because of a lunch break or for other planned reasons; an L is used to designate this.

Using a random sampling approach similar to that for work sampling (Chapter 6), observations are taken over a period of several days and recorded on the chart. Based on the abbreviated data shown in Figure 10-3 (many more observations would be made in a full study), the following can be deduced:

The *lathe* was being set or running on productive work 19 of the 24 hours; this is a utilization rate of 19:24, or nearly 80 percent. The lost time is attributable mainly to waiting for orders (2 hours) and waiting for materials (3 hours). These conditions can be improved by (1) better scheduling and (2) greater coordination in procurement and delivery of raw materials.

The *press* was productive 20 of the 24 hours during the study period. This is a utilization rate of 20:24, or better than 83 percent. The press was observed stopped three times, however, because there was no operator available. Management in this department must ask: Is this an absentee problem? Or is one operator being spread too thinly among several machines?

The *blender* was productive only 12 hours of the 24, for a utilization rate of 50 percent. This is obviously poor performance, and the reason for it is clearly seen. The blender was down for repairs a total of 12 hours, or 50 percent of the time. This machine needs either more effective maintenance or outright replacement. Poorly maintained equipment not only causes loss of time from the machine's designed capacity, it also tends to cause more time to be lost during the start-up period after repairs. Faulty operation may also reduce acceptable outputs by producing products that don't meet quality specifications.

Capacity Improvement Review

Equipment capacities and utilization must be systematically reviewed, focusing on ways to improve utilization. Typical suggestions for improvement include:

- Placement in a more convenient location
- Performance of loading, unloading, and tooling operations by someone other than the equipment operator—or automatically

- Use of fixtures or tools that enable parts to be produced in multiples
- Training of substitute operators for emergencies
- Finding other jobs that the equipment can handle, perhaps by making slight alterations

Preventive Maintenance

This approach is a formalization of the ancient adage "A stitch in time saves nine." Preventive maintenance (PM) depends upon establishment of a policy and procedure for routinely inspecting, lubricating, and installing replacement parts according to predetermined schedules. The intent is that repairs will be made at the time that is least disruptive to operations and before there are unanticipated breakdowns. This work is typically performed during off-hours or slack periods so that it does not interfere with scheduled utilization. Maintenance performed this way is usually done comparatively effectively and quickly.

Time-Life Maintenance

An extension of PM, time-life maintenance schedules replacement of equipment components based upon estimates of their average operating life before failure. Suppose, for example, that a piece of equipment has six parts with an average expected life of 3 months, and on average, one of these six parts must be replaced every 2 weeks. Using the time-life system, all parts would be replaced at the same time—about every 2¾ months in this case. This results in a net savings of replacement time and also helps to avoid breakdowns. A popular aspect of the time-life system is the group replacement of fluorescent light tubes in office buildings, retail stores, and industrial work areas.

Other Time-Saving Maintenance Practices

In addition to PM, there are a number of other ways to save time in maintenance and repair activities. For instance:

- *Reduce travel time.*   Perhaps 25 percent or more of all maintenance-and-repair charges can be attributed to the time it takes for crews to travel to the repair site and back. This time can be reduced by scheduling techniques that group similar work assignments, moving crews sequentially from site to site without having them return to the shop, and providing adequate information so that the necessary tools and parts will be taken along with them. Additionally, the use of equipment such as golf carts and/or paging devices can be effective in speeding up travel and avoiding needless travel.

- *Increase the number of jobs that are scheduled.* As seen above, PM is usually less time-consuming than other maintenance approaches. Accordingly, a target of 75 percent of all jobs to be planned and scheduled should be set.

- *Control work orders.* Crew time simply drifts away unless every repair job is channeled through some sort of dispatching center that makes time estimates and controls job approvals.

- *Establish time standards.* While most maintenance and repair jobs have their idiosyncracies, standard times have been established and are available for a great variety of basic tasks found in pipe fitting, metalwork, carpentry, plumbing, electrical work, and other craft work. Without a time standard (or estimate) to shoot for, maintenance crews are notoriously inefficient.

- *Provide time-saving tools and supplies.* Up-to-date, automatic tools and diagnostic equipment contribute to time savings. For example, self-powered hand tools eliminate time lost in searching for electric outlets.

Time Savings in Process-Flow Management

The way equipment is arranged greatly affects the ease—and speed—with which products, processes, and activities flow through the given space resource. Said another way, the proper layout of desks and machinery can be a great time saver. Prime features of a good layout are (1) orderliness, or the absence of the kind of clutter that impedes flow, and (2) avoidance of backtracking, which causes workers and materials to double their steps.

Process-flow arrangements also help or hinder the moving of parts, materials, products, or supplies from one operation to another. Accordingly, when it comes to material handling, or movement, the following ideas are appropriate:

- *Minimize handling of all kinds.* Picking up and setting down takes time, but such handling does not add to the value of the product or service being processed.

- *Avoid rehandling.* Continuous flow has an obvious advantage, but rehandling can also be avoided in other ways. For example, in the last step of a process, the product can be packaged by the last operator, just as a finished letter can be inserted in an envelope by a typist.

- *Move materials mechanically.* Use gravity chutes, conveyor belts, lift trucks, and the like whenever possible.

- *Deliver raw materials directly to the point of use.* This eliminates the intermediate step of temporary storage in a warehouse or stockroom, with its attendant handling.

Time Savings in Space Management

One of the most effective ways to use time to improve utilization of space is to work a second and/or a third shift. When this is done, rent and many other fixed costs of input are, essentially, free for those shifts. Another approach is to consider space not only in terms of square footage but also as a cube, so that overhead space becomes free, too. It can be used to accommodate point-of-use storage for raw materials, or to provide gravity flows for loading of machines or for delivering supplies to work stations.

Improving the Time Use of Energy and Utilities

The total cost of energy, utilities, and auxiliary services rarely exceeds 10 percent of the costs of goods and services produced by an enterprise. Yet these costs often exceed the amount of profit or operating margin the enterprise generates. Many employees—in fact, many managers and professionals—take these resources for granted. They consider electric power, steam, water, compressed air, sewage, communications systems, and the like as "free." Of course, these resources are not free; they represent either a fixed or a variable cost of operations. When these costs are fixed—that is, when they are paid for over a period of time regardless of the extent of their use—the controllable time factor is limited. When these costs are variable, however, a sizable element of controllable time is often present.

The Energy "Taxi Meter"

Think of the price you pay for utilities as something like a taxi meter. Charges for use of energy and utilities generally are based upon a pressure or volume factor multiplied by the time period of use, or some version thereof. Electricity charges, for example, are usually expressed in rates per kilowatt-hour, where the kilowatt is the unit of electrical energy expended. If your firm is charged for 2500 kilowatt-hours in a month, it means that it has consumed 2500 of these units during the month. From a practical point of view, the conclusion is that the longer the power or lights are on, the greater the usage of electricity. Similarly, for steam or water or natural gas, the longer each is consumed at whatever unit of measure—pounds per square inch (psi), gallons, or cubic feet—the higher the monthly bill will be. Sewage usage rates tend to be linked to water usage, so that the longer the water keeps running, the higher the sewage charges will be.

Energy Reports

It pays, of course, to understand your firm's expenditures for energy and fuels, so that you can pinpoint the areas of most likely waste. A typical budgetary format is shown in the utilities consumption report in Figure 10-4. This is often supplemented by a fuels report, which is essentially a log kept of fuel-tank meter readings. In it, additions and subtractions are metered, and the latter are compared with a standard of fuel usage per unit of output.

Savings in Time-Related Utilities Usage

Most reduction of utility costs comes from decreasing (1) the volume of flow and (2) its duration, or (3) a combination of both. As a simple ex-

Utilities Report				
Dept.: 707	Account No. 27000		Month February	
Utilities Consumed	Unit of Measure	Actual	Budgeted	Variance
Metered				
Electricity	Kilowatt	895	800	+ 95
Water, industrial	1,000 gallons	1,222	1,200	+ 22
Tank gas, welding	100-cubic foot cylinder	15	18	− 3
Allocated				
Compressed air	Dollars ($)	205	200	+ 5
Space heating or cooling	Dollars ($)	185	200	− 15
Sewage charges	Dollars ($)	65	60	+ 5

Figure 10-4. Utilities consumption report.

ample, you cut electrical costs when you use smaller light bulbs and turn them off more often. Variations on this theme include the following:

- Turning down valves and other flow-control devices to the prescribed minimum needed to support the process properly or to maintain the desired environmental conditions. Flows above standard increase consumption unnecessarily.

- Turning off utilities where, or when, the process no longer needs them. This may be as simple as turning off the air conditioning at the close of day. Or it may embrace long-term "null and void" conditions, such as when equipment is taken out of service for a week or two, and the water in the cooling jacket is left running.

- Repairing vessel and pipeline leaks quickly. Even a ¹⁄₁₆-inch hole in a steam pipeline at 50 psi can cost $200 per year. Torn insulation, too, can greatly increase consumption of heated or cooled air.

- Reusing or recycling utilities whenever possible. Rinsing and cooling waters are good targets for what is technically known as a *heat recovery system*. If two rinse tanks are used, for example, the water from the second rinse tank can be used as makeup water for the first. Warmed cooling water from one operation may still be cool enough to use on another, hotter operation. A commonly encountered technique is to use modular ceiling panels that recover heat from lighting and exhaust air and recycle it into the building's heating system.

Support Through Employee Communications

When provided reliable information, employees will respond to the time-saving, cost-cutting methods suggested above. The following methods have been effective in this regard:

- Posting cost-and-usage figures on bulletin boards, as reasonable and attainable conservation goals to be met.

- Placing signs on electric switches that can be selectively turned on or off for janitorial work.

- Placing cost stickers or tags on frequently used water, steam, and air outlets. For example, "This outlet uses 65 cents worth of steam a minute."

- Appointing leak-detection squads to make inspections of washrooms and work areas.

- Forming employee conservation committees to help plan and control use of energy and utilities.

Improving the Time Use of Materials and Supplies

The purchased cost of the materials of manufacture ranges anywhere from 10 to 70 percent of the final cost of the end product. This figure varies according to the industry, the product manufactured, and the extent of the processing performed. An average figure is 20 percent. Looked at this way, for every $1 of finished goods it produces, a company may have to buy 20 cents worth of raw materials, parts, components, and subassemblies. Similar figures might prevail in the construction industries.

Purchased materials that end up in the product are considered *raw materials*. Those that are consumed during the process are thought of as *operating supplies*, or simply supplies. The processing that goes on in most service industries (banks, insurance companies, real estate, etc.) and in public institutions uses relatively few raw materials but may consume large amounts of supplies.

In the retail and wholesale trades, the goods carried and sold are described as *merchandise*. Merchandise makes up the bulk of the materials handled in these trades, but large amounts of supplies in the form of containers and packaging may also be purchased.

In all industries, the conservation of materials and supplies is a necessary activity. It can take any of three general directions: (1) conservation and protection of materials, supplies, and merchandise (all called *stock*) that are under the supervision of the operating departments; (2) inventory control, usually performed by a staff department; and (3) purchasing control, also performed by the staff. Material conservation methods are so extensive, however, that only those that are particularly useful in measuring productivity or are clearly time-related will be discussed below.

Conservation of Materials and Supplies in Process

The following material control reports are especially useful:

1. *Daily materials usage report.* This works like a budget, but it is maintained daily and records (a) actual usage as compared with (b) standard usage for the product or service being produced. Running under the standard is considered good performance. Time, per se, is not necessarily a factor, but the report furnishes a useful measure of efficiency.

2. *Yield measures.* The term *yield* is used to indicate what proportion of the materials of manufacture are actually converted or absorbed into the product. As Figure 10-5 illustrates, the yield measure can point to places where material is lost or wasted. An apparel maker, for exam-

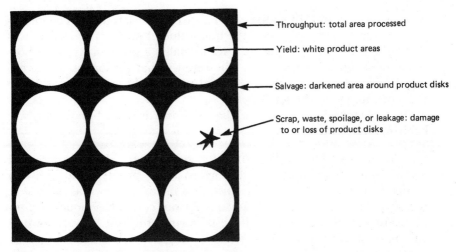

Figure 10-5. Yield relationships in materials usage.

ple, may purchase 100,000 square yards of cloth; 90,000 square yards become part of garments produced, and 10,000 square yards become remnants. The yield is expressed as 90 percent. While yield does not necessarily include a time element, it is an excellent measure of process efficiency.

3. *Spoilage report.* It is important that careful records be kept of spoilage, waste, or defects. While these measures relate mainly to quality, they also reflect upon material utilization. Take the apparel plant. The dress patterns, when perfectly followed, are expected to make 30,000 dresses, each requiring 3 square yards of material. Because of improper cutting and other faulty work, however, the 100,000 square yards of cloth is converted into only 28,500 dresses. Therefore, 1500 potential dresses are scrapped. The spoilage rate is stated as 1500:30,000, or 5 percent. As a consequence, the yield would not be 90 percent; it would be $28,500 \times 3 \div 100,000 = 85,500:100,000 = 85.5$ percent.

4. *Leakage report.* Theft, pilferage, and other unexplained disappearances of goods—whether during processing or from stock—can account for large "leakage" costs each year. Without some sort of accurate inventory system, these losses would go undetected and be absorbed in overall productivity ratios.

Inventory-Time Controls

Any number of inventory controls are time-related. In fact, concerns about time tend to dominate the entire inventory-management process.

The reason for this, of course, is that inventories are easily equated to money, and as a consequence, the time value of money plays an important role in inventory decisions. Additionally, a great many firms borrow money against inventories. The result is that the longer the inventory is held, the greater the amount of money that must be paid in the form of interest to the lenders.

For time-conscious managers, the following areas of opportunity are likely to bear fruit.

1. *Shortening the holding time for inventories.* This includes all inventories: incoming materials, materials in process, and finished goods. In inventory-control parlance, this factor is known as the *cost of carrying.* This cost entails not only the obvious cost of the money tied up in inventories but also most of the following: the cost of warehousing and other storage space, the cost of moving inventories into and out of storage, the potential for obsolescence, and the inevitable costs of spoilage and leakage. Many authorities estimate that the cost of carrying inventories can run as high as 25 percent of initial value per year.

The goal of shortening the carrying time can be approached from several directions:

- *Reduce the ordering lead time.* This requires accurate estimates of (a) how quickly stock in hand will be consumed and (b) how long stock replacement normally takes. Because these estimates are often unreliable, there is a tendency to carry larger levels of stock than necessary (safety stocks), to set unnecessarily early reorder points, and to employ longer lead times.
- *Reduce the levels of safety stocks.* This contributes to shortened lead times, but it also entails risk. The cost of running out of stock, and thus delaying production lines or customer deliveries, must be weighed against the cost of carrying excess stock.
- *Shorten the inventory cycle.* The inventory cycle encompasses the contributing factors of lead time, stock levels, safety-stock levels, and reorder point. It is also highly dependent upon (a) the rate of consumption in the operating processes and (b) the rate at which purchases can be executed and deliveries received. Because of the complexity of the interactions of these factors, it is often simpler to attack each element of the inventory cycle separately rather than to mount an integrated attack, although computer analysis is extremely helpful.

2. *Apply ABC analysis.* This technique, discussed in Chapter 5, effectively divides inventory items into three classes: those few items (class A) that account for the bulk of the total value of the inventory; the great number of relatively inexpensive items (class C) that account for only a small portion of the total value of the inventory; and a small group of medium-value items (class B) that fall somewhere between A and C items in their contribution to the total value of the inventory. For time-

saving purposes, the idea is to concentrate your efforts on the goal of shortening the time that class A items are held in stock. That's where the payoff will be greatest. After the carrying time of class A inventories has been shortened, you can proceed to squeeze time from class B items. In many instances, the class C items won't be worth the effort.

3. *Consider the economic order quantity (EOQ).* The EOQ helps to determine how much should be ordered at one time. In so doing, the *EOQ balances the cost of carrying with the cost of ordering.* The *cost of ordering* covers such expenses as telephone calls, order preparation, order receiving and inspection, and associated record keeping. A basic assumption (one that can encounter many exceptions) is that it costs as much to place and receive a small order as it does a large order. EOQ formulas find the order quantity at which the combined costs of ordering and carrying are lowest. In theory, this quantity should be the optimum figure for an integrated concern for cost and time considerations. It does nothing, however, to reduce the factors that contribute to any of longer times associated with the cost of carrying. Nevertheless, there are numerous computer-driven programs that enable inventory control specialists to test an infinite variety of options in the EOQ formulas—and these can point to opportunities for reducing the time factors.

TIME BYTE 10-3

Speak "Delivery," Not Japanese

When Hewlett-Packard (HP) introduced its JIT program, 21 percent of deliveries were on time. Within 2 years, 51 percent were arriving on time, and early deliveries had reduced inventory costs by $9 million. HP resolved the delivery problem only after breaking it into three parts: (1) communication between the supplier and HP regarding transit time, (2) the suppliers' manufacturing and shipping dates, and (3) the carriers' transportation time. It wasn't easy, however. After months of discussing complaints and countercomplaints with suppliers, HP realized that the main reason for late deliveries was poor communication. HP and the suppliers weren't speaking the same language. For example, suppliers didn't always understand whether the date on the order was the shipment date or a delivery date. Routing instructions weren't clear, either. This was corrected by issuing uniform shipping guides and insisting that suppliers subtract transit times from delivery dates to arrive at their own shipping dates. *Yankee—or even California—ingenuity often has the answers to productivity problems.*

"HP Helps Deliver Just-In-Time," by Dan Marshall, *Harvard Business Review*, July-August 1989, p. 133.

---

4. *Apply the just-in-time (JIT) concept.* This technique, made popular by the Japanese and often called by them *Kanban* (although it has been long known in the United States as *delivery engineering*) works on the principle that raw materials should not be stored at all, that they should be delivered by the vendor directly to the work station—just in time for their use. Admittedly, this can be a very effective time saver. It does require, however, (a) extremely reliable production schedules, along with (b) precise planning of inventory requirements (the best known of these planning techniques is materials requirements planning, or MRP) and (c) intense cooperation on the vendor's part. In fact, negotiation with vendors—vendors who are willing to participate without undue price increases and who are capable of coordinating their production schedules with yours—is one of the most difficult aspects of JIT implementation.

5. *Increase inventory turnover rates.* Accountants and other financial people keep a close eye on this measure. As a financial measure, it compares the annual dollar volume of sales for an enterprise with the average dollar amount of inventories. A similar ratio can be computed for any activity within an operation by comparing the dollar value of its outputs for a given period with the average dollar value of its inventories during that period. With either measure, the higher the turnover rate (or ratio) the better. Higher turnover rates are achieved by shortening the carrying time of inventories at any stage of the process.

PRACTICE TIME 10-1: A Self-Directed Exercise
Leading and Lagging

Background. The inventory specialist for the repair shop of a large dealer in farm implements in Kansas is planning the best way to maintain inventories of an expensive, frequently replaced spare part. He is concerned with establishing minimum and maximum levels that will protect the shop from stock outages of the part during the peak harvest season. He has gathered the following information:

1. The purchasing department has determined that the EOQ for that part should be equal to a 10-day supply at normal usage.
2. The maker of the part requires a lead time for filling the order that is equal to a 5-day supply.
3. The shop manager insists that a safety stock equal to a 5-day supply be maintained at all times to protect against abnormal calls for the part and possible delays in delivery.
4. From mid-August through mid-November, the seasonal demands for the part increase by an amount equal to a 5-day supply.

Assignment—Part 1. What should be the maximum and minimum inventory levels during the harvest season?

Maximum: _____ = day supply
Minimum: _____ = day supply

Assignment—Part 2. The dealer wants to cut stock levels to a minimum, using a modified JIT system. By negotiating with the supplier, the average daily supply of parts on hand during the peak season will be reduced from 12½ days equivalent ($\frac{25}{2}$) to an 8-day equivalent. The average price per part, however, will be increased from $75 to $90. A 1-day supply contains 10 parts. Considering only the cost of the parts held in stock before and after introducing the JIT system, is this a good deal or not?

Yes, because inventory costs are $ _____ less per day
No, because inventory costs are $ _____ more per day

Commentary—Part 1.

Minimum supply in days: 5 to cover safety stock.
Maximum supply in days: 5 for safety stock + 10 for normal usage + 5 for lead time + 5 for seasonal demand = 25.

Commentary—Part 2. It is a good deal. Average daily cost of inventory the old way was 12.5-day-supply × 10 parts per day × $75 per part = $9375. Average daily cost of inventory the JIT way will be 8-day-supply × 10 parts per day × $90 = $7200, or a savings of $2175.

TIME CHECK

Use this action-plan checklist to verify your understanding of the various concepts, ideas, and techniques presented in this chapter and to indicate any need for further action on your part.

	Applies to your situation		Schedule for action	
	Yes	No	Yes	No
1. An eye toward improving productivity by reducing inputs while raising outputs or holding them constant, or by raising outputs faster than inputs.	____	____	____	____
2. Care exercised in making productivity comparisons, especially with the specification of the unit of output and time period.	____	____	____	____

3. A continuing search for application of techniques for improving employee productivity, using methods improvement, motion study, work simplification, automation, and systems analysis.   ____ ____ ____ ____

4. A survey of resources at your command: facilities and equipment, energy and utilities, materials and supplies, money and capital, work force, information and knowledge, and time.   ____ ____ ____ ____

5. Evaluation of the time use of facilities and equipment, using budgetary reports, equipment utilization charts, and/or a capacity improvement review.   ____ ____ ____ ____

6. Implementation of maintenance-time improvement techniques such as PM, a time-life system, and practices that reduce travel time, increase scheduled maintenance, control work orders, establish time standards, and provide proper tools and equipment.   ____ ____ ____ ____

7. Evaluation of process-flow patterns in your operations to (a) eliminate clutter and minimize backtracking, (b) improve material handling, and (c) maximize space utilization.   ____ ____ ____ ____

8. Evaluation of the time use of energy, utilities, and auxiliaries using utilities consumption and fuel reports.   ____ ____ ____ ____

9. Implementation of time-saving practices for utility usage, such as adjusting flows to their specified rates; turning down lights, heating, and cooling when not needed; repairing utility lines promptly; recycling; and establishing an ongoing employee conservation-awareness program.   ____ ____ ____ ____

10. Understanding the high degree to which materials and supplies can contribute to the cost of resources.   ____ ____ ____ ____

11. Evaluation of the time-use of materials and supplies, using a daily materials-usage report, yield measures, and spoilage and leakage reports.   ____ ____ ____ ____

12. Implementation of time-saving
    inventory practices, such as (a)
    shortening the carrying time, (b)
    reducing lead times and levels of safety
    stocks, (c) ABC analysis, (d) EOQ, and
    (e) the JIT method for minimizing
    inventory levels.   ____ ____ ____ ____

11

Improving Scheduling Time

How to make reliable forecasts, and how to prepare and monitor effective time schedules

Plant managers hold production status meetings in which quality, schedules, and costs are discussed. Time after time, a problem with schedules uses up more than its share of the meeting.   H. JAMES HARRINGTON
The Improvement Process

Get me to the church on time.
                    My Fair Lady

The cutting edges of an organization's planning process are the time schedules that specify the sequence in which the department's work is to be performed. These schedules will be only as good as the forecasts upon which they are based and to the degree that you have taken into account all the factors that can affect time estimates. The resulting schedules may follow straight or parallel time paths or—in their ultimate form—a critical path.

Making Dependable Forecasts

Completely reliable forecasts are rare. Justifiable, reasonably attainable deadlines can be set, however, when they are based upon a systematic examination of all the available facts. Two kinds of forecasts are commonly used: historically based forecasts and statistical-relationships forecasts.

Historically Based Forecasts

These forecasts gather historical data, usually in a progression of time in order to see where the trend is most likely to move in the future. This is a simple and useful approach, but it has its dangers. In particular, you should be alert to the potential problems discussed below.

Influence of Time Sequence. Averaging a batch of historically recorded figures, for instance, can be misleading. Take the following sequence of sales orders, recorded sequentially in 1000s over 10 years: 8, 8, 10, 9, 10, 11, 11, 10, 12, 11. The 10 numbers add up to 100. Dividing by 10 yields an average of 10. So your projection for next year might be 10.

Another, much more reliable approach would be to plot the numbers as points on a chart and then draw a smooth line through the numbers that best fit them. See Figure 11-1 for a demonstration of how widely the same set of numbers, recorded in different sequence, might vary. In

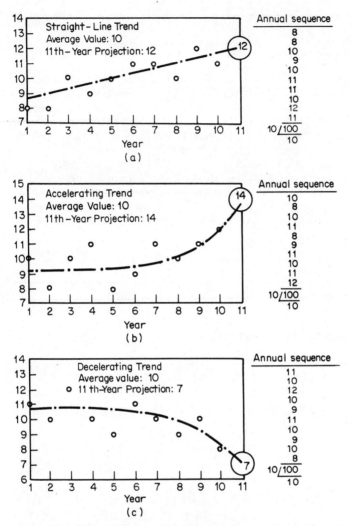

Figure 11-1. Effect of the sequence of data on forecasts. In (a), (b), and (c) the numerical average for the 10-year period is always 10. The annual sequence patterns vary, however, indicating projections for the eleventh year of 12, 14, and 7.

Figure 11-1*a*, a straight line indicates a projection of 12. A curved line, as in Figure 11-1*b*, gives a projection of 14 if the sequence of numbers is rising; if the sequence is falling, however, as in Figure 11-1*c*, the projection is 7.

Adjustments of Time Series. Statisticians describe historically based data—data recorded at regularly spaced intervals of time—as a *time* *series*. They advise that development of projections (or *trend lines*) from this data can be influenced by more than just the sequence of occurrences. A true indication of a trend line in a time series will not be derived, warn statisticians, until the data have been adjusted for the following factors:

1. *Seasonal variations.*   We all know about peaks and valleys in temperatures and their impact on the sale of clothing and many other goods. For a trend to be viable, the inherent seasonal variations must be excluded from the data. One technique for "smoothing" the data is the use of *moving annual totals.* Take a series of data for 12 consecutive months, ending in May 1989. When the 1990 data for June come in, June 1989 is dropped from the total and June 1990 is added in. The moving annual total is plotted for 12 consecutive months, continually dropping the oldest and adding the newest.

2. *Irregular and chance variations.*   It is all too easy to be overly impressed by some random movement of data, either up or down. Either occurrence may cause panic to set in. With the help of statistical analysis, these irregularities can be identified for what they are and smoothed out of the data. To make this determination, statisticians examine *standard deviations* and *probability distributions*. These provide measures of the probability of a seemingly abnormal figure (a figure which deviates from the expected one) being normal or of having significance. More information about these techniques can be found in *The Manager's Guide to Statistics and Quantitative Methods.**

Statistical-Relationships Forecasts

Careless analysis of either time series or of freshly gathered primary data can lead you to jump to some very misleading conclusions, especially if a number of factors can be seen to influence the data. Suppose, for example, that you have several time series at hand: one shows sales of a particular product, another reports population shifts in your marketing area, another shows the number of building starts, and still another traces trends in interest rates. (All these series are available from the U.S. Department of Commerce or from the Bureau of Labor Statistics.) In terms of forecasting next year's sales, it would be very helpful to find some connection between sales trends and any of the other time series, each of which is provided by the government. Such connections are called *correlations*. If you were to simply "eyeball" the various series

*Donald W. Kroeber and R. Lawrence LaForge, *The Manager's Guide to Statistics and Quantitative Methods*, McGraw-Hill, New York, 1980, "Measures of Variability," pp. 57–61, and "Probability Distributions," pp. 75–93.

looking for correlations, the chances are that you could easily be con-
fused or misled. Here again, statistical analysis comes to the rescue.
Multivariate analysis, aided by computer programs, is the principal
technique used for identifying the presence or absence of correlations.
Multivariate analysis helps to determine to what extent a change in one
condition is related—if at all—to a change in another condition. For instance, it can be used to see whether a rise in the sale of household furniture is related to (and can be predicted by) the number of new homes
being built.*

Factors That Affect Time Estimates

From the discussion of time measurements in Chapter 9, it might appear that calculations of the time needed to complete a project or an
assignment are cut and dried. This is far from the truth. Because so
many variable factors influence the calculations, even the most careful
approaches produce only rough estimates. To help you understand
how this can be true, each variable factor is examined below.

Inherent Time

Computers to the contrary, few things are accomplished instantly. Inherent in the conversion or operating processes are a number of essen-
tials. An individual or a machine (frequently both) must work on the
material or service involved. The material or document must be moved
from work station to work station. Finally, the finished product or document is ready for shipment and delivery. The time between receipt of
an order (or assignment) and its fulfillment is called the *manufacturing
cycle*, the *order-delivery cycle*, or simply the *process time*.

Whatever the term used, the point is that, inescapably, the time will
be consumed. Furthermore, an allowance for such inherent time must
be incorporated into time estimates if the estimates are to be reliable.
Knowing the actual time required for a certain procedure may be absolutely necessary in order to make reliable time estimates. For example,
time studies may show that the time needed to perform several hundred individual tasks in an assignment adds up to only 48 hours, or 6
days. The actual process time, however, may easily be 10 days, or even
15 or 20. How can this happen? Such inherent time is created by the
inevitable delays in processing and issuing work orders, in moving ma-

*Kroeber and LaForge, "Multivariate Analysis," pp. 131–161.

terials and documents from station to station, in time lost waiting for available machine time, and in the realities involved in coordinating a great many activities.

Inherent time can be shorted, of course, by many of the techniques of methods improvement, work simplification, and other approaches discussed in the section entitled "Improving Employees' Use of Time" in Chapter 10.

TIME BYTE 11-2

Fast Starts for Harley's HOGs

When Harley-Davidson achieved its great turnaround in the late 1980s, it attributed much of its success to its ability to make model changeovers quickly. This was especially necessary because Harley promotes bikes that have been "customized" to suit the individual tastes of the riders of its HOGs. (HOG was originally the acronym for Harley Owners Group; later it became the nickname for Harley's huge motorcycles.) Harley stresses these five rules for achieving remarkable reductions in setup times:

1. Move mainline setup steps to off-line preparation stations.
2. Minimize movement and travel time for setup teams.
3. Replace nuts and bolts on setup equipment with quick-action fasteners.
4. Preset tools and fixtures before moving them into place.
5. Standardize dies, tooling, fixtures, and parts design so that match-ups between parts and tooling can be made with minimum adjustment.

Shortened setup times are often the key to a time-saving production schedule.

Well Made in America: Lessons from Harley-Davidson on Being the Best, by Peter C. Reid, McGraw-Hill, New York, 1990, pp. 152–153.

Setup Time

Also known as *makeready time,* setup time is sometimes considered broadly to include both the beginning and the end of an operation. It may then be called *setup and teardown time* or *makeready and put-away time.* Makeready is obviously an important contributor to inherent time. Even though the makeready effort is ardently pursued, it does not add value to a product or service; yet it must be performed. Before beginning to paint, a painter mixes the paint, sets up a ladder, and spreads a drop cloth. After the painting is completed, the cans of paint are capped, the ladder is taken down, and the drop cloth is removed. Such setup and put-away tasks are necessary and time-consuming, and they must be taken into account in estimating the time for a job.

Shortening Setup Time. Improving coordination of orders and schedules helps to cut down on the number of times a process must be made ready. For example, setups are minimized by:

- Ganging up several similar orders so that the same tooling can be used on many consecutive jobs.
- Minimizing cleaning of color- or chemical-contaminated processing equipment by scheduling orders progressively from lighter to darker colors and from lower to higher contamination tolerances.
- Assigning work selectively to operators who have performed it before so that they can get started faster—in other words, applying the principle of specialization.
- Arranging operating layouts according to product flow, rather than process flow. That is, each product moves along its own assembly or processing line, without having to move—with dissimilar products—from process to process along a universal processing layout.

It should be noted that great advances have been made in computer-controlled processing equipment, so designed that changeovers from piece to piece or from document to document are made automatically and almost instantly. Be that as it may, there are still thousands of cases in which such equipment is either not available or not economically feasible for the particular conditions of the operation.

Learning Time

Learning time can be viewed as a special version of setup time. It is typically associated with starting up—starting up a new process, a new product, a new operation, a new organization, or a new employee. Output rates are always slower when starting up than after things are running smoothly. Employees have to learn the new operation or the new machine. "Bugs"—unanticipated difficulties—show up and must be eliminated. Operations have to be coordinated. Statistically, when someone is learning a new job, there is a uniform percentage drop (such as 10 percent) in the time needed to produce a single unit of output every time the total number of units of output is doubled. Here is an example of the output of a records-entry department working on a new entry system in a government tax agency.

Effect of Doubling Output	
Minutes per form	Number of entries completed
10.0	200
9.0	400
8.1	800
7.3	1,600
6.6	3,200
5.9	6,400
5.3	12,800

When the times per entry (vertical scale in Figure 11-2) is either not available or not economically feasible (horizontal scale—essentially a time scale), a *learning curve* is created. Because learning is equated to the accumulation of experience over a period of time, the curve is often called an *experience curve*, especially when it applies to organizationwide learning.

Caution: In this example, the learning-improvement rate was estimated at 10 percent for each doubling. While this is a good average figure, the rate can vary greatly according to the difficulty and complexity of the new operation.

Rule of Thumb. Based on the 10 percent improvement—or learning—rate, here is a useful rule of thumb: *It will take an operator or an oper-*

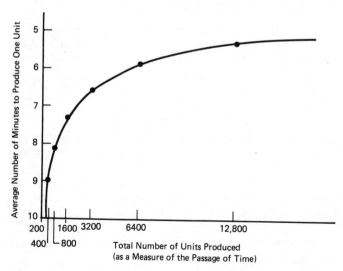

Figure 11-2. Learning (or experience) curve.

ation about half as much time per unit to produce a unit the sixth time the output is doubled as it did to produce the first unit. In other words, if it takes 1 hour to make the first part, it will take only a half-hour to make the sixty-fourth part.

$$1 \times 2 = 2 \qquad 2 \times 2 = 4 \qquad 4 \times 2 = 8$$

$$8 \times 2 = 16 \qquad 16 \times 2 = 32 \qquad 32 \times 2 = 64$$

It is important to note that in the example above, the sixty-fourth part will be made some time after the thirty-second hour is worked (64 parts × ½ hour per part = 32 hours). This means that it will take more than four 8-hour days to get up to normal running speed. For a part that took only 10 minutes to make, getting up to speed would take more than 320 minutes (5 hours and 20 minutes).

$$64 \text{ parts} \times 5 \text{ minutes} = 320 \text{ minutes}$$

Lost Time

Lost time is sometimes overlooked when time schedules are prepared. Lost time is worth your attention, however, since it includes all the time that is irretrievably lost due to:

Personal time. Time anticipated for washup, rest breaks, and lunch periods, plus the time allotted for holidays and vacations. It has been estimated that the average worker will also lose about half an hour a day on unscheduled personal activities.

Technical time. Unanticipated delays due to machine breakdowns, material shortages, gaps in scheduled job orders, power outages, and communications and/or computer failures.

Costly Time

Certain practices and shortcomings in planning and coordination cause an organization to buy time at a costly price. These situations are identified as follows:

Crash time, which occurs when a product or service is forced into a schedule out of turn and hastened through the process with special attention and handling—on "red-rush" or as-soon-as-possible (ASAP) status. Such instances arise from attempts to mollify favored customers, meet a competitor's delivery offer, or make good on a delay caused by improper scheduling or by an oversight. These jobs cost more time to produce (often at overtime rates) because they do not flow through normal channels.

Expediting time, in which a supervisor or specialized clerk must trace down so-called lost orders and/or walk them through the process. Obviously, this is a costly use of valuable time. It often occurs in conjunction with crash time and rush jobs.

Overtime, which entails the use of costly labor-hours beyond 8 in a day and 40 (or 35 for some companies) in a week. For all nonexempt employees, a U.S. company must pay a premium either in dollars (an additional 50 percent of the hourly wage for hours over 40) or in equal time off later in the same work period. There is always the likelihood, too, that productivity will be less during overtime hours than during regular hours.

Time-Saving Schedules

Plans and procedures are the outcome of the planning process, but they have little real bite until they are converted into schedules. And it takes a specific schedule, at that, to pin down squarely the various time elements in a plan. Schedules can be developed in several ways and forms. Among these are (1) straight-line scheduling, (2) parallel scheduling, and (3) network (or critical path) scheduling.

Straight-Line Scheduling

Using this technique, tasks, jobs, assignments, or activities are arranged in the sequence in which they are to be performed. The process is somewhat like stringing a series of graduated beads, being careful to make sure that each operation is in the right sequence. No step is scheduled ahead of a step that must be completed before the next step can be made. For example, in assembling an auto, the wheel must be mounted to the hub before the hub nuts that hold the wheel in place can be positioned and tightened. The "calendar control chart" that you prepared as a Practice Time exercise in Chapter 3 (Figure PT 3-1) was essentially a straight-line schedule.

Straight-line scheduling (see Figure 11-3 for the technique at its most basic) is simple to carry out and easy to follow. It is often the best way. It has a serious drawback, however, in that it does not allow for having two tasks performed at the same time—which can be a great time saver.

	Straight-Line Scheduling		
Process _Address 1,000 envelopes and insert brochures in them for mailing_			
Step Number	Task to Be Performed	Time Needed for Each Operation (in Hours)	Cumulative Time Needed (in Hours)
1	Go to stockroom, get 1,000 brochures and envelopes, deliver to addressing work table	½	½
2	Set up addressing table and semiautomatic addressing machine	½	1
3	Address 1,000 envelopes	2	3
4	Clean up and put away addressing machine	¼	3 ¼
5	Deliver addressed envelopes and brochures to inserting table	¼	3 ½
6	Set up inserting table and semiautomatic inserting machine	½	4
7	Insert brochures and seal envelopes	1	5
8	Clean up and put away sealing machines	½	5 ½
9	Deliver stuffed, addressed envelopes to mailroom	½	6
	Total Elapsed Time _____ Hours		

Figure 11-3. Straight-line scheduling at its simplest.

Parallel Scheduling

This approach may start with the same information about the process as does straight-line scheduling, but it adds one valuable feature. As in Figure 11-4, it seeks to overlap one or more of the steps in such a way that two things are accomplished during the same time period. If, for example, in furniture manufacturing, a worker can prepare one set of chair rungs for gluing and insertion while the previously inserted set is drying, the processes overlap a little and time is saved. Similarly, if two employees can work on the same product simultaneously, it makes no sense to schedule them in such a way that one stands by waiting for the other to finish.

Gantt Production Control Chart.　Many refinements can be made in parallel scheduling. The most commonly encountered is the Gantt chart for production control. This chart is seen almost everywhere. It is used, in one form or another, in many businesses to coordinate the progress of a number of orders and projects. You will recognize it as a sort of horizontal timetable, with each of its stripes assigned to mark the progress of a separate project toward its deadlines. You may see it in an advertising agency, for example, to track the development of an ad from its conception to its insertion date. Or it may appear on an office

Parallel Scheduling

Process: _Address 1,000 envelopes and insert brochures in these for_
mailing

Tasks To Be Performed			Cumulative Elapsed Time
Step 1 ½ hour	Step 2 ½ hour		½ hour
Step 3 2 hours			2½ hours
Step 4 ¼ hour	Step 5 ¼ hour	Step 6 ½ hour	3 hours
Step 7 1 hour			4 hours
Step 8 ½ hour	Step 9 ½ hour		4½ hours
Total elapsed time—parallel planning: 4½ hours Total elapsed time—straight-line planning: 6 hours			

(a)

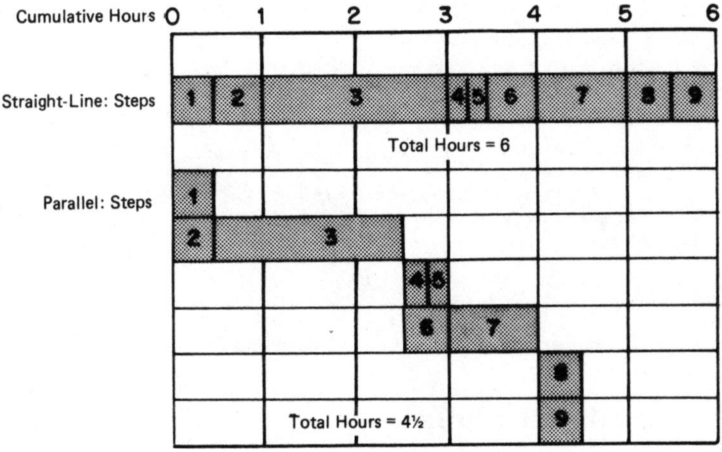

(b)

Figure 11-4. Comparison of (a) parallel scheduling with (b) straight-line scheduling.

wall to display work schedules and deadlines. It is most often used for scheduling production orders in manufacturing plants, as shown in Figure 11-5a. As you can see, it is simply a special application of parallel planning. It sets a *time standard* by reserving in advance whatever block of time is needed to complete a job or order. Various marking schemes are then used to indicate the degree of completion of the various jobs at any point in time, as shown in Figure 11-5b. Thus, the chart fulfills its other function as a *time control*.

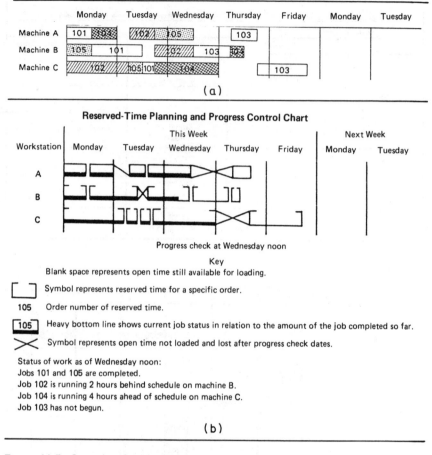

(a)

Reserved-Time Planning and Progress Control Chart

Progress check at Wednesday noon

Key

Blank space represents open time still available for loading.

Symbol represents reserved time for a specific order.

105   Order number of reserved time.

Heavy bottom line shows current job status in relation to the amount of the job completed so far.

Symbol represents open time not loaded and lost after progress check dates.

Status of work as of Wednesday noon:
Jobs 101 and 105 are completed.
Job 102 is running 2 hours behind schedule on machine B.
Job 104 is running 4 hours ahead of schedule on machine C.
Job 103 has not begun.

(b)

Figure 11-5. Gantt chart for (a) scheduling production and (b) monitoring progress.

Critical Path Scheduling

The ultimate in parallel (or overlapping) schedules is created by means of network planning, which produces the program evaluation and review technique (PERT) chart and utilizes the critical path method (CPM). Its great value lies in its (1) ability to arrange overlapping schedules in highly complex, one-of-a-kind projects, such as building a bridge or launching a new product, and (2) to identify the critical bottlenecks beforehand so that they can be eliminated or circumvented.

A breakthrough in time planning and control was brought about by the development of PERT and especially its successor, CPM. CPM helps to pinpoint the critical 10 to 20 percent of tasks in complex, one-of-a-kind projects that ultimately control the total time needed to complete a project. Once these critical tasks have been identified, either (1) the plan can be modified to work around them or (2) extra effort and resources can be applied to these tasks in order to shorten the time it takes to complete them.

Creating a CPM Schedule

To apply CPM time control, you follow these five steps:

1. *List in sequence, as in straight-line planning, all the tasks necessary to complete the project.* It is important that the sequence properly represent the need to complete certain tasks before the next one can be started. For example, the roof cannot be put on a house until the framework has been erected. The framework cannot be erected until the foundation has been poured. The foundation cannot be poured until the excavation has been completed.

2. *Estimate the time needed to complete each task under ordinary conditions.* Table 11-1 shows how steps 1 and 2 are combined to provide a table of tasks and time estimates for the activities to be performed in purchasing and installing a large piece of industrial equipment.

3. *Construct an "arrow diagram" (also called a network diagram) that shows the interdependency of the various tasks, as shown in Figure*

Table 11-1. Tasks and Time Estimate Table for CPM Planning Project for Purchasing and Installing a Piece of Industrial Equipment

Task or activity to be performed	Weeks needed to perform task or activity	
Decide to buy equipment.	0	Starting point
Prepare purchase specifications, and place order.	1	
Prepare specifications and drawings for tooling.	3	
Delivery of equipment.	4	
Prepare drawings for equipment installation.	2	
Prepare drawings for utilities installation.	3	
Manufacture tooling.	9	
Excavate foundation pit.	1	
Construct forms for foundation.	2	
Pour and set concrete foundation.	1	
Install water-supply equipment.	2	
Install drains for equipment.	3	
Purchase and install electrical-supply equipment.	8	
Install equipment on foundation.	1	
Connect utilities to equipment.	2	
Try out equipment.	2	
Turn over to operating department.	0	Finishing point
Total number of weeks to perform tasks and activities.	44	

11-6. The length of the connecting arrows is not important, but their direction indicates the required sequence. The diagram is constructed (usually by specialists in the process) by answering three questions for each task in turn: (a) What task or events immediately precede this task? (b) What immediately follows? (c) What other tasks can be performed at the same time as this one?

On Figure 11-6*a*, *each arrow represents a task or activity* needed to move the project (or some part of it) from one point to another. Each activity is marked with a *time-to-complete figure*, taken from Table 11-1. *Each circle represents an event*—a deadline indicating a completed activity or group of activities. Each event is marked with a capital letter.

4. *Add the times of all the tasks that appear along each of the diagrammed paths in order to find the critical path.* On Figure 11-1*a*, there are four possible paths, each with a different total time:

Path	Weeks
1. A–B–C–F–J–K–L	18
2. A–B–C–D–G–H–I–J–K–L	12
3. A–B–I–J–K–L	10
4. A–B–E–K–L	15

The longest path (path 1, 18 weeks) is the *critical path.*

5. *Look for ways to shorten the critical path.* Note that the electrical task represents the critical time (8 weeks) between events F and K. Water and drains can be installed in 2 and 3 weeks respectively, but event K must wait until the electricity is in place. One solution would be to find a contractor who, at a premium, could finish the electrical connections in 4 weeks instead of 8. This would cut the time on that path by 4 weeks so that the project could be completed in 14 weeks. If this were done, however, path 2 would be the critical path because its total time is 15 weeks. You would then have to focus your efforts on shortening the new bottleneck task—"Prepare toolings"—between events E and K to a time of 7 weeks or less. By shortening the time of each ensuing bottleneck task, the critical path can be continually compressed. An optimum is reached when the cost of the resources applied to shortening the total time is no longer equaled by the value of the time saved.

6. *As a further extension of CPM, construct a parallel diagram of the network on a time scale.* An example is shown in Figure 11-6*b*.

Milestone Charting

A simpler method than either the Gantt chart or the CPM method, the *milestone chart*, is often used to provide a visual indication of deadlines

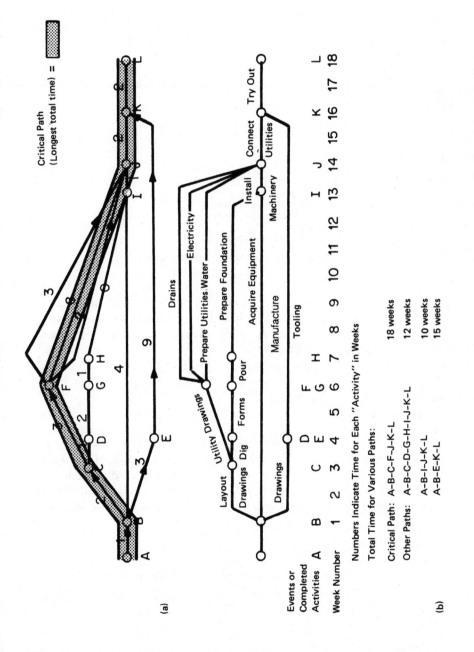

Figure 11-6. CPM chart. (a) PERT or arrow diagram illustrating the critical path from A to L. (b) The same chart as in A placed on a graphical time scale in order to follow and control progress.

Critical Path
(Longest 'total time') =

Events or Completed Activities A B C D E F G H I J K L

Week Number 1 2 3 4 5 6 7 8 9 10 11 12 13 14 15 16 17 18

Numbers Indicate Time for Each "Activity" in Weeks

Total Time for Various Paths:

Critical Path: A–B–C–F–J–K–L   18 weeks
Other Paths: A–B–C–D–G–H–I–J–K–L   12 weeks
             A–B–I–J–K–L   10 weeks
             A–B–E–K–L   15 weeks

Drawings
Utility Drawings
Layout
Dig
Forms
Pour
Prepare Foundation
Prepare Utilities Water
Electricity
Drains
Acquire Equipment
Manufacture
Tooling
Install
Machinery
Connect
Utilities
Try Out

(a)

(b)

221

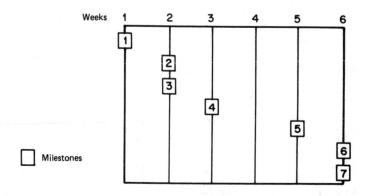

1. Complete data gathering from client.
2. Approve placement plans and schedule.
3. Present sample copy and art.
4. Approve final copy and art content.
5. Prepare finished art and complete typesetting.
6. Give final approval.
7. Deliver to scheduled newspaper media.

Figure 11-7. Milestone chart for planning a newspaper advertisement.

(or "milestones") for completion of the various tasks that make up a project. The focus of a milestone chart is on completion dates rather than on starting times. A milestone chart for preparing a newspaper advertisement is shown in Figure 11-7.

Keeping Time Schedules on Time

Implementation is what makes or breaks plans and schedules. Schedules need constant surveillance. Otherwise, slippage occurs. If you have responsibility for ensuring that schedules are met, you will have to become actively involved in supervising them. Here's a helpful list of things you can do routinely each day to keep things moving on schedule:

Before each day begins:

1. Check the production schedule and/or work orders for the day.
2. Check to make sure that equipment to be used is ready for operation.
3. Check the supply of material, stock, forms, etc., that will be needed to complete the work.

4. Line up a firm work schedule for the day, and plan your job assignments accordingly.

At the start of the shift:

5. Check attendance. Assign employees to work stations or specific orders or projects.
6. If necessary because of absences, balance the work force by rearranging assignments, securing additional help from other departments, or hiring temporary help, if available.
7. For all new, special, or temporary projects or assignments, make it clear when the work should be completed.

During the day:

8. Stay on the floor or in the shop immediately before and after rest and lunch breaks and for a full 15 minutes before quitting time.
9. Check periodically to make sure that employees are at their work stations and not roaming aimlessly.
10. Check periodically to make sure that employees are not idly waiting for materials, instructions, or assignments.

At the close of the day:

11. Make a list of unsolved problems that have come up during the day. Think of ways to solve or minimize them tomorrow.
12. Think ahead about what must be done the next workday: (a) check the production schedule and/or work orders coming up; (b) check the equipment and materials that will be needed; and (c) make a clear plan for tomorrow's job assignments.

PRACTICE TIME 11-1: A Self-Directed Exercise

Get It Going the Earliest!

Debbie thought that she had finished her assignment. She had been asked to draw up a plan for installing a vendor-rating program for the purchasing department. She had done this and had outlined it according to the schedule shown on page 224. When her boss saw the schedule, however, he expressed disappointment. "Why, this will take 12 weeks. Can't you get it done sooner?" Debbie demurred, saying that she intended to go about her plan, step by step. She did acknowledge that if she were to overlap some of the essential activities, she might be able to shorten the deadline date for installation. "Well," said the manager, "just do it! Get it going the earliest you can."

Instructions. Examine Debbie's plan, which is outlined below, and see what you can do to convert it from a straight-line to a parallel plan and, thus, get on-stream earlier.

Step	Estimated number of weeks needed for step
1. Design vendor-rating form.	2
2. Present tentative rating specifications to suppliers for their suggestions.	2
3. Gather rating-specification suggestions from suppliers, consolidate them, and present them to purchasing manager for approval.	4
4. Revise rating form. Confirm to suppliers. Present to purchasing manager and general manager for approval.	2
5. Formally announce installation date to suppliers and to company's production, receiving, and quality control departments.	2
Total time needed	12

Assume that the time needed to complete each step will be the same as before.

Assignment.

    a. Which steps can be overlapped? _____ To what extent can they be overlapped?_____

    b. What will be the new total time needed?_____

Commentary.

    a. Step 2 can be advanced by at least 1 week, since by that time Debbie should have a good idea of what specifications might be considered. Debbie has complete control over form design, so she needn't wait until it is completed. This automatically advances the whole procedure by a week. Step 5 can also be advanced by at least 1 week, since this step is also under Debbie's control, and there is no reason she can't begin to prepare the announcements before the final approval is received.

    b. The new deadline for installation will now be 10 weeks. You may have arrived at a rationale for overlapping different steps. If so, you've got the idea of the advantages inherent in parallel planning. Note, however, that it is easier to move up starting dates for proce-

dures over which you personally have control than for procedures
that involve other people.

PRACTICE TIME 11-2: A Self-Directed Exercise
Moving It Up

The makers of a new faxing machine have assumed a 10 percent learning
(or experience) curve for its design and manufacturing departments.
Accordingly, they expect to be up to normal production rate of under
11.0 hours per machine by the time they have made 32,000 machines.
Here are their calculations:

Hours per machine	Number of machines completed
20.0	500
18.0	1,000
16.2	2,000
14.6	4,000
13.1	8,000
11.8	16,000
10.6	32,000

The calculations at the 10 percent rate are as follows:

20.0 hours $\times$ 0.90 = 18.0 hours $\times$ 0.90 = 16.2 hours and so on.

Instructions. The designers and manufacturing people have worked
together and found a way to simplify and speed up the process so that
the learning rate will now be 15 percent. They ask you to make
calculations as above, multiplying each rate by 0.85.

Assignment.

a. How many machines will be made
   before the production rate drops
   below 11 hours per machine?   _____ machines

b. What will that production rate be?   _____ hours per machine

Commentary.

    a. The rate will surely drop to below 11 hours per machine after 8000
machines are made, or somewhere between the 4000 and 8000 level.

    b. The rate at 8000 machines will be 10.43 hours per machine.
Calculations:

Hours per machine	Number of machines completed
20.0	500
17.0	1,000
14.5	2,000
12.3	4,000
10.4	8,000

TIME CHECK

Use this action-plan checklist to verify your understanding of the various concepts, ideas, and techniques presented in this chapter and to indicate any need for further action on your part.

	Applies to your situation		Schedule for action	
	Yes	No	Yes	No
1. Use of historical forecasts in making planning projections, while making necessary adjustments in time-series data.	___	___	___	___
2. Application of statistical techniques before making assumptions of correlation among data used for forecasting.	___	___	___	___
3. Time estimates adjusted for the influence of inherent time, setup time, learning time, lost time, and costly time.	___	___	___	___
4. Knowledge of how to calculate learning time based upon various percentages of improvement.	___	___	___	___
5. Scheduling approaches chosen for the suitability of either straight-line, parallel, or network scheduling.	___	___	___	___
6. Opportunities sought to overlap tasks and operations where possible, so that two things can be done at the same time.	___	___	___	___

7. Application of Gantt chart
   start-and-stop techniques for
   scheduling and control of small jobs
   and projects.   _____ _____ _____ _____

8. Understanding the value of CPM for
   identifying and minimizing
   time-consuming bottlenecks in large,
   complex, one-of-a-kind projects.   _____ _____ _____ _____

9. Use of the milestone chart to display
   deadlines and measure progress of
   small projects.   _____ _____ _____ _____

10. Continual surveillance of progress
    toward fulfillment of schedules.   _____ _____ _____ _____

12
Time Savings in Key Functions

How to conserve time in the vital functions of production and operations, quality assurance, marketing and sales, and financial matters

Management needs something more than
men, materials and machines to make profits.
It needs a system which prevents the waste of
time and effort, i.e., waste of money.
CHARLES F. "BOSS" KETTERING,
LEGENDARY INVENTOR AT GENERAL MOTORS

In the major functions of a business enterprise, time is most likely to be saved or wasted in huge chunks. These areas—production or operations (including quality assurance), marketing, and finance—offer the greatest payoff for a manager's time-savings efforts. While there are universal approaches to time conservation that are applicable everywhere, certain techniques are especially needed, and effective, in operating, marketing, and financial management. The techniques and approaches presented in this chapter do not exhaust every possibility. Instead, they have been selected either because they provide a basic point of view or because they are unusually effective. Many specialized time-saving approaches described here and in previous chapters are also useful in organizations in the not-for-profit and public sectors.

Production or Operations Time

The accepted convention is to use the term *production* to describe activities involved in making a product and the term *operations* for those involved in providing a service. Increasingly, however, *operations* is used as the umbrella term for both product and service activities. You will, of course, encounter variations in usage according to local preference.

 TIME BYTE 12-1

Changeovers Like Six-Dimensional Chess

Four years is the usual time it takes an automaker to change over to a new engine design. Ford Motor Co., however, has bet $1 billion on cutting that time in half. To do so, Ford (1) reduced the number of parts by 25 percent, (2) specified 350 parts, such as pistons, so that they can be used in several different models, and (3) designed engine blocks so that they can be made of either cast iron or steel (for high performance). At the heart of the concept is a building-block design that allows a factory to equip itself to manufacture several different models with the same tooling. The ultimate assembly scheme has been described as "like playing six-dimensional chess." *Even if an accelerated changeover system is as simple as checkers, the payoff can still be impressive.*

"A Dozen Motor Factories under One Roof," by David Woodruff, *Business Week*, Nov. 20, 1989, p. 90.

Saving Time in Production

Concerns for time compression in the production functions tend to focus on scheduling and schedule-related problems. These problems manifest themselves in several ways, each with a time-wasting feature.

1. *Excess capacity.* When facilities are underutilized and equipment stands idle too often, excess capacity exists. There are three possible solutions: (a) produce stock to inventory, (b) shut the equipment down temporarily and reassign its operators in order to make their time productive, and (c) sell the equipment and subcontract its work to other firms.

2. *Undercapacity.*   Equipment overloading is an indicator of under-capacity. Such a condition almost always induces use of one or more of the following, not very attractive, solutions: (a) working overtime and increasing labor costs by one-half; (b) working a second shift on the same equipment and staffing up temporarily; (c) adding equipment, which may ultimately be underutilized; (d) subcontracting work to another firm at premium rates; and (e) purchasing parts or materials instead of making them. In the long run, the most effective solution is to find ways to improve the process so that it will produce more in a shorter time. (See Chapter 10 for ideas about improving the time use of employees, equipment, and utilities.)

3. *Long changeover and start-up times.*   When items must be scheduled in bits and pieces, lot sizes (or batches) are small, or production runs are of relatively short length, changeover and start-up times are especially troubling. Two approaches are often used to cope with this condition. *First,* focus on scheduling improvement by grouping (or ganging up) several common product sizes, selected from different orders, into one consolidated run. *Second,* look for technological improvement. The solution may be as simple as using tools and dies that incorporate a series of progressive size changes in a single set. That way, several different sizes can be produced from a single setup, transforming a series of short runs into longer runs. Increasingly, however, quicker changeovers are achieved with computer-controlled equipment that offers a wide variety of options.

4. *Job-shop priorities.*   Manufacturing, contract, and service shops that work on many custom products and one-of-a-kind orders—job shops—search endlessly for time-effective ways of scheduling orders and equipment. Over the years, a number of rules of thumb have evolved for determining which jobs should come first. While the rules are often conflicting, they do provide a rationale that assigns highest priorities to:

- The job with the earliest due date
- The job with the least "slack time" (time remaining until the due date minus the time needed to complete the job) left before its due date
- The job with the earliest due date at a particular machine
- The job with the least slack time for each of its remaining operations

In many instances, however, preoccupation with due dates and slack times obscures what is often the simplest and most time-effective scheduling method: *assigning jobs in order of their estimated processing time, with the shortest job in the batch given the highest priority.*

TIME BYTE 12-2
Portable Electronic Notebooks

Hand-held computers now substitute for pencils and clipboards when employees work away from their desks or in the field. These electronic marvels were first designed to speed up inventory taking. Today, they are used in a multitude of places to gather and record data—more of it and faster. For example:

- At Avis Inc., garage staffs use them to print customer receipts to speed up rental returns.
- At Federal Express, drivers report parcel deliveries with electronic scanners.
- At Otis Elevator Co., service personnel responding to emergency calls use hand-held computers to query service files.
- In the Newark, New Jersey, Police Department, patrol officers enter license numbers into hand-held computers to detect stolen cars and scofflaws.

Anything that speeds up clerical operations will be welcomed.

"Hand-held Computers Help Field Staff Cut Paper Work and Harvest More Data," by Gilbert Fuchsberg, *The Wall Street Journal*, Jan. 30, 1990, p. B1.

Saving Time in Clerical Operations

Traditionally, clerical operations have defied measurement and control. Only in recent years has it become accepted that clerical operations generate products, too—nebulous ones like decisions and advice, but also very tangible ones like reports, documents, and forms. In their own way, these products, usually called services, contribute to, or detract from, an organization's productivity. This is true whether they are provided as internal services or directly to customers. Accordingly, the time taken to perform clerical operations warrants the same scrutiny given production operations, and in much the same way. There are, however, differences of focus and technique that apply uniquely to clerical operations.

1. *Technological time savers.* A study made by Booz Allen & Hamilton, a consulting firm, confirmed the widespread evidence that offices are notoriously unproductive—often operating at less than 50 percent effectiveness. What was unusual about the Booz Allen study, however, was its revelation that office workers spend from 15 to 40 percent of their time on activities that are totally unproductive. Most of

these activities, the study concluded, could be eliminated or speeded up by readily available technological means. For example:

- Time wasted in seeking the status of an order can be reduced by desktop access to an information tracking system.
- Time lost in hunting for information on sources of supply can be reduced by on-line access to external supplier databases and internal records of supplier performance.
- Time consumed in making extensive corrections and revisions in reports and correspondence can be minimized by access to word-and-graphics processors.
- Time spent on tracking down colleagues by telephone can be eliminated by a desktop keyboard system in connection with electronic or voice mail.
- Time spent in meetings can be greatly reduced by video-conferencing.
- Time spent in scheduling meetings can be minimized with desktop displays of executive calendars and automated coordination and reminder systems.

2. *Time analysis and improvement.*   Analysis for potential time savings in clerical work can be accomplished in three steps:

First, break down the office services provided into discrete categories, such as reports, forms, entries, studies, searches, advice, and decisions. List the items that appear in each category.

Second, examine each item for any of these nine potential time-saving improvements:

- Eliminate it entirely if it is no longer needed.
- Defer it to a more convenient date, at which time it can be performed more efficiently.
- Reduce the quality standard to what is actually required.
- Reduce the amount of detail to what is actually needed.
- Reduce the frequency of the report or activity.
- Combine it with another item so that two services can be accomplished at the same time.
- Substitute some other, less time-consuming, service.
- Improve the way the service is performed, through either process redesign or office automation.
- Transfer work that is unsuitable for one office's resources ("misplaced work") to an office with facilities that will be more effective in performing it.

Third, identify for each item the options that are easiest and least costly to implement. Take action selectively on the items with the biggest payoff.

Quality Assurance Time

It has become increasingly clear in the last decade that in order to assure and control quality, you must be able to identify all the factors that contribute to quality rather than being misled by bits and pieces of it. An ideal way of looking at the total problem of quality assurance is to divide it into four interrelated parts:

1. *Prevention.* This basic step is most often overlooked. It is essentially an inexpensive one, rarely exceeding 10 percent of all quality costs. Prevention includes (a) modification in the quality of design as it affects manufacturing or operations, (b) studies of process suitability, (c) development of test and inspection equipment and procedures, and— most important—(d) awareness of quality, and training programs. Efforts to prevent quality problems often save great amounts of time that might otherwise be needed later on to correct them.

2. *Appraisal.* This is the technical term for test and/or inspection. It typically can account for about 25 percent of all costs of quality assurance. Appraisal describes all the efforts taken to assure the quality of conformance. Appraisal does not add value to a product or service. It simply passes judgment. If the product or service matches the quality standards specified, the product or service can move forward. If the product or service does not measure up to the standards set for its condition or performance—that is, if a *defect* or an *error* has been found— the product or service must be judged a failure. It is the correction or disposal of failed products or services that is so expensive, and so time-consuming.

TIME BYTE 12-3

On-Time Measure Unfair?

When the U.S. Transportation Department singled out USAir as having the worst on-time performance among major airlines in 1989, the company cried "Foul!" Using the same on-time quality measure for all airlines, the company contended, works against USAir. Its routes are shorter, and as a result, its flights must make many more takeoffs and landings than other airlines. USAir claimed that on the majority of days, when weather was good, 90 percent of its flights had arrived on time. The record had been spoiled on bad days, when poor weather had caused pyramiding of delays. Additionally, if an airplane from United, for example, flies from New York to Chicago direct, it has to contend with weather at only two airports. If USAir were flying along that route, it might have to contend with takeoffs and landings at from three to five cities—doubling or tripling the statistical probability of a delay.

Still another problem is triggered when rescheduled departure times are posted. The airline controls the listing, but when overly optimistic dispatchers announce "improved" but unofficial times that can't be met, the already-delayed plane will be hit with another mark against its on-time record.

It's not unusual for quality standards to have two dimensions: what customers expect and what the producer would like to deliver.

"USAir Compiles Worst On-Time Arrival Record," by Martha M. Hamilton, *Washington Post*, "Washington Business," Jan. 15, 1990, p. 5.

---

3. *Internal remedial actions.*   When inspection or tests reveal a product deficiency—an error or a defect—there are two courses of action, both of them expensive and time-consuming:

- *Rework,* which entails anything from repairing, reshaping, or refinishing a part or product to retyping a letter or rekeyboarding a computer entry. Rework also includes costly time in searching for the source of the error and devising a means for rectifying it.

- *Disposal,* which usually entails a partial or total loss of the resources that have already gone into the product or service at that stage of operations. Costs can sometimes be partially recovered by selling wastes for *scrap value.* But even this recovery requires additional time for collecting, certifying, baling, and otherwise preparing the scrapped materials for sale.

4. *External remedial actions.*   These, too, include a variety of costly and time-consuming efforts, such as field inspections and field services, product recalls, warranties, complaint handling, and litigation. Bad publicity can be the result, and so can—in many instances—loss of business.

Taken together, the costs of correcting or disposing of internal and external failures account for about 65 percent of all the costs of quality assurance.

Mistaken, Time-Wasting Notions

Obviously, the costs of quality assurance can be enormous. There is thus an understandable tendency to rush at the problem helter-skelter, often on the basis of widely held misconceptions. Philip Crosby, the man who conceived of Zero Defects, the program that ensured the quality of products and components needed to put the first man on the moon, suggests that any of the following notions will waste time in trying to assure quality:

- *Mistaken notion:* Good quality is a condition that is readily recognized and agreed upon by any well-intentioned individual.

To the contrary: Quality is a prescribed set of characteristics established by the enterprise that produces the product or service. Without such prescriptions, the meaning of quality is always in dispute.

- *Mistaken notion:* Quality represents an economic condition that cannot always be afforded.

  To the contrary: Quality is an essential part of the design and pricing of a product or service. As such, it is a necessity, not a luxury.

- *Mistaken notion:* Most, if not all, problems of quality originate from poor workmanship.

  To the contrary: Quality problems are just as likely to have their source in any of the following: unfeasible design specification, improper tooling and equipment, faulty materials, unclear or inadequate instructions, erratic power and utility supplies, poorly coordinated schedules, misfiring computer programs, irrational management, and garbled communications all along the line from shop and office floor to the customer.

- *Mistaken notion:* Most, if not all, quality problems can be solved by routine activities of the quality-assurance department, or by special controls devised and installed by this same department.

  To the contrary: Quality is everybody's business. At best, quality engineers and other quality-control specialists can only analyze, advise, and assist. Achieving true quality assurance takes organizationwide (1) awareness of the problems and (2) acceptance of responsibility for solving them.

Shortening the Appraisal Time

Since appraisal procedures account for about one-quarter of the total cost of quality assurance, the inspection and test processes represent a prime target for improvement in time usage. In order to assess this potential, it helps to examine each of the four categories into which the appraisal process is cast.

Product or Service Inspection. The core of appraisal is product or service inspection. Conformance to quality standards can be determined by (1) gauging, by weight or other dimension; (2) visual comparison with a standard part; (3) testing, for fit or operational function; and (4) breaking or opening to examine concealed interiors and construction, a process that usually destroys the product. *Product or service inspections can be speeded by*:

Prepositioning parts and components for ease of inspection.

Inspecting and testing at the process work station rather than by removing the part to a test bench.

Using various *nondestructive test devices,* such as shadowgraphs for display of enlargements of tiny parts; x rays, magnetic inspection, spectography, or ultrasonic waves; and an almost infinite number of automatic, electronic, and/or computer-driven detection and recording systems.

Providing automatic feedback of performance and conformance to production or clerical operators so that there are no delays waiting for inspection results.

Enabling production and clerical operators to perform inspections as part of their assigned duties. Great progress can be made this way, not only in saving of inspection time but also in improved quality of workmanship.

Process Inspection.   Similar to inspection of products or services, process inspection is focused on the conditions or functioning of the process. Measurements are made against standards of temperature, pressure, humidity, vibration, movement, acceleration, and the like—including time. Automatic inspection systems are most used in process inspection, and are commonplace in chemical plants and oil refineries. They are also commonly built into devices as simple as copying machines that report defects—such as jamming or outage of paper—instantly to the user.

Tool and Equipment Inspection.   Just as the product and process must be inspected for conformance, so must the tools and equipment that make the product or carry on the process be regularly appraised against quality standards. This kind of appraisal lends itself to inspection by the operator, thus eliminating the need for intervention by another party, while also providing instant feedback to the person who controls the operation.

Location of Inspections

The place, or sequence in the process, at which an inspection is made is critical in minimizing the cost of failures. There are several guidelines:

1. *First-part inspection.*   The earlier an inspection is made, the better. A faulty part or an error at the start of the process increases the cost of disposal or correction the longer the process goes on. A simple application of this principle is first-part inspection, wherein the process is not allowed to go forward until the first unit of output has been shown to conform to the standard.

2. *Receiving inspection.*   Raw materials, component parts, and operating supplies should be inspected when received and before they are

allowed to enter the process. Receiving inspection is one of the best time investments that can be made.

3. *Key-point inspection.* Inspections should be made at the points where the greatest consequences of error or defect exist, in terms of both the costs of damage to the product and/or the cost of performing the operation itself.

Extent of Inspection

A fundamental question is whether every part and piece of a process should be inspected—*100 percent inspection*—or whether inspection of a representative sample—*sampling inspection*—is good enough. The answer is that, where there are a great number of parts and pieces, sampling is not only reliable enough for most purposes but is also the least expensive method by far. Another argument is that 100 percent inspection is not 100 percent reliable; fatigue and boredom do take their toll. And, without question, if saving time is an objective, sampling inspections are the quickest. Accordingly, sampling is the generally preferred method. It relies upon statistically sound techniques for drawing a random sample from a lot or batch. Studies show that sampling, when properly prescribed and performed, is equivalent in accuracy to 100 percent inspection.

A natural outgrowth of sampling inspections has been the use of *statistical quality control (SQC)* as an adjunct of product, processing, and tooling inspections. The difference is this: a sampling inspection takes a static picture of a batch of parts of materials after the batch has been accumulated; SQC takes a moving picture of a batch as it is being produced. As a consequence, SQC enables an operator to adjust the process, the tools, or his or her own workmanship so as to keep the units in the batch within the quality control standards. The adjustments are based upon observations made at random intervals. By tracking these observations, the operator can tell whether any variations from standard in a unit's measurements are "normal" or whether they represent significant deviations that must be controlled.

A concordant development in recent years has been to shift the emphasis of all inspections from inspection to *audit.* The *audit concept* changes the punitive aura associated with the term *inspection* to a more positive emphasis on confirming that the quality of product, process, and workmanship conforms to established standards.

Quality-Time Awareness

In the determined effort to improve the quality of goods and services produced in the United States, management has had to accept it that quality cannot be "managed in," "engineered in," or even "controlled in." Quality must be *built in*, and this can be accomplished only through the concerted efforts of all members of an organization. This awareness of the comprehensiveness of the quality problem and acceptance of a broader base of responsibility can be traced to two developments in particular, Zero Defects and Quality Circles. Both programs set prevention as the prime target, knowing that time, effort, and money invested in prevention greatly reduce the need to spend time, effort, and money on appraisal and on correction of failures.

The starting point for a time-saving approach to quality improvement, therefore, is an ongoing quality awareness program. To be effective, however, such a program must include *every member* of an organization, from top to bottom.

Marketing and Sales Time

Marketing and sales are inextricably tied into time constraints imposed by forces in the marketplace. Customers' impatience for delivery of merchandise, a product's life cycle, introduction of new products, and the time needed to effect a sale are the time-related forces examined below, together with suggestions for coping with them.

We-Want-It-Now Time

Waiting time is something most consumers don't enjoy. Accordingly, a major attraction in a product or service is ready availability. This quality is called *time utility*. It takes time, of course, to manufacture a product or to produce the service. Advertising, promotion, and selling are time-consuming, too. There are also a number of other expensive and/or time-consuming functions associated with marketing. These include order processing, storage and warehousing, and distribution.

Order Processing. Once entirely a manual operation, order entry now lends itself to automatic systems, and a wide variety of proprietary programs can be tailored to each firm's requirements. Consequently, there is no good reason for delay at this phase of marketing.

Storage and Warehousing. Like other aspects of inventory control, storage and warehousing can be handled using up-to-date, sophisticated techniques. (See Chapter 10 for examples.) Transportation time to and from warehouses, however, adds another dimension to the problem. Optimum placement of warehouses and distribution centers reduces transfer and delivery times. Preferred locations can be selected by using mathematical techniques such as linear programming.

Channels of Distribution. Before a product or service is placed in the hands of a buyer, it must often flow through a long line of intermediaries, such as wholesalers, distributors, jobbers, and retailers. All these intermediaries can provide valuable services to the buyer as well as the seller. Any steps, however, that can be taken to shorten the distribution time are welcome. Three approaches, in particular, warrant special consideration:

1. *Eliminate the number of intermediaries.* The simplest approach is to eliminate either a wholesaler or a retailer, thus eliminating one step in the handling of goods on their way to the customer. The producer usually suffers a loss of services, but this loss is more than compensated for by the savings in time, commissions, and transportation charges.

2. *Have the shipments bypass the intermediary.* Under this arrangement, known as *drop shipping*, the intermediate sales agent or broker makes the sale and files the order, and the producer ships directly to the customer.

3. *Engage in direct marketing.* For many companies, the ultimate way to shorten the chain between the producer or supplier and the customer is direct marketing. A direct marketing company acts as its own sales agent, using a variety of techniques such as direct mail, radio and telephone advertising, and telephone. If the supplier (like a department store or catalog sales firm) is independent of the producer, the product may be drop-shipped without ever passing through the supplier's hand.

Altering the Product's Life Cycle

In principle, at least, the fortunes of a successful product or service begin modestly, as shown in Figure 12-1, gradually rise to a peak of sales and prosperity, and then inevitably descend. Each phase of the product's life cycle has its own characteristics, discussed below.

Introduction. During this phase, profits are nonexistent, and advertising expenditures must be heavy in order to attract consumers' attention.

Growth. As the product obtains consumer acceptance, it also begins to be profitable. Advertising must be continued to sustain momentum.

Maturity. Profits peak early in this period, while sales don't reach their maximum until toward the end. The reason for this dichotomy is that

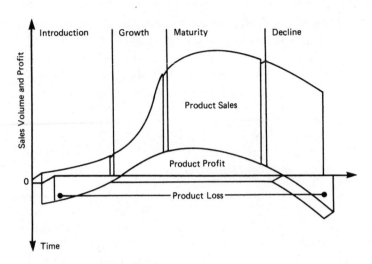

Figure 12-1. Stages in a product's life cycle.

success attracts competition, and along with competition come lower prices and higher advertising expenses.

Decline.   Profits decline rapidly and often disappear. A company faces three choices at this stage: (1) drop the product from its line while milking it for any remaining returns, (2) invest in upgrading the existing product, or (3) begin looking for a replacement.

From a timing viewpoint, a manager will keep careful watch over a product's life cycle. Using knowledge of the product's current stage in its life cycle, the manager can take appropriate action. Action may be taken for the following reasons:

1. *To shorten the introduction stage.*   Ordinarily, the faster the product gets to market and obtains a leadership position, the more difficult it is for new competitors to enter the market successfully. Introduction is accelerated by having advertising, promotion, and distribution channels firmly in place at the start.

2. *To accelerate the growth stage.*   As experts Al Ries and Jack Trout advise about the timing of advertising expenditures in their best-selling book, *Bottom-Up Marketing,** "When you're a big winner, pour it on! If marketing were a race horse, you could clearly see the importance of breaking out of the pack early."

3. *To prolong the maturity stage.*   It is important that advertising be

---

*Al Ries and Jack Trout, *Bottom-Up Marketing*, McGraw-Hill, New York, 1989, p. 207.

sustained during this period. Otherwise, decline will set in earlier than normal. Other actions are also called for, such as (a) finding new uses or applications for the product or service, (b) finding unoccupied niches into which to push it, and (c) repackaging it to give it the aura of a new product.

4. *To minimize the impact of decline.*   When there is no longer any hope of profit, the product should probably be dropped from the line. Before that time, however, a search for new products should begin, as discussed next.

TIME BYTE 12-4
Slow-Footed Product Start-Ups

The winning products these days are the ones that get out of the gate fastest. While this fact is easily recognized, it's difficult to act on. The bureaucracy in many companies seems to make them too slow-footed when it comes to getting a new product on line. Gillette Co.'s Sensor razor is a case in point. A bright young engineer came up with the idea for a floating cartridge for a disposable razor in 1977. The idea, however, was passed back and forth, up the line and down, for years, until the product finally reached the market on Super Bowl Sunday in 1990. Reasons for the 13-year delay? Internal squabbles about design and price, a need to register 22 patents, R&D expenditure of $75 million, and another $125 million for development and tooling. Even then, it took a radical organizational change to move the project off dead center. A new vice president was put in charge in 1988, and he set firm goals for a final design and a deadline for product release by Super Bowl time.

Other big companies tend to have similar problems in new-product development. Ford, for example, will take 8 years to release a new version of the Taurus. Meanwhile, the Honda Accord is being revamped every 4 years. And even the president of laid-back Apple Computer has been criticized for the company's lack of innovative new products. The president's response was to pledge to shorten the time to develop a new computer from 18 months to 12.

Shortening the introduction stage of a product's life cycle helps it to reach the profit level sooner.

"How a $4 Razor Ends Up Costing $300 Million," by Keith H. Hammonds, *Business Week*, Jan. 29, 1990, p. 62.

Faster New-Product Introductions

The difficulties involved in trying to make an early start in development of a new product are underscored in Time Byte 12-4. The process is almost always an extended one that proceeds through several stages: exploration or research, product screening, business feasibility analysis, product development and design, market testing, and market placement. A primary objective is to reduce the time for each stage and for the process as a whole.

One particularly revealing study, by Tom Peters,* shows that it takes about 9 percent of the total process time for exploration and screening, 7 percent for the feasibility analysis, 43 percent for development and design, 20 percent for market testing, and 21 percent for market placement. In *Thriving on Chaos*, Peters pinpoints the first three stages as representing the crucial bottlenecks. Specifically, he urges: "Aim for a 75 percent reduction in *time to first tangible test* for the average product." That would have the effect of cutting total product-introduction time by almost half.

Speeding Up Sales Calls

Like the workers on the factory floor and the clerks at the office keyboard, salespeople—in retail shops, on the telephone, or out in the field making calls—represent the cutting edge of most marketing efforts. Good salespeople are self-motivating and self-directing. In a typical sales force, however, there are others who need considerable direction and control—and if they don't get it, the time they waste will outweigh the value of the sales they make. The three approaches discussed below—sales-call budgets, sales-call reports, and sales-call controls—can provide the needed time-saving direction and control.

Sales-Call Budgets.   To determine the number of possible selling days in a year, you can subtract nonselling days (holidays, vacations, trade shows, sales meetings, etc.) from total business days. Then deduct a realistic contingency allowance of between 10 and 20 percent from the total possible selling days, which will leave approximately 170 projected selling days. The sales-call budget is determined by multiplying projected selling days by the number of calls expected per day. Using an estimated figure of 6 calls per day, for example, the annual sales-call budget will be 170×6, or 1020 calls. Finally, a monthly budget can be derived by dividing the total by 12, or 85 calls a month.

Sales-Call Reports.   A properly designed sales-call report not only advises the sales manager of what's going on in the field, but also helps force salespeople to plan their calls and itineraries in advance. Salespeople often disdain both controls and paperwork, even if it helps them

---

*Tom Peters, *Thriving on Chaos*, Harper and Row, New York, 1987, p. 275.

save time. The best reports, therefore, use a brief, time-saving format. Good ones are available from a number of proprietary form publishers.

Sales-Call Controls.   Based upon data gathered from sales-call reports and travel expense vouchers, sales-call controls analyze three performance measures: calls per day, sales per call, and cost per call. *The number of calls per day can often be increased by*:

- Better routing of the salesperson by the sales supervisor
- More efficient design of sales territories
- Better planning of the time spent during sales calls, such as establishing beforehand primary and fall-back goals for each call, opening remarks, benefits to be presented, and closing arguments
- Reduction of paperwork and administrative chores
- A more effective home-base support system

Financial Time

Nowhere else in the business and personal world is the saying "Time is money" truer than in finances. Whether borrowing or lending, paying bills or collecting for them, or judging the worth of your financial position, time is a critical and inescapable factor.

Time Value of Money

The time value of money is measured by how much you must pay for it in the form of interest over a stipulated period of time. When you borrow $1000, for instance, at a simple interest rate of 12 percent, the price you pay in interest for the use of that money for a year is $120. It is important to remember that, at the end of the year, you must also repay the sum that was borrowed—the principal. Some methods of financing ask the borrower to pay the interest up front. That way, although you've contracted to borrow $1000, you get only $880. If you pay the 12 percent rate monthly on the unpaid balance, the true rate may be closer to 22 percent.

None of this is an academic exercise. It points up several important facts:

1. Through the magic of compound interest, money invested together with its annual interest payments multiplies geometrically over a period of years. For example, a company may have two choices: invest $100,000 in a new piece of equipment expected to last 15 years, or in-

vest the money in a bond that pays 12 percent compound interest over the same period. Money invested and compounded in the bond will accumulate to $547,000 at the end of 15 years. As you can see, time plays a heavy role in the decision-making process.

2. Because of the effect of compound interest upon financial planning, $1 in the hand today is considered to be worth more than $1 a year from now. Money managers always look at investments from that point of view. In the example of $1000 borrowed at 12 percent, the present value of the loan is $1000; its value a year from now is only $880. The money manager says that the $1000 must be "discounted" by its interest rate to determine its value in the future.

3. The difference between present and future values of money implies the following rule of thumb for borrowing and repayment: Borrow when interest rates are low (future value is high), and repay when interest rates are high (future value is low).

4. The inevitability of inflation also makes a future dollar worth less than today's. Under an annual inflation rate of 3 percent, for example, $1 today will be worth only 97 cents a year from now. Accordingly, a borrower always has the advantage that (quite aside from consideration of interest rates) loans are paid back with money that is cheaper than what was originally obtained from the lender.

5. On the other hand, the longer the repayments are stretched out, the more expensive a loan will be. That's because you are using the lender's money—and paying interest for the use of it—over a longer period of time.

6. A popular and convenient way to judge the value of an investment in an item of equipment is its payback period. The payback period is determined by dividing the cost of the investment by the profit it is expected to return each year. For example, an investment of $5000 in a machine that is expected to yield a profit of $1000 per year would have a payback period of 5 years. The payback period is misleading because it does not take into account the cost of the money invested, which at 12 percent interest would be $600 a year.

Corporate Borrowing Time

Corporations raise money in two ways:

1. *Equity financing.* Corporations sometimes sell a share of ownership and profits with no guarantee that the money will ever be returned to the investor. *Hence, time doesn't enter this equation, either in the form of interest or as periodic repayments of the investment.* The investor simply waits for dividends or appreciation of the value of the shares.

2. *Debt financing.* Corporations may borrow money under terms that require interest payments as well as periodic repayment of the borrowed principal. *Time plays a very large role in this kind of arrangement.* The leveraged buyouts of the 1980s, for example, were financed mainly by borrowing with the expectation that repayments would be made from future profits at less costly money. In many instances these expectations did not materialize, and the combined burden of heavy interest payments and debt-reduction payments sent these firms into bankruptcy.

Credit Time

Bankers and other lenders are completely aware of the time value of money. They fully understand that money allowed to sit idle without drawing interest is costly money.

Companies that extend credit should take a tip from the bankers: *Invoices that remain unpaid allow a customer to use the vendor's money without paying interest.* Take, for example, a company that has $100,000 in its receivables account, and assume that this money has been outstanding an average of 30 days, with commercial interest rates at 12 percent. Under these circumstances, the company is literally giving away $1000 a month ($100,000 × 0.12 ÷ 12 months).

Of course, this practice can work both ways. If you are the buyer, the longer you can put off paying your bill without a penalty, the cheaper your purchase will have been. This is becoming increasingly difficult to manage, however. Purchases made with credit cards and under most formal arrangements build an interest rate into the contract. Many suppliers, however, still offer a bonus (such as a 2 percent discount) for early payments, even if a penalty is imposed for late payments.

From a credit control viewpoint, accountants and credit managers watch two time-related financial measures:

Receivables turnover, which is calculated by dividing the net sales for the period by the accounts receivables figure. If, for example, net sales were $300,000 and receivables $40,000, the turnover would be 7.5 times.

Collection period, which converts the number of times that receivables are turned over into a figure that shows, on average, how long it takes a company to collect its bills. The collection period is calculated by dividing the number of days in the year (the figure used is 360, the same figure the Egyptians used!) by the turnover figure. In this example, 360 ÷ 7.5 = 48 days.

Cash Flow

Corporations and individuals, too, should be well aware of the need for prudent control of cash flow. It was stated succinctly by Mr. Micawber in Charles Dickens's *David Copperfield*:

> Annual income twenty pounds, annual expenditure nineteen pounds six; result happiness. Annual income twenty pounds, annual expenditure twenty pounds ought and six; result misery.

Today, there are many methods for analysis and control of cash flow. The simplest technique, and the most useful, is the preparation of a cash-flow budget, as shown in Figure 12-2. The cash-flow budget tracks and reconciles the time flow of (1) revenues from every source and (2) payments of all kinds. Its special value is that it enables an organization to plan ahead for:

Times of excess cash—positive cash flow—when money might be switched from a checking account to a savings certificate or money market fund so that it earns interest.

Times of cash shortage—negative cash flow—which will usually require borrowing to pay bills.

TIME CHECK

Use this action-plan checklist to verify your understanding of the various concepts, ideas, and techniques presented in this chapter and to indicate any need for further action on your part.

	Applies to your situation		Schedule for action	
	Yes	No	Yes	No
1. Action taken to correct conditions of either excess capacity or undercapacity, both of which are wasteful of time.	____	____	____	____
2. Improvements made to shorten changeover and start-up times.	____	____	____	____
3. Application of prioritizing techniques to production schedules in job shops, with highest priorities given to jobs with the shortest processing time.	____	____	____	____

Month	J	F	M	A	M	J	J	A	S	O	N	D
Sales budget in cash revenues	40*	40	40	40	80	100	50	20	30	50	60	100
Expense budget in cash payments	30	30	80	70	60	50	20	30	80	60	40	50
Cash excess (+) or shortage (−) each month	+10	+10	−40	−30	+20	+50	+30	−10	−50	−10	+20	+50
Cumulative cash excess (+) or shortage (−)	+10	+20	−20	−50	−30	+20	+50	+40	−10	−20	0	+50
Cumulative excess cash												
Cumulative cash shortage to be filled by short-term borrowing												

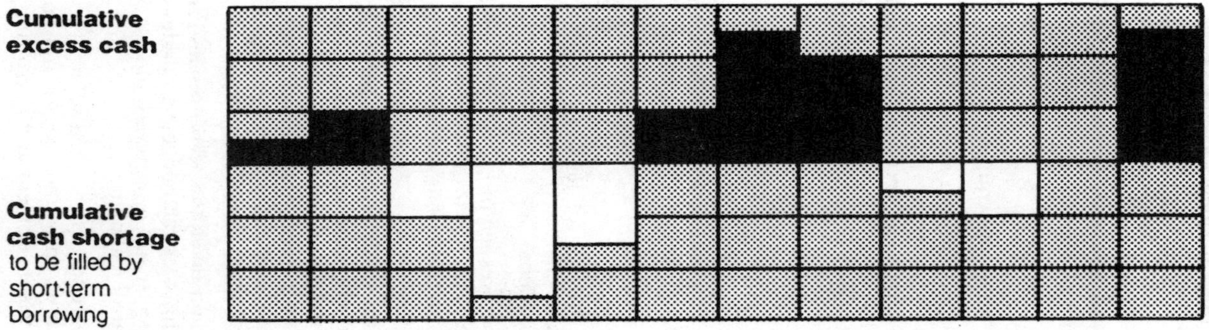

* All figures are in thousands of dollars.

Figure 12-2. Example of a cash-flow budget showing cumulative monthly excess or shortage.

4. Segmentation of clerical work into discrete categories, and examination of each item for possible application of any of nine time-saving improvements. ___ ___ ___ ___

5. Knowledge of the four interrelated aspects of quality assurance: prevention, appraisal, internal remedial actions, and external remedial actions. ___ ___ ___ ___

6. Implementation of a time-saving appraisal program, including time-conserving inspections of (a) product or service, (b) processes, and (c) tools and equipment. ___ ___ ___ ___

7. Inspections that are located (a) as early in the process as possible, using first-part and receiving inspections and (b) at critical points in the process where the cost of potential damage is greatest. ___ ___ ___ ___

8. Time and cost of inspections reduced by using sampling inspections, shifting emphasis to audits (which imply a more positive, proactive tone), and introducing SQC techniques. ___ ___ ___ ___

9. Understanding of the power to improve both quality and productivity of the strongly participative approach, which characterizes Quality Circle programs. ___ ___ ___ ___

10. Compression of the time consumed in marketing by order processing, storage and warehousing, and physical distribution. ___ ___ ___ ___

11. Study made of each product's life cycle with the goals of shortening the introduction stage, accelerating the growth stage, prolonging the maturity stage, and minimizing the impact of decline. ___ ___ ___ ___

12. Action taken to speed up sales calls by using sales-call budgets and sales-call reports, and by applying time-saving control techniques. ___ ___ ___ ___

13. Awareness of the time value of money and of compound interest and how it affects investment and borrowing decisions. ___ ___ ___ ___

14. Awareness of corporate methods of financing through equity (which has no time implications) and debt (in which time plays a large role.) ____ ____ ____ ____

15. Continuing surveillance of internal credit practices so that bills are (a) paid promptly without an interest penalty and (b) collected within the shortest possible collection period. ____ ____ ____ ____

16. Maintenance of a cash-flow budget so as to anticipate periods of excess cash (which can be invested at interest) and periods of cash shortages (when borrowing is necessary). ____ ____ ____ ____

Index

About the Author

Lester R. Bittel, professor of management and Virginia
Eminent Scholar at James Madison University, has devoted
his entire career to management. He is the recipient of
numerous awards, including the Frederick W. Taylor Award
for his contributions to management literature and the
Centennial Medal, both given by the American Society of
Mechanical Engineers. An internationally respected writer,
he is a five-time winner of the Jesse H. Neal Award for
Outstanding Business Journalism. Among his many
successful guides for managers are *What Every Supervisor
Should Know*, Sixth Edition, *Handbook for Professional
Managers*, and *The McGraw-Hill 36-Hour Management
Course*, all published by McGraw-Hill.